VIOLINS OF HOPE

VIOLINS
of HOPE

Violins of the Holocaust—
Instruments of Hope and Liberation
in Mankind's Darkest Hour

JAMES A. GRYMES

HARPER ◉ PERENNIAL

NEW YORK • LONDON • TORONTO • SYDNEY • NEW DELHI • AUCKLAND

HARPER ⬤ PERENNIAL

HarperCollins books may be purchased for educational,
business, or sales promotional use. For information please
e-mail the Special Markets Department at SPsales@
harpercollins.com.

FIRST EDITION

Designed by Fritz Metsch

Library of Congress Cataloging-in-Publication Data
has been applied for.

ISBN 978-0-06-224683-7

HB 06.19.2023

We played music for sheer survival.
We made music in hell.

—HEINZ "COCO" SCHUMANN

CONTENTS

CONTENTS

VIOLINS OF HOPE

PROLOGUE

———

AMNON'S
VIOLINS

Amnon and Moshe Weinstein repairing a double bass in their
workshop, ca. 1965. Amnon continues to make and repair string
instruments in this same workshop in Tel Aviv. *(Courtesy of Amnon
Weinstein.)*

Amnon Weinstein's earliest memories are of his immediate family sitting around the table at major Jewish holidays like Rosh Hashanah and Passover in the late 1940s. There were four of them. Amnon, his little sister Esther, and their parents Moshe and Golda. And four hundred ghosts. These were the ghosts of the relatives who had been left behind when Moshe and Golda had immigrated to Palestine in 1938.

Moshe was a violinist, a violin teacher, and a violin repairman. He had been fascinated by the violin ever since he was seven years old, when he had heard a traveling Klezmer ensemble playing at a wedding in his hometown of Brest-Litovsk. Since there were no suitable violin teachers in Brest-Litovsk, Moshe traveled to Vilna, a Lithuanian city that was a capital of Jewish culture. There Moshe attended the same conservatory that Vilna native and violin virtuoso Jascha Heifetz had attended just a few years earlier. Moshe even won an award for performing Mendelssohn's difficult violin concerto—the same work with which Heifetz had made his debut. It was in Vilna that Moshe met his future wife Golda, who accompanied him on the piano.

After finishing their studies at the Vilna conservatory, Moshe and Golda decided to move to Palestine. They were Zionists, followers of a Jewish movement that called for a home and a national identity for Jews in the Land of Israel. Their four hundred relatives remained behind in Europe. Some, like Moshe's father Yaakov—a rabbi—considered the secular Zionist movement to be sacrilegious. They believed that returning to Israel prior to the arrival of the Messiah was contrary to God's will. Others simply waited too long to secure the finances and paperwork necessary to travel to the Holy Land. When Germany invaded the Soviet Union on June 22, 1941, they became trapped in Nazi-occupied Eastern Europe.

Knowing that he would not be able to make a living as a violinist in Palestine, Moshe decided to become a violin repairman. The violin is a very popular instrument in Jewish culture, and Moshe wisely predicted that the tens of thousands of Jews who were immigrating to Palestine would create a market for an outstanding craftsman who could fix their instruments. In order to develop his skills, Moshe traveled to Warsaw to apprentice with Yaakov Zimmerman, a respected Jewish violinmaker.

Zimmerman is remembered as an outstanding artisan who was also very kind, especially toward young Jewish musicians. Famous violinist Ida Haendel, who was seven years old when her father brought her to Warsaw to study at the Chopin Conservatory, describes Zimmerman as a selfless person who would often repair instruments for free. Former concertmaster of the Berlin Philharmonic Michel Schwalbé, who also trained in Warsaw, recalled how Zimmerman gave him everything he needed to play the violin, including instruments, strings, and bow hairs.

Zimmerman even found a room in the apartment of Warsaw industrialist Shimon Krongold in which Schwalbé could practice. For Jewish children like Haendel and Schwalbé, this level of support was life-changing. Zimmerman disappeared during the Holocaust. It is assumed that he died in the Warsaw Ghetto.

Upon moving to Palestine, Moshe found a job picking oranges alongside numerous other immigrants in the agricultural community of Petah Tikvah. By 1939, he and Golda—who was also known as Zahava, the Hebrew form of her name—had earned enough money to move six and a half miles west to Tel Aviv. Moshe opened his violin shop and quickly established himself as a prominent figure in Tel Aviv's burgeoning music scene. He was a peaceful man who thought that all children should learn to play the violin. People who played music, he believed, could be neither evil nor violent. While the exploitation of music during the Holocaust would prove him wrong, Moshe himself exemplified the noble principles behind his convictions by arranging scholarships that helped promising young talents like Pinchas Zukerman and Shlomo Mintz travel to the United States to receive the best training in the world at the Juilliard School.

Moshe and Golda also started a family. Their son Amnon was born in 1939. Their daughter Esther came along five years later.

By the end of the Holocaust, Moshe and Golda had heard very little from the relatives they had left behind. At first they had received a few letters asking for help with securing visas from family members who had hoped to join them in Palestine. But all communication had stopped once Germany had invaded the Soviet Union in June 1941.

Then a Holocaust survivor visited Moshe in Tel Aviv and told him how his entire family had been killed.

Before the war, Moshe's family had moved to Volkovysk, which was occupied by the Nazis shortly after the German invasion. The Germans had started massacring Jews immediately. On November 2, 1942, all of the remaining Jews from Volkovysk and the surrounding areas were marched to a former prisoner-of-war camp. A number of Jews who tried to escape were caught and executed. One of them was Moshe's brother, who was shot on the spot. By the end of the year, all but two thousand of the twenty thousand Jews in the camp would be sent to the Treblinka death camp. Everyone else was sent to Auschwitz on January 12, 1943.

The horrific stories were too much for Moshe to handle. That night, he suffered the first of many heart attacks that would ultimately cause his death. Moshe never spoke of his family again.

It was just as hard for Golda to talk about her family. They had remained behind in Vilna, which was occupied by the German army on June 24, 1941. The troops were quickly followed by death squads that began rounding up Jews and taking them to the nearby Ponary forest. Ponary had once been a popular weekend getaway for Vilna's Jews and gentiles alike. Now it would become the site of one of the most brutal massacres in the Holocaust. There were fifty-seven thousand Jews living in Vilna during the German invasion. By the time the Red Army liberated the city on July 13, 1944, only a few thousand remained. Like Moshe, none of Golda's relatives survived.

Racked with survivor's guilt, Golda threw away the letters she had received from her family. The memories were like voices she could no longer bear to hear. When young Amnon asked about his grandparents, aunts, and uncles, she would struggle to find words that could explain why he would never be able to meet them. The best she could do was to bring out a book she had found about the Vilna ghetto and the Ponary massacre. "This is where your grandparents are," she would tell him, pointing to the ghastly photos of the dead. "This is my family." She would break down in tears, unable to explain further.

Although they could never bring themselves to discuss their dead relatives, the guilt and sorrow Moshe and Golda felt over their devastating losses permeated the Weinstein household, and with it Amnon's childhood.

There were tangible reminders, as well.

Since Moshe was the president of the Association of Vilna Immigrants, the Weinstein apartment was the first stop in Palestine for survivors from Vilna who were hoping to start a new life in the land of their biblical ancestors. Moshe welcomed them all into his apartment for home-made meals and warm beds until they could find homes of their own. Young Amnon was frightened by the emaciated guests who were startled by every noise. He could not understand why they hid leftover bread under their pillows and blankets. Years passed until the sounds of the visitors crying themselves to sleep stopped resonating in his own nightmares.

As a young man, Amnon tried to forget about the catastrophe that had robbed him of his extended family and replaced them with terrifying strangers. He busied himself with establishing a career as a luthier—a maker and repairer of string instruments. Growing up in his father's violin shop, Amnon had watched as Moshe had helped countless young violinists launch their performing careers. Moshe had given the poorest students violins, bows, and strings, just as his mentor Yaakov Zimmerman had done for Jewish children in Warsaw. Amnon wanted to make the same impact on the lives of musicians. After apprenticing with his father, he moved to Cremona, Italy, to learn old-world craftsmanship in the city made famous by violinmakers such as Amati, Guarneri, and Stradivari. In Cremona, Amnon studied with master luthiers Pietro Sgarabotto, Giuseppe Ornati, and Ferdinando Garimberti before moving to Paris to learn from renowned violinmaker Étienne Vatelot.

When Moshe passed away in 1986, Amnon took over the family business. In 1998, he continued the dynasty that his father had initiated by starting to train his own son Avshalom, who may be the first third-generation Jewish luthier in history. By that time, Amnon had established himself as one of the finest luthiers in the world and an important figure in Israeli culture. His wife Assi also enjoys prominence as a journalist and as the daughter of one of the heroic Bielski brothers, who were commemorated in the film *Defiance*.

Despite Amnon's efforts to ignore the Holocaust, it continued to haunt him. In the late 1980s, a man who had played the violin in Auschwitz visited Amnon's workshop. The survivor had not touched his instrument since leaving the death camp. He now wanted to get it restored for his grandson. The top of the violin was damaged from having been played in the rain and snow. When Amnon took the instrument apart, he discovered ashes inside that he could only assume to be fallout from the crematoria at Auschwitz. The very thought of what that violin and its owner had been through together shook Amnon to his core, but he quickly pushed those gruesome thoughts aside. It was still too difficult for him to think about the Holocaust.

By the 1990s, around the same time he started training his son Avshalom, Amnon was finally ready to reclaim his lost heritage. Five decades after his family had been destroyed, he started reflecting not only on the Holocaust but on the role that music—specifically the violin— played in Jewish lives throughout that dark period. He began locating and restoring violins that were played by Jewish musicians during the Holocaust.

Some of the instruments that Amnon has tracked down were damaged during the Holocaust, and had been unplayable ever since. But once he brings them into his workshop, Amnon pours his heart, his soul, and his considerable expertise as a master luthier into breathing new life into them. The painstaking restorations can take up to eighteen months. When Amnon is done piecing the violins back together, they are ready for performances in the world's finest concert halls. Although some of the musicians who once played the neglected and severely damaged instruments were silenced by the Holocaust, their voices and spirits live on through the violins that Amnon has lovingly restored.

The Violin in the Holocaust

The violin has formed an important aspect of Jewish culture for centuries. Many of the world's greatest violinists have been Jewish. This includes—but is certainly not limited to—the nineteenth-century dedicatees of the revered violin concertos by Brahms and Mendelssohn; twentieth-century masters Jascha Heifetz, Yehudi Menuhin, and Isaac Stern; and contemporary virtuosos Itzhak Perlman, Pinchas Zukerman, and Shlomo Mintz. Some scholars have even attributed the violin's invention to Jews who fled to Italy after Spain expelled its entire Jewish population in 1492. Since then, the instrument has played a vital role in professional life as a popular choice for classical Jewish musicians, as well as in communal life as an essential component of the enduring Klezmer tradition.

During the Holocaust, the violin assumed extraordinary new roles within the Jewish community. The instruments introduced in this book chronicle just a few of those functions.

For some musicians, the violin became a liberator that freed them and their families from Nazi tyranny. In 1936, Bronisław Huberman recruited seventy-five Jewish performers to form a new orchestra in Palestine, providing them with the legal and financial means to move safely out of Europe before it was too late (chapter 1). Ernst Glaser, the Jewish concertmaster of the Oslo Philharmonic Orchestra, used his musical influence to escape a Nazi riot during a concert in Bergen in 1941. He eventually fled occupied Norway to Sweden, where he spent the remainder of the war performing and raising money for the Norwegian freedom fighters camped out along the border (chapter 4).

For many, the violin was a comforter in mankind's darkest hour. Erich Weininger was imprisoned in Dachau before being transferred to Buchenwald. After the British Quakers engineered his release in 1939, the Nazis allowed him to leave for Palestine, where Weininger and 3,500 other illegal immigrants were intercepted by British warships. They were deported to the island of Mauritius, where they were confined until the end of the war. Throughout those five years, Weininger brought comfort to himself and to his fellow prisoners by playing the violin in an orchestra with other detainees (chapter 2).

For others, the violin was a savior that spared their lives in concentration camps and ghettos. The members of the orchestras in Auschwitz played as the work details marched in and out of the concentration camp every day. In exchange, they often received lighter work details and better food—providing them with their best chances for survival (chapter 3). In the ghettoized Romanian territory of Transnistria, Feivel Wininger performed at weddings and parties in exchange for leftovers that he could bring back to his family. By playing the violin, Wininger was able to spare sixteen family members and friends from starvation (chapter 5).

In at least one case, the violin was an avenger that brought retribution for murdered family members. After his parents and sister were executed, Mordechai "Motele" Schlein joined Uncle Misha's Jewish Group, a band of Jewish combatants who were fighting the Nazis in the dense forests of Poland and Ukraine. In August 1943, Motele infiltrated a Nazi Soldiers Club, where he was hired to provide entertainment during meals. Every night, Motele would hide his violin in the Soldiers Club and take home an empty violin case. He would return the next morning with a few pounds of explosives hidden in that case. When high-ranking SS officers arrived for a visit, Motele blew up the building (chapter 6).

For the family of Shimon Krongold, a violin is one of the only remaining mementos of their beloved relative. After Shimon died of typhus in Central Asia, a survivor brought the instrument to Shimon's brother in Jerusalem. The violin and a picture of Shimon holding the instrument are the only items of Shimon's legacy that survived the Holocaust (epilogue).

Although today Shimon Krongold's Violin and the other Violins of Hope serve as memorials of those who perished, during the Holocaust they represented optimism for the future.

Wherever there were violins, there was hope.

1

THE
WAGNER
VIOLIN

Arturo Toscanini (center left) and Bronisław Huberman (center right) at the public dress rehearsal of the Palestine Orchestra on December 25, 1936—one day before the ensemble's debut. (*Photograph by Rudi Weissenstein, Pri-Or PhotoHouse. Courtesy of the Murray S. Katz Photo Archives of the Israel Philharmonic Orchestra.*)

In the early twentieth century, Jews living in Germany were participating in the intellectual and cultural life of their county in ways that would have been inconceivable in previous eras. In 1925, Jews comprised 16 percent of physicians, 15 percent of dentists, and 25 percent of lawyers in the German state of Prussia, even though they formed less than 1 percent of the general population. In addition to holding prominent positions in the banking industry and on university faculties, Jews were disproportionately represented in Germany's artistic scene, representing 3 percent of professionals in music and theater, 4 percent in the film industry, and 7 percent of visual artists and writers.

Tragically, the increase in Jewish success in professional life was accompanied by a rise in anti-Semitism. Discrimination against Jews was, of course, not limited to Germany, and it was certainly not anything new. Ever since the birth of Christianity, gentiles had looked upon Jews with suspicion, blaming them for everything from the death of Jesus Christ to natural disasters. The persistent myth of the "blood libel" even accused Jews of using the blood of Christian children for religious rituals, particularly the making of the unleavened bread for Passover.

In the years following World War I, right-wing Germans blamed the Jews for their demoralizing losses on the

battlefield, as well as for the social and economic turbu-
lence that followed. Jews were falsely accused of stabbing
the country in the back by failing to adequately support
the war effort. The right wing maintained that it was this
betrayal, not weaknesses in the military, that had ultimately led to Germany's defeat. They contended that the
only way to restore Germany to its former glory was to rid
the country of the Jews who were responsible for its ruin.

The assimilation of Jews into German society was also
blamed for a perceived decline in German culture. Germany had dominated classical music from J. S. Bach in
the early eighteenth century to Richard Wagner in the
late nineteenth century. The end of that two-hundred-
year supremacy was attributed to the Jewish composers
and composition teachers who eschewed traditional Germanic tonal structures in favor of modernist composi-
tional processes. The international Jewish influences that
championed atonality, it was argued, had undermined
German culture. One prominent conservative composer
even drew a parallel between the "impotence" and "de-
cay" in German musical tastes and the decline in German
society that had led to the country's otherwise inexplicable
military defeat.[1]

Immediately after Adolf Hitler was appointed chancellor of Germany on January 30, 1933, he and his Nazi
Party initiated an agenda to rid Germany of the Jewish
influences that they blamed for the country's downfall.
On April 7, Hitler ratified the Law for the Restoration
of the Professional Civil Service. The new law called for

the removal of Jews from all public positions, but its interpretation was later expanded to exclude employment at private institutions, as well. It mandated the dismissal of Jewish personnel at police and fire stations, post offices, libraries and museums, and especially at cultural institutions. Jewish musicians who worked for music conservatories, orchestras, and opera companies quickly found themselves out of work.

Ernst Böhm had been serving as the solo contrabassist for the West German Radio Orchestra in Cologne for seven years when he received instructions to stay away from the radio building until further notice. The order claimed that the injunction was just temporary, but Böhm would never play with the orchestra again. On June 29, the Reich Broadcasting Association sent the West German Radio a list of "non-Aryan" and "politically unreliable" employees who were to be fired in keeping with the Law for the Restoration of the Professional Civil Service.[2] Böhm's name was at the top of that list. He was officially dismissed exactly one month later.

The decisions over which musicians would keep their jobs were left to the newly created Reich Chamber of Music. Founded by Minister of Propaganda Joseph Goebbels as one of seven departments within the Reich Chamber of Culture, the Chamber of Music oversaw all professional musical activities in the country. To assist with the restoration of Germany's musical supremacy, the Chamber of Music made sure that only "good German music" such as the compositions of Bach, Beethoven, Brahms,

Haydn, Mozart, and Wagner were performed. Strictly forbidden was "Degenerate Music" such as jazz, atonal works, and any compositions by Jewish composers such as Mahler, Mendelssohn, and Meyerbeer. The chamber also controlled who performed the approved music. To earn money by performing, one had to be a member of the Chamber of Music. To be a member of the Chamber of Music, one could not be a Jew.

Given the Jewish propensity for string instruments—especially the violin—it is not surprising that Jews had been especially overrepresented in the string sections of professional orchestras. Once the dismissals began, their absence was felt immediately in those ensembles. German composer Georg Haentzschel once remarked that he noticed that the Jewish musicians were disappearing, "because the violin sections were getting thinner and thinner."[3]

A minority of internationally renowned Jewish musicians were fortunate enough to have the means to leave Germany. Arnold Schoenberg, the Jewish composer who is considered to be the father of atonal music, had little choice but to flee. He ended up in the United States, along with former concertmaster of the Berlin Philharmonic Szymon Goldberg, virtuoso violin soloist Fritz Kreisler, and a number of other famous conductors, performers, and composers. All in all, the United States served as the sanctuary for approximately half of all Jewish immigrants from Germany and Austria, including 465 musicians.

Many outstanding performers stayed behind. While they were indeed well trained and highly skilled, they

had not yet established the level of international prestige
that would have attracted offers from orchestras outside
of Germany. Others might have been able to secure employment, but lacked the resources to move abroad. Jews
who wished to emigrate with their families had to secure
the sufficient travel funds up front. They would then have
to navigate through an intentionally difficult Nazi bu-
reaucracy for the necessary tax clearance certificates and
exit permits. Finally, they would be able to leave Germany
only if the immigration quotas established by their destination countries had not already been met.

There was also a subset of the Jewish population
that simply did not want to leave their homes. Some—
especially those who were decorated veterans of World
War I—were patriotic Germans who refused to believe
that they would really be in danger in their beloved homeland. They convinced themselves that their country's experiment with Nazism would be so short-lived that any in-
conveniences would be temporary. Tragically, they could
not have been more wrong.

The Jewish Culture League

Percussionist Kurt Sommerfeld was one of the hundreds
of Jewish musicians who were dismissed from their orchestral positions. After being fired when the Berlin Municipal Orchestra was purged of its Jewish performers,
Sommerfeld registered with the employment office, where
he found little sympathy. "That's no problem," the clerk

told him sarcastically. "Go to the Jewish cemetery and become a Jewish gardener."[4]

Determined to make his living as a musician, Sommerfeld answered an advertisement for a drummer in a coffeehouse band. The gig was going fine until a man in the audience stood up and shouted, "Waiter, a round of beer for the band, except for the Jew back there. No beer for him!"[5] Sommerfeld walked off the stage, quitting the job on the spot.

Sommerfeld was out of work again, but not for long. In September 1933, he became the first of many unemployed Jewish orchestral musicians to find refuge in the Culture League of German Jews.

The Culture League of German Jews was founded in 1933 by Kurt Baumann, a twenty-six-year-old production assistant who had worked for the capital city's most prominent opera houses: the Berlin State Opera, the People's Theater, and the Municipal Opera. Baumann realized that the 175,000 Jews who lived in Berlin—approximately a third of Germany's Jewish population—could support their own cultural activities as well as any medium-sized city could. He worked out a plan for a Jewish culture league and presented it to his mentor Kurt Singer, a charismatic former deputy director of the Municipal Opera who had already been thinking along the same lines. Their plan was bold: to maintain a presence for Jewish culture in Germany while also providing modest incomes for out-of-work Jewish artists.

By May 1933, Baumann had convinced the Nazi authorities to allow him to create a league that would sponsor high-quality productions by Jewish musicians, actors, and lecturers. There were, of course, several stipulations designed to segregate what was happening in the Jewish community from the rest of Germany. The staff and presenters would be composed exclusively of Jews, and their activities would be reported only in the Jewish press. The audience would also be limited to Jews, who would be registered, monthly subscribers with photo identifications—no tickets could be sold at the door. The subscribers were especially important since the league would not receive the government subsidy enjoyed by Aryan organizations. The texts, music, and exhibits were increasingly limited to non-German works that had to be approved by the Interior Ministry at least one month in advance. In addition to gaining control over Jewish cultural activities, the Nazi authorities gained a valuable propaganda tool. Any international questions about Germany's treatment of the Jews could be answered by pointing to the cultural organization that the Nazis had created especially for the Jews.

By providing both culture and inspiration, the culture league became very popular within the city's Jewish community. By early 1934, the association had twenty thousand members. Audiences flocked to culture league performances to briefly escape the problems they increasingly faced in their daily lives. But the culture league provided much more than a diversion. It was a source of spiritual resistance in the face of Nazi oppression. "For those who played, it was something very special—after all, nothing else was available," violinist Henry Meyer explained. "We were born to perform and when we did that we really lived."[6]

The culture league in Berlin inspired offshoots in Frankfurt, Cologne, and Hamburg. While the Berlin league staged theatrical productions, operas, and orchestral concerts, the league in Frankfurt hosted only an orchestra. The leagues in Cologne and Hamburg limited their scopes to theatrical performances. Smaller league branches were also established in dozens of other German cities.

One of the musicians in the Frankfurt Culture League orchestra was Günther Goldschmidt. Günther was a flute student at the conservatory in Sondershausen before being expelled in 1934 because of his Jewish heritage. He transferred to the Karlsruhe music academy, but was removed a year and a half later for the same reason. Kicked out of school and unemployed, Günther agreed to play two concerts with the Frankfurt Culture League orchestra, substituting for its sick principal flutist, Erich Toeplitz. Günther escaped to Sweden shortly after the performances, but traveled back to Frankfurt six months later to permanently replace Toeplitz, who had immigrated to Palestine. Although it meant returning to Nazi Germany, Günther was eager to reunite with violinist and violist Rosemarie Gumpert. Günther and Rosemarie had met during Günther's first rehearsal with the Frankfurt orchestra. They had quickly fallen in love.

In 1935, the Nazi government consolidated all forty-six independent culture leagues under the umbrella of the Reich Association of Jewish Culture Leagues, with Singer as its leader. The change in name from the Culture League of German Jews to simply the Jewish Culture League reflected an increase in government-sponsored anti-Semitism. A person could either be a German or a Jew, the Nazis maintained, but there was no such thing as a "German Jew."

Of course, it was not just Jewish musicians who were subjected to escalating anti-Semitism. The Nazis were continuing to implement policies that discriminated against Jews in all walks of life. In September 1935, Nazi Germany further marginalized Jews by enacting the two notorious legal measures known as the Nuremberg Laws. The first, the Law for the Protection of German Blood and German Honor, prohibited marriages and extramarital intercourse between Germans and Jews. The second, the Reich Citizenship Law, robbed Jews of their German citizenships, stripping them of their rights and providing the legal justification for further ostracism. Jews lost access to state hospitals and universities. They were no longer allowed to enter public libraries, parks, and beaches. They were officially Germans no more.

In the years that followed the passage of the Nuremberg Laws, the culture leagues struggled to stay afloat. Their memberships dwindled as Jews continued to emigrate. Those who remained behind were increasingly unable to pay their monthly dues as new laws went into effect banning them from employment. By early 1938, at least half of

Jewish workers in Germany were out of work. In response to the shortage of subscribers, the Nazis shut down the various branches of the culture league throughout Germany, leaving intact only the original chapter in Berlin.

With the shuttering of the Frankfurt Culture League, Günther and Rosemarie joined the orchestra of the league in Berlin. Just as Günther had been able to join the Frankfurt orchestra when Erich Toeplitz had immigrated to Palestine, numerous departures from the Berlin orchestra had opened up positions there.

At that time, the Nazis were content to solve the "Jewish Question" by simply removing Jews from German society. The first step had been to segregate the Jews by removing them from public life and stripping them of their civil rights. The second step was to intimidate the Jews into leaving the country—a policy that ironically overlapped with that of the Zionists who dreamed of creating a Jewish nation in Palestine. It was not until 1942 that Nazi Germany would fully enact the "Final Solution to the Jewish Question" by annihilating the Jews who remained behind.

The problems of sustaining the culture league while so many of its members were emigrating can perhaps best be seen in the string of first-rate conductors who led the orchestra in Berlin. The first conductor was Michael Taube, who had served as Bruno Walter's assistant at the Berlin Municipal Opera. After Taube immigrated to Palestine at the end of 1934, Joseph Rosenstock took over. Rosenstock, who had succeeded Otto Klemperer at the

Wiesbaden State Opera before becoming the music director of the Mannheim National Opera, left for Japan in 1936, ultimately immigrating to the United States. He was succeeded by Hans Wilhelm Steinberg, who had previously directed the opera house in Frankfurt. Motivated by the success of the Berlin Culture League, Steinberg had founded its counterpart in Frankfurt in 1934 before transferring to Berlin. Steinberg conducted the Berlin Culture League orchestra for only three months before fleeing to Russia and then to Palestine. The ensemble's final conductor was Rudolf Schwarz, who had served as the music director at the state theater in Karlsruhe.

One of the most infamous anti-Semitic demonstrations during this period took place between November 9 and the morning of November 10, 1938. On that riotous night, Nazi Brownshirts stormed the streets shouting, "Perish, Jewry" and "Kill the Jews!"[7] They destroyed hundreds of synagogues, looted thousands of Jewish-owned businesses, and physically assaulted every Jew they could find. At least ninety-one Jews died that night. Another thirty thousand Jews—including Günther's father—were arrested and sent to the Buchenwald, Dachau, and Sachsenhausen concentration camps. The shattered glass on the ground reflected the flames of the burning buildings, earning the riots the name "Kristallnacht," or "Night of Broken Glass." The large-scale violence forced many European Jews—and the rest of the world—to finally start to grasp how ruthless the Nazi regime could truly be.

Nazi Germany's persecution of the Jews intensified

after Kristallnacht. Jews were no longer allowed to own businesses of any kind. They were forced to sell any land, stocks, jewels, and works of art for whatever prices they could manage. Jewish children were expelled from public schools. Jews were banned from attending public concerts, plays, movies, museums, and sports events. All Jewish newspapers and publishing houses were shut down. The culture league in Berlin became the only source of culture, entertainment, and news for Jews in all of Germany.

It was in this climate of increasing oppression that the Berlin Culture League orchestra continued to perform. Their concerts brought an ongoing sense of normalcy to the performers and audience members. The performances also provided a form of spiritual resistance—even if it was within a system tightly controlled by the Nazis. "This is why I practice, this is why I perform," Günther thought to himself. "This is what I'm meant to do. And for as long as I can, I must continue to make beautiful music. In an ugly time, the best protest is beauty."[8]

By 1941, the Jewish Culture League was on its last legs. The majority of the performers who were in the primes of their careers had left the country, leaving behind musicians who were unable to sustain the high quality of performances. Since Jewish musicians tended to prefer string instruments, it was especially difficult to find wind players to balance out the instrumentation. The audiences had also shrunk considerably, through emigration as well as through poverty and incarceration. Some musicians and audience members were murdered at the hands of the Nazis. Others, such as former Munich Philharmonic violinist Josef Lengsfeld, committed suicide. Fully immersed in a world war and no longer making a pretense of supporting Jewish society, the Nazis disbanded the culture league in August 1941.

By this time, Günther and Rosemarie had gotten married and had immigrated to the United States. An American benefactor had provided the required sponsorship by guaranteeing that they would be gainfully employed. He had even raised the six hundred dollars they had needed for the journey. A friend in the American embassy had helped them apply for visas. They had left Berlin on June 1, 1941, and had started their new lives in America three weeks later as George and Rosemary Goldsmith. They performed all over the country before settling down in Missouri, where Rosemary played with the St. Louis Symphony while George worked as a bookseller. In 1967, they moved to Ohio so Rosemary could join the venerable Cleveland Orchestra, a position she held until her retirement in 1981.

Bronisław Huberman

While Günther and Rosemarie were able to immigrate to the United States thanks to an American patron, a number of Jewish musicians and their family members were rescued from Nazi persecution by Jewish violinist Bronisław Huberman when he founded what is now the world-famous Israel Philharmonic Orchestra.

Born in Częstochowa, Poland, in 1882, Huberman established himself from a very young age as a violinist of extraordinary talent. He was six years old when he started taking lessons at the Warsaw Conservatory. By the age of ten he had been accepted as a pupil of the legendary violinist Joseph Joachim in Berlin. Huberman started touring Europe at the age of eleven, including a performance of Brahms's Violin Concerto in 1896 that impressed even the concerto's famously cynical composer. Huberman spent the next five decades touring the world. In addition to establishing himself as one of the most electrifying violinists of all time, he became beloved for his compassion and humanitarianism by performing free concerts for the poor and by organizing a benefit concert for the victims of the devastating earthquake and tsunami in Messina, Sicily, in 1908.

In the 1930s, Huberman committed himself to protesting the injustices of Nazism. When conductor Wilhelm Furtwängler invited him to appear with the Berlin Philharmonic, Huberman refused. "It is not a question of violin concertos nor even merely of the Jews," he explained in a letter to Furtwängler that he also released to the press. "The issue is the retention of those things that our fathers achieved by blood and sacrifice, of the elementary preconditions of our European culture, the freedom of personality and its unconditional self-responsibility unhampered by fetters of caste or race."[9] Huberman vowed to never set foot in Nazi Germany.

Huberman would later publish an open letter to German intellectuals in the British newspaper the *Manchester Guardian* that would become widely circulated throughout the world, even in Germany. The letter offered a scathing critique of not only the Nazi thugs directly responsible for heinous crimes against Jews, but also of the German intellectuals who were watching the injustices unfold without interfering. Huberman accused the Germans who were standing idly on the sidelines of being the ones who were the most culpable for Nazi crimes.

At the same time that he was becoming outraged by what was happening in Germany, Huberman was growing increasingly enchanted with Palestine.

Huberman had first performed in Tel Aviv in 1929. When he returned in 1931, even he was unable to articulate why he had come back, other than to say that he was hoping to strengthen the connection between Europe and the Jewish community in Palestine. By his third visit in 1934, when he gave twelve sold-out concerts over eighteen days, Huberman was clearly growing quite attached to Palestine—and vice versa. Huberman's enthusiasm for the Jews in Palestine was reinforced by the rise of anti-Semitism in Europe. While he had initially been skeptical of Zionism, he was now starting to see the Jewish colonization of Palestine as an extension of the European culture he loved rather than as an abandonment of it.

Huberman's newfound excitement for Palestine was also fueled by the remarkable enhancements to the music scene that had occurred over the preceding months. Thanks to a handful of professional musicians who had fled Nazi Germany, Tel Aviv now had a modest orchestra with which Huberman played concertos by Bach, Mozart, and Beethoven. One of the orchestra's conductors was Michael Taube, who had been the founding conductor of the Berlin Culture League orchestra. If a population could make such rapid progress in such a short time span, Huberman posited, then its potential for future greatness was unlimited.

Before leaving Palestine for the third time, Huberman penned a letter to Meir Dizengoff. In addition to serving as the first mayor of Tel Aviv, Dizengoff was the president of the Palestine Philharmonic Symphony Union, which sponsored the orchestra. In his lengthy missive, Huberman outlined a proposal to bolster the quality of the orchestra by hiring wind players from Germany. Recognizing that it would be impossible to pay a reputable conductor enough to spend the entire concert season in Palestine, Huberman recommended dividing the responsibilities among two or three Jewish conductors from Europe and the United States. He even contacted two of them: Issay Dobrowen, who was serving as the conductor of the San Francisco Symphony, and Hans Wilhelm Steinberg, who at that time was leading the culture league orchestra in Frankfurt. Huberman's letter to Dizengoff also proposed a number of bold initiatives, such as regular performances in Jerusalem and Haifa in addition to the primary concerts in Tel Aviv, as well as a concert tour of Egypt. In a discussion with other musicians, Huberman further recommended the creation of music schools that could cultivate homegrown talent.

After growing frustrated when Dizengoff and the other leaders of the Symphony Union did not agree with all his suggestions, Huberman did something even more audacious. He decided to establish his own orchestra. The historic opportunity was simply too good to pass up. First-rate musicians who had been dismissed from their positions in Europe were in desperate need of employment. Why not put those virtuosos to work in a new orchestra in Palestine?

Huberman envisioned a world-class orchestra composed exclusively of Jewish musicians. Such an ensemble, he maintained, would be the greatest weapon against the Nazis who were claiming that Jews were incapable of great art. "Can you imagine a pro-Jewish or pro-Zionist propaganda more effective than a concert tour of the Palestine Orchestra, undertaken in a couple of years throughout the civilized world and acclaimed both by Jews and by gentiles as amongst the best in existence?" he asked. "To beat the world campaign of anti-Semitism it is not enough to create material and idealistic prosperity in Palestine, we must create there new gospels and carry them throughout the world. And the symphony orchestra, as I visualize it, would be perhaps the first and easiest step towards that highest aim of Jewish humanity."[10]

Huberman's return to Palestine in December 1935 increased his eagerness to create an orchestra for the Jewish pioneers. Over the course of two recitals in Tel Aviv, he performed for three thousand audience members. The first performance was for classical music aficionados. The second was for common laborers, who, Huberman was happy to note, were just as enthusiastic and respectful as any audience. He later remarked that he had never felt so proud of being Jewish as he was during his performance for the workers. Indeed, it was this music-loving environment that made Palestine so endearing. Huberman estimated that the percentage of concertgoers within the general public was six to eight times higher within the Jewish community of Palestine than it was in European cities.

By this time, Huberman had fleshed out his plans for the Palestine Orchestra, which he shared with the *New York Times* in a February 9, 1936, article titled "Orchestra of Exiles." The ensemble's first concert would take place that October 24 in Tel Aviv. The ambitious concert season that followed would include sixty concerts over the next eight months in Tel Aviv, Jerusalem, and Haifa, in addition to twenty concerts in smaller agricultural communities. Each program in the larger cities would be performed twice: once for affluent subscribers and once for common laborers. Adolf Busch—a non-Jewish virtuoso violinist who had left his German homeland several years earlier in protest of the Nazi regime—had agreed to appear as a soloist during the first season. Other leading artists were being invited.

By performing for workers and insisting that his new orchestra do the same, Huberman provided a fascinating insight into his beliefs on the role of music in public life. He took a very democratic approach by maintaining that everyone—regardless of income—should have equal access to great music. He was especially careful to contend that performances for common laborers should be held to the same high standards as those for elite subscribers. The only difference between the two should be the price of admission. While many of his contemporaries felt that concerts for workers could be taken less seriously, Huberman believed the opposite to be true. Musically educated listeners are capable of enjoying substandard interpretations because they have the training to focus less on the skill of the performer and more on the craft of the composer, he argued. It is the untrained ear that is in the greatest need of flawless performances.

Two weeks after reporting the creation of the Palestine Orchestra, the *New York Times* publicized Huberman's greatest coup of all: Arturo Toscanini, the conductor of the New York Philharmonic, who was widely considered to be one of the finest musicians in the world, would lead the first performances of the Palestine Orchestra. Toscanini had refused to conduct in his homeland of Italy ever since the rise of fascism there. In addition to boycotting Nazi Germany, he was also speaking out about the country's persecution of the Jews. As Huberman pointed out, Toscanini's decision to conduct for the nascent Jewish community in Palestine while refusing to set foot in the culturally advanced countries of Italy and Germany constituted "a historical mark both in the struggle against Nazism and in the upbuilding of Palestine."[11]

On April 20, Huberman created yet another buzz about the creation of his new orchestra by announcing that Toscanini would be conducting two movements from Mendelssohn's incidental music to *A Midsummer Night's Dream*. This represented yet another protest of Nazi discrimination. The musicians who had been expelled by the Nazis would be playing music that had been banned by the Nazis.

In his discussions with the conductors who would lead the Palestine Orchestra, Huberman expressed an interest in pieces by Jewish composers, although such works would only end up constituting a very small percentage of the orchestra's repertoire. Huberman was, however, very deliberate in discouraging the conductors from programming pieces by composers with connections to the Nazi regime. When one conductor suggested a piece by the controversial German composer Richard Strauss, Huberman forbade it, writing, "We cannot hold a place for a man who, on the one hand has a Jewish daughter-in-law and a Jewish librettist, but on the other hand for materialistic reasons served as president of the Nazi's Reich Chamber of Music until the moment they kicked him out."[12]

As the excitement about the orchestra intensified, Huberman increased his efforts to raise money for the ensemble. During a concert tour of the United States, he traveled to Seattle, Los Angeles, and San Francisco, performing, organizing fund-raising committees, and collecting donations. On March 30, 1936, he attended a fund-raising banquet that was hosted by Albert Einstein, who also wrote personal letters on Huberman's behalf soliciting donations. Huberman canceled several European concerts

to continue his fund-raising efforts for three weeks after
the Einstein dinner. By the time he left the country on
April 23, he had raised $15,500 in donations, $2,000 in
allocations, and $7,000 in pledges. This was a consider-
able amount of money, considering that the average yearly
family income in the United States was $1,524. Huberman
felt that if he had stayed in America for one more week he
could have raised another $10,000.

Recruiting the Musicians

Huberman's successful fund-raising changed his plans for
recruiting musicians. At first he had planned to hire string
players who were already in Palestine and focus his efforts
on attracting Jewish wind players from Europe. But by
1935, Huberman had raised so much money that he decided to also replace the string players in Palestine with
the very best ones from Europe. "From now on, only truly
first-class musicians will be considered," he resolved.[13] In
addition to reaching a musical goal by raising the quality
of the ensemble, recruiting string players would serve a
humanitarian function by providing employment to Jewish string players who were out of work in Europe.

When Toscanini signed on to conduct the orchestra,
Huberman had to raise his sights even higher. Huberman had originally planned for an orchestra of around
sixty musicians, which would suffice for works from the
eighteenth century and early nineteenth century. But
Toscanini was likely to program masterworks from the

late nineteenth and early twentieth centuries that would require a larger ensemble. Asking Toscanini to conduct an incomplete orchestra was out of the question, so Huberman was compelled to increase the size of the ensemble from sixty to seventy-five musicians.

Since Huberman refused to return to Germany for any reason, he put Hans Wilhelm Steinberg in charge of selecting German musicians for the orchestra. Steinberg had conducted the culture league orchestras in Frankfurt and Berlin. He therefore had contacts in two ensembles that had already amassed outstanding Jewish musicians. Joining the Palestine Orchestra ended up saving these musicians' lives. Many of the culture league musicians who remained behind perished in the Holocaust.

One of the musicians Steinberg recruited from the Berlin Culture League was trombonist Heinrich Schiefer. Born and raised in Berlin, Schiefer had made a living in his hometown by playing in coffeehouses, in silent-movie theaters, and in the German Film Orchestra before being dismissed from all of his positions in 1933. After accepting various jobs in Spain, the Netherlands, and Switzerland, Schiefer joined the Berlin Culture League orchestra in 1934. But by March 1936, the increasing discrimination had convinced him to leave Germany for good.

Schiefer auditioned for Steinberg in Berlin's elegant Hotel Fürstenhof that May. The entire process lasted just five minutes. Steinberg asked Schiefer to perform an excerpt from Wagner's opera *Tristan und Isolde* that Schiefer had never seen before. After listening to Schiefer's interpretation, Steinberg had him play it again. This time Steinberg conducted Schiefer to see if he could adjust to Steinberg's interpretation. That was all Steinberg needed to hear.

Steinberg accepted Schiefer into the orchestra on the spot, but the trombonist already had two other job offers on the table. One was from a former colleague from Berlin who was starting a jazz band in Argentina. The other was from a symphony orchestra in Baku, the capital of the Azerbaijan Soviet Socialist Republic. Two of Schiefer's colleagues from the Berlin Culture League orchestra joined the jazz band in South America, but Schiefer opted to join Huberman's orchestra. He was convinced by Steinberg's urgings, as well as by the prospect of later bringing his parents to Palestine. "Enough with the jazz and communists," his father advised him. "Stick with the Jews."[14]

Another performer from Berlin was Horst Salomon. Salomon had studied the French horn at the music conservatory in Berlin for five years before the purging of the conservatory's Jews in the spring of 1933 had prohibited him from taking the final examination. He joined the Berlin Culture League orchestra that fall as principal horn and played under Steinberg's baton. Since Steinberg was already familiar with Salomon's playing, the hornist was admitted into the Palestine Orchestra without an audition.

In addition to Schiefer and Salomon, Steinberg was able to recruit violinist Basia Polischuk and percussionist Kurt Sommerfeld from the Berlin Culture League orchestra. As with Salomon, Steinberg vouched for Sommerfeld's playing and waived his audition. From the orchestra in

Frankfurt came clarinetist Heinrich Zimmermann, violinist Rudolf Bergmann, violist Dora Loeb, and cellist Ary Schuyer, as well as bassist Ernst Böhm, who had joined the ensemble after being fired from the West German Radio Orchestra.

Also recruited from the Frankfurt orchestra was flutist Erich Toeplitz. Toeplitz was studying piano and music education at the music conservatory in Cologne when that institution expelled its Jewish students in 1933. He was readmitted shortly afterward under a quota system, but was isolated and ostracized by his Nazi schoolmates. He made up his mind to leave Germany as soon as he completed his studies.

To make himself more employable, Toeplitz started taking lessons on the flute, an instrument he had played informally since his childhood. In the spring of 1934, he answered an advertisement for the new culture league orchestra in Frankfurt. He auditioned in Cologne and was appointed principal flutist. A year later, he heard a rumor that Huberman was starting an orchestra in Palestine. He asked Steinberg to recommend him. Steinberg replied that he had already done so, and that Toeplitz would be given a position. When Toeplitz left Frankfurt, he was replaced in the culture league orchestra by Günther Goldschmidt.

The relationship between the culture league orchestras and the Palestine Orchestra was friendly at first. There was even talk of having the Berlin orchestra visit Palestine and for the Palestine Orchestra to undertake a tour of Jewish communities in Germany. Not surprisingly, this idea was quickly rebuffed by Huberman. "I am utterly opposed to giving concerts in Germany, in the same way that I am opposed to collaborating with Jewish institutions of the German ghetto in general," he maintained. "Besides, it would be against my sense of self respect to ask permission from the German authorities and then get denied. As far as I am concerned, the entire idea is out of the question."[15]

Kurt Singer and other culture league leaders later sent a telegram to the Palestine Orchestra congratulating them on their inaugural performance. But the goodwill would not last long. As the Palestine Orchestra continued to recruit musicians from the culture leagues, Singer naturally became resentful of having his musicians poached by a foreign orchestra. He was also rightfully worried about the future of his ensemble. "Everything now depends on keeping our orchestra intact," Singer wrote to Sommerfeld, who had already immigrated to Palestine to join the orchestra. "For this reason I have addressed an urgent appeal to your conductor, my friend Steinberg, requesting that no more musicians from our orchestra be recruited to Palestine. We can barely find young talent in Germany anymore, and I do not want to unnecessarily complicate the work of our hard working and highly talented [conductor] Rudolf Schwarz."[16]

Huberman himself conducted the auditions in Vienna. Although Austria was still independent of Nazi Germany, anti-Semitism was on the rise. Both the Vienna Philharmonic and the Vienna Symphony retained their Jewish musicians, but had stopped accepting additional Jews into their ensembles. In response to the growing anti-Semitism, Huberman gave up his residency at Vienna's Hetzendorf Castle and discontinued his masterclass at the Vienna State Academy in the summer of 1936. He then appointed three of his finest masterclass students—Heinrich Haftel, David Grünschlag, and Alfred Lunger—to the first violin section of the Palestine Orchestra.

For the initial screenings of musicians from Warsaw, Huberman turned to Jacob Surowicz, a violinist in the Warsaw Philharmonic Orchestra. At first, Surowicz assumed that Huberman was interested in his orchestra's section members. He asked whether the very best musicians in his orchestra should also audition for the Palestine Orchestra. Huberman smiled and responded, "not also, but *only* the very best musicians should apply."[17] Huberman was committed to establishing an ensemble that would rival the top two or three orchestras in Europe. Surowicz himself ended up joining the Palestine Orchestra, along with six of his colleagues from the Warsaw Philharmonic.

Instead of waiting for Huberman to come to them, several musicians traveled to Palestine in the hopes of auditioning for him there. Not knowing Huberman's travel schedule, they arrived on tourist visas that sometimes expired before they had the chance to meet him. To them, it was well worth the risk. A successful audition carried with it the promise of a permanent visa. During Huberman's successful tour of Palestine in December 1935, musicians waited for him in hotel lobbies, hoping for auditions. Although Huberman's schedule was already full, he made time to hear them all.

The Palestine Orchestra provided a safe haven for musicians who were already planning on leaving Europe, as well as for a few performers who otherwise may have never considered emigrating. Eighteen-year-old Hungarian violinist Lorand Fenyves did not even know what he was auditioning for when his teacher Jenő Hubay told him to play for Huberman. Several days later, Fenyves received a telegram from Huberman instructing him to be ready to leave for Palestine within a week. Fenyves's parents wanted him to honor the contract he had already signed to become the concertmaster of the Gothenburg Symphony in Sweden, but conductor Felix Weingartner convinced him to not pass up the once-in-a-lifetime opportunity to play with the best Jewish performers from Europe under Toscanini's baton. Lorand's sister Alice Fenyves came with him to Palestine, joining the orchestra's viola section.

Although Huberman was not able to attract every musician he wanted to join his orchestra, the performing backgrounds of those he was able to recruit were remarkable. Of the seventy musicians who are listed in the orchestra's first program, fifty-two had once been members of leading orchestras such as the Budapest Philharmonic, Leipzig Gewandhaus Orchestra, Vienna Concert Orchestra, and Warsaw Philharmonic. Of those fifty-two, an impressive thirty had held leadership positions in their orchestras. The final roster of musicians would include performers from Argentina, Austria, Czechoslovakia, France, Germany, Hungary, Italy, Latvia, the Netherlands, Poland, Russia, Switzerland, the United States, and Yugoslavia. Huberman was creating not just an orchestra of exiles, but an orchestra of all-stars.

Huberman was also aware that he was doing more than just building a world-class orchestra. He was saving lives. When the president of the Hebrew University of Jerusalem expressed concern about the long-term viability of the orchestra, Huberman countered by outlining a rationale for bringing musicians to Palestine under any economic circumstances. "Why should we dread to think of that future when the present state of about fifty musicians (out of the seventy-five to compose the orchestra) is right now worse off in Germany and Poland than we could imagine them at the worst in Palestine?" he asked.[18]

Immigration Visas

Once the musicians had been recruited, all that was left was to secure immigration visas for the orchestra members and their families. This turned out to be much more difficult than Huberman had anticipated. It also proved to be the most important thing he accomplished.

Jewish immigration to Palestine had been on the rise ever since the British government—which had controlled the territory since 1917—had issued the Balfour Declaration on November 2, 1917. This was the document that confirmed England's support for the establishment of a national home for Jews in Palestine. In the 1920s, the British had issued unlimited immigration visas to Zionists from all over Europe, as well as to Jews fleeing persecution in Poland and Russia.

By 1929 tensions between the Jews and Arabs in Palestine had escalated into Arab attacks on Jews and Jewish property. England had responded with the Passfield White Paper of 1930, which had called for a limit to Jewish immigration. Since then, the British government had scaled back the number of visas it allocated to the Jewish Agency for Palestine, the organization responsible for coordinating Jewish immigration. The Jewish Agency was forced to adopt a selective policy that carefully scrutinized every candidate for immigration, including the musicians who were coming to Palestine for Huberman's orchestra.

Had the musicians been wealthy, there would not have been any problems with securing visas. The Jewish Agency was granting unlimited visas to "capitalists" who owned assets totaling at least 1,000 Palestinian pounds. At the time, this was equivalent to approximately 20,000 reichsmarks—a good deal of money considering that members of the Berlin Culture League were only making around 200 reichsmarks a month. Huberman was well aware that musicians were unlikely to have that kind of money. He quickly dismissed the capitalist certificates as an option. He preferred to find a solution that would not cause financial difficulties for members of the orchestra. He was specifically interested in workers certificates, which allowed their holders to also bring their spouses and underage children.

In the absence of potential applicants who would qualify as capitalists, the Jewish Agency only agreed to offer the musicians visas for one year. The agency believed that the performers would not want to stay in the country for very long. They preferred to award the few permanent visas they had been allocated to workers who would be more likely to settle in Palestine. This was another plan that Huberman found to be unacceptable. He insisted that he could not ask musicians to leave their jobs and homes in Europe and move their families and belongings to Palestine without securing full immigration rights. To make matters worse, a temporary visa would require the musicians to pay customs charges on their families' furniture. If this was the only option, Huberman threatened, then he would not proceed any further with his plans to establish an orchestra.

Throughout the process of securing immigration visas for the musicians, Huberman was always careful to look out for their families. When Polish musicians were struggling to cover the cost of moving their families, Huberman arranged for the orchestra to pay for half of the travel expenses of their wives and children. Those who could not afford to pay the other half of the expenses would receive it from the orchestra as an advance. Knowing that the initial costs of moving were the greatest, Huberman deducted the advance from the musician's salary in ten monthly installments, starting with the third month of employment. Musicians with children even received an increase in salary of half a pound per child every month.

While Huberman was struggling to find an answer to the visa problem, another development threatened to put an end to his plans: the escalation of the conflict between the Arabs and the Jews in Palestine. Another Arab revolt had begun on April 21, 1936, after six rival Arab leaders had come together to rally against the continuation of mass Jewish immigration. A general strike and a boycott of Jewish businesses quickly intensified into a severe economic and political crisis, as well as bloody attacks on the Jews and the British. The British authorities responded by further restricting the number of visas they would issue for the remainder of the year and by calling in military reinforcements from Egypt and Malta.

Concerned about bringing musicians to Palestine in the middle of a civil war, Huberman had no choice but to delay the orchestra's first concert. After learning that Arab unrest tended to subside in November, when the Arabs had to return to work for the beginning of the orange-picking season, Huberman postponed the inaugural performance from October 24 to December 26. The first rehearsal was also delayed for two months, from early September to early November.

In the meantime, the Jewish Agency continued to propose solutions to the problem of immigration visas. One idea was to offer temporary visas that were valid for two years instead of one, but Huberman again insisted on permanent visas. Another suggestion was to admit the musicians as "small capitalists" whose instruments would be accepted as proof that they owned assets worth at least 250 Palestinian pounds (5,000 reichsmarks). Huberman rejected this as well, since some musicians did not possess their own instruments. Those who did would not be able to pretend that their instruments were anywhere near that valuable.

Failure was not an option. As Huberman explained to Chaim Weizmann, the president of the World Zionist Organization and the future first president of Israel, an inability to help the musicians immigrate would not just embarrass the Zionist community but would hand the Nazis an unexpected victory.

It was not until August 11, after the British high commissioner for Palestine intervened on Huberman's behalf, that the Immigration Office announced that the Jewish Agency would receive forty visas specifically earmarked for musicians of Huberman's choosing, along with those musicians' wives and children. By the end of the month, the British authorities would also approve visas for the parents and siblings of members of the orchestra. Additionally, workers visas were granted to musicians' adult children over the course of September. Once Huberman exceeded his allocation of forty permanent visas, he completed the orchestra with musicians on one-year visas that were converted into permanent visas in the following year.

The significance of solving the immigration problem cannot be understated. Through his uncompromising dedication, Huberman had saved an entire orchestra of musicians and their families from Nazi tyranny. Without his help, they may have never been able to leave Europe. The vast majority of them might very well have died in the Holocaust.

The Musicians Arrive

Although the musicians had been guaranteed their visas, it was still not clear when they would arrive in Palestine. Rumors were rampant in the summer of 1936 that the British were going to capitulate to Arab demands that all Jewish immigration be suspended. This prompted Zionist offices throughout Europe to start urging all prospective immigrants to leave immediately. Huberman considered asking the musicians to move up their arrival dates to early September, but this would have created a financial crisis. The musicians would not have been able to support themselves and their families without getting paid for the two months prior to the first rehearsals. Once again, the high commissioner came to Huberman's defense by promising him that the musicians would be able to immigrate in October regardless of any changes to England's overall immigration policies.

All of this uncertainty caused a great amount of confusion and anxiety among the musicians. Erich Toeplitz had yet to receive a contract on July 15, 1936, when he received a letter from Huberman announcing that the first rehearsals and performance had been postponed by two months. Two weeks later, another letter inquired whether it would be possible for Toeplitz to leave prior to November 1. One week after that, a third letter informed Toeplitz that there was no need to arrive early, after all. It was not until September 1 that a contract was sent.

Toeplitz finally arrived at the Palestinian port of Haifa on November 2, along with ten other musicians from Austria and Germany. They had sailed aboard the SS *Tel Aviv*, which was making its final journey from Italy to Palestine. Like so many other Jewish enterprises during that time, the Palestine Shipping Company, which owned the ocean liner, had proved to be a failed venture. At least the trip had been a success. During the voyage, many of the musicians had come together for a benefit concert for the Jewish National Fund, which financed the purchase of land in Palestine.

At Haifa, the musicians boarded a bus to Tel Aviv, which was no easy journey in those days. Since there was no direct road along the coast from Haifa to Tel Aviv, the bus had to travel through the Arab-controlled West Bank. Their journey had already been delayed for two months by the Arab revolt. Now they were heading into Arab territory during a general strike. The Arabs were protesting the signing of the Balfour Declaration exactly nineteen years earlier. To the musicians who were accustomed to the cosmopolitan atmosphere of European capitals, even the desolate, rocky landscape across which the bus traveled seemed hostile.

When the musicians reached Tel Aviv, everything changed. After living in constant fear in Europe and traveling through the unwelcoming West Bank, they gazed at the blooming citrus groves and the young people strolling leisurely through the streets. The disparity in the landscape reminded the musicians of how far the Jewish community in Palestine had come in such a short time. It was in this same pioneering spirit that Huberman had established a major symphony orchestra in less than three years.

In addition to quickly familiarizing themselves with a new location with tropical weather and exotic food, the musicians had to acclimate to each other in a very short period of time. Every orchestra has a distinct sound that allows careful listeners to distinguish one ensemble from the others. When a new musician joins an orchestra, he or she has to quickly adapt to the practices of the existing ensemble to blend into that sound. In this case, the entire orchestra was composed of musicians from different countries, with dissimilar educational backgrounds, who had never played together before, and who did not even speak a common language. It was no easy task to achieve a uniform sound in the weeks prior to Toscanini's arrival.

At first the orchestra rehearsed in smaller sections: strings, woodwinds, and brass. This allowed the individual instrument families to establish their own sounds. It also gave the city of Tel Aviv the time it needed to complete their concert hall. The presence of a professional symphony orchestra and the appearance of superstar conductor Arturo Toscanini required a stage and a seating capacity larger than had ever existed in Palestine. To accommodate this demand, the 1,500-seat exhibition hall in which Huberman had performed in December 1935 was combined with an adjacent hall to form one concert hall that could seat 2,500 audience members. The creation of such a hall in such a short time span represented yet another testimony to the passion and resourcefulness of the Jewish community.

On December 4, the orchestra moved into the new hall and finally played together for the first time. United in exile, the musicians started to sense the strong collaborative relationship that results in a cohesive sound. But there were concerns about the acoustics in the hall. Huberman was concerned that the first violins—which by all rights should have been the strongest section in a Jewish orchestra—were not projecting properly. They tried raising the chairs, but this did not help. The problem persisted until Toscanini arrived one week prior to the inaugural concert. He seemed to fix the problem by lowering the chairs, but it was difficult for the musicians to tell whether the sound improved because of the new seating arrangement or because of Toscanini's inspirational conducting. Regardless, Toscanini wasted little time in developing a beautiful orchestral sound, accomplishing in one week what usually takes many years.

Up until Toscanini's arrival, the orchestra had been conducted by Steinberg, who at Huberman's insistence had been drilling the orchestra over the course of more than sixty rehearsals in less than two months. Despite such a great amount of preparation, everyone was still nervous about Toscanini's arrival. The conductor was legendary for temperamental outbursts. The musicians were worried about how he would react to their imperfections.

Many skeptical musicians and community members were convinced that Toscanini would leave after the first rehearsal, if he came at all. But Toscanini was patient with the eager performers as they learned how to play together. According to one musician, Toscanini found the Palestine Orchestra to be more responsive to his instructions than the established ensembles he usually conducted.

At first, Toscanini simply listened as he conducted Brahms's Second Symphony, which was the first piece he had chosen to rehearse. As the first movement unfolded, he started to interact with the musicians in his native language of Italian, occasionally mixed with German. "Oboe: singing!" "Trumpet: a little louder" "A little softer . . . shh . . . shh . . . piano, piano, pianissimo." By the second movement, the orchestra already sounded completely different. In the third movement, Toscanini started to demand perfection. He spent several minutes with the oboist on the grace note that precedes the third note in the very first measure. Again and again he called out, "Music is not played, it is sung, it is sung!" To make his point, he sang along with the orchestra, placing his hand on his chest when the orchestra did not meet his high standards. In the fourth movement, he chastised the ensemble for not playing fast enough, rapping his baton on his music stand and crying out, "Follow, follow!" As the rehearsal continued, Toscanini became increasingly animated, stomping his feet to spur the violinists into playing "with fire" and yelling "macaroni pie" when they got lost.[19] The antics worked. The entire orchestra sounded better than ever.

The success of Toscanini's first rehearsal generated a great deal of excitement in the Jewish community of Palestine. Skeptics who had previously been reluctant to purchase tickets now stormed the box office, snatching up all of the subscription tickets and available seats. The demand was so great that the police were brought in to protect the orchestra staff from the mob of ticket seekers. "What has been happening around the Toscanini concerts these past few days was to a large extent not enthusiasm, but a psychosis," wrote one member of the orchestra staff. "At times I have gotten the impression that the individuals involved have lost track of what they are asking for as they scream, beg, and threaten."[20] The plans for the seating in the new hall were continually revised to squeeze in more audience members.

The public's overwhelming interest and the orchestra's proficiency in the earliest rehearsals convinced Toscanini to open up the final two rehearsals to agricultural workers, as well as to musicians, teachers, actors, and writers. The colonists were moved to tears by what they heard. They had never dreamed that their adopted homeland would be able to assemble an orchestra of such renowned musicians. They could have never imagined that Toscanini would conduct the opening concerts.

The first official performance of the Palestine Orchestra took place in the evening of December 26, 1936. The hall was packed with 2,500 audience members, including British and Jewish luminaries from Tel Aviv, Jerusalem, Haifa, and elsewhere throughout Palestine. Several hundred music lovers stood in the drizzling rain outside of the auditorium, pressing themselves against the wall and even climbing onto the roof to hear the concert. They had come to witness the birth of their orchestra under the baton of the celebrated conductor Arturo Toscanini. They were not disappointed.

When Toscanini took the stage, he was welcomed with a thunderous standing ovation. Then the concert began.

The first piece on the program was Rossini's Overture to *The Silken Ladder*, a work with fiendishly difficult violin parts that showed Toscanini's faith in his first violins. The entire orchestra rose to the challenge. Next were the two German masterpieces: Brahms's Second Symphony and Schubert's *Unfinished* Symphony, in which the musicians played at their very best. As a calculated protest of Nazi Germany's prohibition against Jewish composers, Toscanini followed Brahms and Schubert with the Nocturne and Scherzo from Mendelssohn's *A Midsummer Night's Dream*.

The audience listened in silent admiration and then responded to each piece with prolonged applause and shouts of "bravissimo!" When the concert concluded with Weber's *Oberon* Overture, the orchestra received yet another standing ovation. The only sour moment came when Toscanini was angered by a photographer's flashes and refused to return to the stage for the curtain calls the audience enthusiastically demanded.

It was perhaps the musicians who were most thrilled with the performance. After being dismissed from the orchestral positions they had earned through years of practice, after being unemployed and humiliated, and after moving their entire families to a strange country, they were not just making music again. They were doing so under the baton of a true master. "Under his conducting problem spots simply disappear. The music rises and falls, sings and laughs, thrills our hearts and brings us to tears," wrote cellist Thelma Yellin. "We play as never before. It sounds as if we—the Palestine Orchestra—have been playing together for years, not weeks. The eyes of those of us who hold music dearest of all are wet with tears. We have finally arrived at our destination: we have become an instrument in the hands of the greatest artist of our time."[21]

Ever since its first concert, the orchestra has continued to be the crown jewel of Israeli culture. By giving exceptional performances for subscription holders and workers alike in Tel Aviv, Haifa, and Jerusalem, as well as in various settlements throughout the country, the orchestra quickly became the pride and joy of the Jewish community in Palestine. When the State of Israel declared its independence in 1948, the orchestra was there to perform "Hatikvah" (The Hope), the nineteenth-century Zionist hymn that had become Israel's national anthem. Today the orchestra that is now known as the Israel Philharmonic Orchestra is widely recognized as one of the very best orchestras in the world—just as Huberman intended it to be.

But the ensemble's greatest legacy can be found in the

lives it saved during the Holocaust. By helping the musicians as well as their family members immigrate to Palestine, Huberman saved an estimated one thousand lives between 1935 and 1939.

The Wagner Violin

Many orchestra members brought top-quality, German-made instruments with them to Palestine. After the war, when they learned of the atrocities that the Germans had committed during the Holocaust, they refused to play on their instruments any longer. They simply did not want to have anything to do with Germany ever again. This included continuing the unofficial ban that had been in place since Kristallnacht on playing the music of Richard Wagner, whose anti-Semitic writings and nationalist compositions had become powerful symbols of the Nazi regime.

Several violinists destroyed their German instruments. Others sold theirs for pittances to Moshe Weinstein, who could not bear to think of any instruments being damaged—even German ones. The first violin Moshe purchased was made by the eighteenth-century German violinmaker Benedict Wagner. "Not only was it made in Germany, but the maker's name is Wagner," its owner complained, even though the two Wagners were not related. "If you don't buy it from me I'm going to throw it away."

Unsellable in Israel, the violins remained in Moshe's workshop until they were passed to Amnon. By the time Amnon took over the business in 1986, 52 of the 110 violins in the shop's inventory were German, as were 16 of the 19 violas and 12 of the 19 cellos. In the 1990s, Amnon became curious about the Wagner Violin and the other German instruments his father had purchased decades earlier but had never sold. He realized that, contrary to modern opinion, the German instruments were just as good as those made in Italy and France at the same time. Moreover, the German virtuosos who had founded the Palestine Orchestra had actually preferred violins made in Germany over the ones made elsewhere, even though there was no difference in price—at least before the Holocaust.

So why did Italian and French violins eclipse German instruments in prestige and cost in the second half of the twentieth century? The answer is simple. The market for musical instruments is driven by demand, and that demand is based on the types of instruments played by the leading virtuosos. Since the greatest violinists tended to be Jews who would only play on instruments made in Italy or France, the rest of the music world followed suit, creating a run on those instruments and ignoring their German counterparts. Today, German instruments are sold at fractions of the prices demanded by comparable instruments that just happened to be made in Italy or France.

In 1999, at the invitation of a German bowmaker who had seen the German violins in the Weinstein collection, Amnon gave a lecture on his German instruments at a conference in Dresden for the Association of German Violinmakers and Bowmakers. The success of the presentation and Amnon's insatiable curiosity inspired him to begin searching for other violins with connections to the Holocaust.

This was the start of the Violins of Hope project.

2

ERICH
WEININGER'S
VIOLIN

The Beau Bassin Boys, ca. 1941–45. Erich Weininger is the violinist on the far left. *(Courtesy of the Ghetto Fighters' House Museum, Israel.)*

Butcher and amateur violinist Erich Weininger was twenty-five years old and living in Vienna on March 11, 1938, when Austrian chancellor Kurt Schuschnigg delivered an earth-shattering address over the radio. In a trembling voice, Schuschnigg announced that he would be resigning and handing over power to the Nazis. Schuschnigg's efforts to suppress the rise of Austrian Nazism had failed, as had his attempts to establish peace with Hitler. With no foreign powers willing to come to Austria's aid, Schuschnigg had no choice but to peacefully surrender to the Nazis in the hopes of avoiding a bloody German invasion. Schuschnigg bade farewell to his country with the words "God save Austria!"[22]

The radio followed Schuschnigg's address with the theme from the slow movement of Haydn's String Quartet in C Major, op. 76, no. 3. The melody is one that Haydn wrote in 1797 in honor of Holy Roman Emperor Francis II. In 1938, the tune served as the national anthems of both Austria and Germany. Austrians who were hoping to avoid being annexed by Nazi Germany would have instantly noted the irony of broadcasting a song they knew to begin with the words "Blessed be, without end, wonderful homeland." Pro-German Nazis no doubt appreciated the manifestation of the song they knew as "Germany, Germany, above all."

The German army marched into Austria later that

night, but by that time the Nazi takeover was already complete. Immediately after the closing bars of Haydn's anthem, Austrian Nazis took to the streets, shouting and waiving swastika flags. "One people, one Reich, one Führer," they chanted. "Die, Jews!"[23]

The Nazi marauders commandeered Jewish-owned vehicles and businesses. They vandalized Jewish homes and shops. They grabbed Jews off the streets, pushed them onto their hands and knees on the sidewalks, and forced them to scrub away the slogans for Austrian independence that had been painted there just days earlier. "At last, the Jews are working," the mob taunted. "We thank our Führer, who has created work for the Jews!"[24]

The anti-Semitic regulations that the Nazis had systematically implemented in Germany over the previous five years were extended into Austria virtually overnight. Jews could neither attend schools and universities nor practice any professions. They were forced to relinquish their businesses and property for compensation that was nominal at best. They were forbidden from eating at public restaurants, visiting public baths, entering public parks, and going to public theaters, and were regularly subjected to ridicule and intimidation. Over the next three months, seventy thousand Austrian Jews were arrested, principally in Vienna. Most were harassed and tortured for a few hours or days before being released.

The Nazis quickly began turning their attention from humiliating and terrorizing the Jews to expelling them from Austria. On April 1, all of the prominent Jewish leaders in Vienna were sent to the Dachau concentration camp. In May and June, an additional two thousand Jewish intellectuals who had been specifically targeted by the Nazis were arrested, beaten, and placed on three trains to Dachau. This included Erich Weininger, who arrived at the concentration camp on June 3, 1938.

Dachau

One of the first Nazi concentration camps, Dachau was established in March 1933, just weeks after Hitler came to power in Germany. The camp was constructed on the site of an abandoned World War I munitions factory ten miles northwest of Munich. Initially built to accommodate five thousand German inmates, its original detainees were political prisoners such as communists and social democrats. The ranks soon grew to incorporate other factions that the Nazis deemed undesirable, including homosexuals, Roma (Gypsies), and Jehovah's Witnesses. When Erich arrived in Dachau, he was among the first non-Germans to be detained in a concentration camp. He was also among the first to be imprisoned simply for being Jewish.

Erich was arrested by the Austrian police at the end of May along with several hundred other Jews, including the famous psychologist Bruno Bettelheim and the composer and conductor Herbert Zipper. They were taken to a detention center in a converted school on Karajan Street—named after the personal physician of Emperor Franz Joseph I who was the father of the already famous conductor Herbert von Karajan. They expected to be released within a couple of hours or days, as many of them had been after previous arrests. But this time, they would not be allowed to return home.

After a few days, the Jews were loaded into police vans and taken to Vienna's western train station. When the van doors flew open, they were greeted by SS guards who ordered them to run. The Nazis savagely struck the prisoners with fists, clubs, whips, rifle butts, and bayonets. They corralled them through the station and toward a train, dragging anyone who stumbled by the hair. Those who resisted were shot. Those who survived sustained serious injuries. Bettelheim was savagely beaten in the head and stabbed with a bayonet. Zipper suffered severe facial trauma and two broken ribs.

It took thirteen hours for the train to travel the three hundred miles to Munich. The trip was continually interrupted for sessions of torturous exercise and brutal beatings. The passengers were ordered to sit up straight with their hands on their laps. They were forced to stare straight into blinding lights that hung from the ceiling. Several faltered during the night and were beaten or shot to death. When the train arrived in Munich the next morning, the Jews were packed into cattle cars—150 in each car—for the final leg of the train ride to Dachau.

Upon their arrival in the concentration camp, the prisoners were stripped of their remaining possessions, shaved, and dressed in ill-fitting striped uniforms. Prisoner life was governed by very strict rules. Breaking them would result in severe punishment. "Everything in Dachau is prohibited," the camp commandant announced. "Even life itself."[25] Although Dachau was technically an internment center and not a death camp, its prisoners were subjected to starvation, beatings, torture, and grueling forced labor. During the Holocaust, at least 31,591 of its 206,206 detainees died from malnutrition, exhaustion, disease, suicide, and murder at the hands of the SS guards.

Although the prisoners were closely watched most of the time, the guards often left them unsupervised on Sundays. Some took advantage of their free time to socialize with other captives or read newspapers. Others wrote to their families. They were allowed to send two short letters each month. Herbert Zipper did something quite extraordinary: he formed a clandestine orchestra.

Shortly after arriving in Dachau, Zipper had met several excellent musicians, including a number of outstanding string players. He had also heard that there were one or two violins and just as many guitars that had somehow been brought into the camp. These discoveries inspired Zipper to form a makeshift ensemble. Given the low number of instruments available in Dachau, it is very likely that Zipper's orchestra included Erich, who had managed to bring his violin with him from Vienna. To complete the ensemble, Zipper convinced two instrument makers in the camp wood shop to secretly build instruments out of stolen wood. He even persuaded an SS guard to smuggle in some violin strings.

Zipper's fourteen-piece orchestra performed in a latrine building that was still under construction. Their repertoire consisted of well-known classical works as well as music that Zipper composed in his head each week during forced labor. He wrote out the pieces late at night, making sure to accommodate the odd instrumentation and the varied skill levels of the musicians, when he was supposed to be cleaning toilets. Zipper notated the music on strips of paper that fellow prisoners would tear from the margins of Nazi newspapers and painstakingly paste together.

There was only room in the unfinished latrine building for twenty to thirty people at a time, so the orchestra played in shifts of fifteen minutes to allow as many audience members as possible to rotate through the performances. The prisoners filed in quietly and remained in conspiratorial and awed silence throughout the brief concerts. In a tightly controlled concentration camp like Dachau, where such pursuits were strictly forbidden, the musicians and the audience members risked torture or even death for participating in these unsanctioned concerts.

In addition to providing a source of emotional comfort for the detainees, the music served as an inspirational reminder of the humanity that Dachau had taken from them. When they listened to the music, they were no longer weak, demoralized, and humiliated. They were dignified and strong, united in their spiritual resistance to Nazi persecution. If only for fifteen minutes a week, they were surrounded not by the ugliness of the concentration camp but by the beauty of music.

In 1938, the Nazis were still more concerned with expelling Jews than with killing them. Their solution to the
"Jewish Question" continued to be coercing Jews into emigrating. They were even willing to release concentration
camp prisoners who agreed to leave the country. Most
of Dachau's detainees, especially those who promised to
surrender their property and move away, were released
after several months. More than 1,200 others, including
Weininger, Bettelheim, and Zipper, were packed into
four cattle cars and transferred to the Buchenwald concentration camp on September 23, 1938, to make room in
Dachau for an influx of Jews from the German annexation of the Sudetenland. A convoy of 1,100 Jews followed
one day later.

Buchenwald

Established five miles north of Weimar in 1937, Buchenwald was one of the largest concentration camps on German soil. Like Dachau, Buchenwald was designed as an
internment facility and not specifically a death camp, as
Auschwitz would later become. But Buchenwald's harsh
conditions—far worse than those at Dachau—nevertheless
claimed the lives of 43,045 of its 238,980 prisoners during
the Holocaust. Many died of starvation, while others were
literally worked to death under the Nazis' brutal "Extermination Through Labor" policy. Still others succumbed
to disease or were simply murdered by the SS guards.

Erich brought his violin to Buchenwald, but there was

no possibility of participating in performances—even clandestine ones. Immediately upon arriving, the prisoners were told that gatherings of any kind were strictly forbidden. If any of them witnessed anyone breaking those rules, they were to report it immediately or risk being punished themselves. Such punishment typically involved being stretched out on a whipping post and beaten on the back twenty-five times with a whip or a club.

When Erich arrived in Buchenwald, there were about ten thousand prisoners, living in unbearable conditions. Unlike Dachau, which had been systematically clean and orderly, Buchenwald was filthy. There was no running water until January 1939, forcing the detainees to go for months without bathing or brushing their teeth. The appalling hygiene was exacerbated by the nonstop rain and the unpaved roads, which covered everything and everyone with slimy mud. The toilets were four large ditches, twenty-five feet long, twelve feet wide, and twelve feet deep. Since there was nothing to hold on to while they were relieving themselves, exhausted prisoners often fell or were thrown by SS guards into the foul trenches, where many of them died.

The situation in Buchenwald grew even worse on November 10, 1938, when the prisoner population was instantly doubled with the addition of ten thousand Jews who had been arrested on Kristallnacht. Five additional barracks had been built in the preceding weeks, but they were hardly enough. Each night, eight hundred detainees were locked in barracks built for four hundred. Many died of suffocation overnight. Others died of starvation from only receiving half of the already paltry food rations. Still others succumbed to typhus when an epidemic ran rampant through the cramped and unsanitary camp.

Throughout their incarceration in Buchenwald, the prisoners were subjected to various forms of torture. This included "sport" sessions in which the SS guards would force a few of them to exercise until they died of exhaustion. Sometimes the torture was inflicted on the entire camp at the same time, as when the guards would make the detainees stand at attention in the freezing cold. On December 14 and 15, 1938, the captives stood from 5 p.m. to noon the next day as punishment for two prisoners who had escaped. Several dozen of the flimsily clad detainees died of exposure while countless others, including Bettelheim, suffered frostbite as the temperature dropped to 5 degrees Fahrenheit overnight.

At this time, the Nazis were still promoting mass emigration as a comprehensive method of ridding Germany and Austria of their Jewish populations. In August 1938, Adolf Eichmann established the Central Office for Jewish Emigration in Vienna to expedite the expulsion process. Jews who were able to pay a hefty Reich Flight Tax and other fees were allowed to emigrate, but only after surrendering all of their wealth and possessions to the Nazis, and only if they agreed to leave the country as soon as possible. Even those in the concentration camps were released if third parties paid the fees and obtained the requisite paperwork on their behalves. The 9,370 Jews who were released from

Buchenwald in the winter of 1938–39 included Zipper, who returned to Vienna on February 20, 1939, after his family secured the documents necessary to immigrate to Uruguay. Bettelheim was released on April 14, after obtaining a passport, visa, and ticket to the United States.

Zipper and Bettelheim were fortunate to secure their departures in early 1939. By that August, the Nazis were no longer issuing exit permits to male Jews between the ages of eighteen and forty-five. Within the next two years, they would put a stop to all Jewish emigration. The very last group of Viennese Jews who were allowed to leave Austria departed for Portugal in October 1941. By then, the Nazis had concluded that the "Final Solution to the Jewish Question" was not the expulsion but the extermination of the millions of Jews who remained in Nazi-occupied Europe. One year later, the Nazis would order all Jewish prisoners remaining in Buchenwald to be transferred to Auschwitz.

The Jews who were able to emigrate prior to 1940 were assisted by numerous international relief organizations. The American Jewish Joint Distribution Committee and England's Council for German Jewry each provided funds for one hundred thousand or more Jews to leave Germany, Austria, and Czechoslovakia. The German Emergency Committee, established in London by Quakers, rescued another six thousand Jews.

Among those whom the German Emergency Committee freed from the concentration camps was Erich, whose sister-in-law was a Quaker who had emigrated from Vienna to London one year earlier. First, she was able to pressure the Nazis into releasing her husband—Erich's brother Otto—and then she got them to free Erich. Thanks to the Quakers, Erich was released from Buchenwald and was allowed to return home to Vienna. From there he was able to leave Nazi-occupied Europe—becoming one of the last Jews to escape the Holocaust.

Erich's father Karl, conversely, decided not to leave. He was reluctant to undertake the arduous process of emigrating, especially since he was among the many German and Austrian Jews who were convinced that the Nazis would not be in power for very long. His decision would prove to be fatal. One day, Karl wore an overcoat on top of the jacket onto which he had sewn his Star of David. In the cold Vienna winter, he had briefly forgotten that Jews were required to visibly display the yellow badge at all times. A close family friend who had often dined at the Weiningers' home informed on the elderly Weininger to the Nazis. Karl was arrested, taken to a police station, and pistol-whipped to death.

Bratislava

By the end of 1939, half of the 525,000 Jews who had been living in Germany before the Nazis took over had left the country. Half of Austria's 200,000 Jews had also fled. Some went to North America, South America, Eastern Europe, or Asia. Others, like the musicians who formed the Palestine Orchestra, had immigrated to the Holy Land.

By that time, however, there were fewer and fewer places left to go. The countries that had been accepting Jews since 1933 had become overwhelmed with refugees. Some began instituting strict quotas. Others closed their borders altogether. Even Palestine ceased to be an option for most Jews after Great Britain responded to ongoing Arab unrest by issuing the White Paper of 1939, which greatly reduced the numbers of Jews who could immigrate there. Such limits placed severe restrictions on Jewish immigration just at the time when European Jews needed asylum the most.

There may be no story that encapsulates the frustrating impracticalities of the emigration process better than the saga of the MS *St. Louis*. The ocean liner left Hamburg on May 13, 1939, with 937 immigrants bound for Cuba, where most planned to stay only until their American visas came through. The majority of the passengers were German Jews, including Günther Goldschmidt's father Alex and uncle Helmut. Many of them had been imprisoned alongside Erich in Dachau and Buchenwald. When the *St. Louis* arrived in Havana, its passengers learned that the Cuban landing permits for which they had paid inflated fees had been revoked. Cuba was closing its doors to immigrants. By this time, one of the original passengers had died of congestive heart failure, leaving 936. Of those, 28 passengers who had paid five-hundred-dollar bonds were allowed to disembark, while the remaining 908 passengers were denied entry.

In the hopes of protecting his passengers, the German

captain rerouted the *St. Louis* to Florida, only to be turned
away by the U.S. Coast Guard. The United States had
already filled its quota of German immigrants for the
year, and refused to accept any more. The captain reluc-
tantly set sail back to Europe, docking the *St. Louis* in
Belgium instead of returning to Nazi Germany. Great
Britain welcomed 287 refugees. One Hungarian businessman returned home. The remaining 620 passengers found
refuge in France, Belgium, and the Netherlands. Being
outside of Nazi Germany brought a reprieve from danger,
but only briefly. As Germany occupied more and more of
Europe, the 620 refugees on the continent found themselves in danger once more. By the end of the Holocaust,
254 of them would be dead, including Alex and Helmut
Goldschmidt.

Erich and the other Jews in Germany and Austria were
well aware of the difficulties with emigrating. With few
options at their disposal, thousands of them decided to
immigrate to Palestine illegally. Many of them had been
fully assimilated into European culture and would have
never otherwise considered moving to Palestine. Even
some of the staunchest Zionists were reluctant to risk
breaking the law in such tenuous times, especially if doing
so would weaken the relationship between Jews and Great
Britain. But they could not find any alternatives. There
was simply nowhere else to go.

A number of Jews sought assistance from the Zionist
organization Hechalutz (Pioneer), which prepared young
Jews for immigration to Palestine. Erich was one of many

hopeful colonists who lived on training farms sponsored by Hechalutz. These camps offered instruction in agriculture and other trades to give future settlers the skills they would need to successfully integrate themselves into the Jewish community of Palestine.

When the Hechalutz office in Vienna was unable to secure passage to Palestine, Erich and many others turned to Jewish financier Berthold Storfer, who had been named director of the Committee for the Transportation of Jews Overseas by Adolf Eichmann himself. For the Nazis, facilitating illegal immigration killed two birds with one stone: it would rid Europe of more Jews while also irritating the British government, which was struggling to maintain peace between the Arabs and the Jews who were already in Palestine. Viennese Jews would begin lining up at Storfer's office before midnight, hoping that the next day would bring the paperwork that would enable them to emigrate. Since some certificates expired quickly, the Jews would have to return every two months until their transports could be arranged.

While they waited for Storfer to orchestrate their emigration, the Jews continued to be terrorized. Nazi hooligans would grab them off the streets—sometimes while they stood in line in front of Storfer's office—and force them to wash their cars, polish their boots, or scrub the pavement to the delight of jeering onlookers. The Jews could not even feel safe in their own homes. The Gestapo could knock on the door at any minute. "They came at night, hauled us out of bed, beat me, the wife, and the children, broke up the furniture, and threw the pieces out the window," recalled one victim.[26] Others were taken into "protective custody," which meant torture and sometimes death.

After several months of anxious anticipation, the first group of Austrian and German Jews aided by Storfer's committee left Vienna on December 15, 1939. The plan was to take the train to Bratislava, the capital of the newly formed Slovak Republic. After staying in Bratislava for a few days, the Jews would be transported down the Danube by the Nazi-owned Danube Steamboat Company, naturally in exchange for exorbitant fares. Once they reached the Black Sea, the Jews would board the Greek steamship *Astrea*, which Storfer had chartered to sail to Palestine.

Nothing went according to plan.

The Jews arrived in Bratislava at midnight. They were met by members of the Hlinka Guard, which served as the internal security force for the pro-Nazi Slovak government. They were taken to the Slobodárni, a cheap hotel near the train station that was already filled with Czech Jews who had arrived a few days earlier. Some of the new arrivals staked their claim to floor space in overcrowded hallways and lounges as the remainder of the Jews from Vienna began to arrive. Others were taken just outside of town to the Patrónka, a hodgepodge of derelict huts and barracks that had once been a bullet factory and was now the home to 190 Czechs.

The German and Austrian Jews in the Slobodárni and Patrónka quickly learned from their Czech counterparts that the Danube had frozen over, leaving no possibility of sailing to the Black Sea. Any hopes of finding another method to continue their trip were dashed several days later, when they learned that the *Astrea* had sunk during a storm. For at least the foreseeable future, the Jews would have no choice but to remain in Bratislava in conditions that could hardly be considered ideal. Their Slovak transit visas were only valid for limited periods of time, forcing them to continually renew their paperwork by bribing corrupt officials. Until they could find a way to leave, the sojourners would be confined to the Slobodárni and the Patrónka by the Hlinka Guard. To add insult to injury, the Jews were forced to pay for the substandard lodgings in which they were being detained.

The Slobodárni was an ugly five-story building that the city had built as a boardinghouse for single men. It was never designed to hold hundreds of refugees. In one overcrowded lounge, 120 men shared sixty soiled and worn-out mattresses. There were only two toilets and one sink, and no place to wash clothes or dishes. The several hundred occupants of the Slobodárni were taken outside twice a day, when they were allowed to slowly amble around a small courtyard for fifteen minutes.

Life in the Patrónka was even worse. The 190 Czechs, 200 Austrians, and 400 Germans detained there slept on wooden bunks covered in straw. The roof of the abandoned factory often leaked, soaking the straw beds. The windows were either broken or missing altogether, giving the tiny iron stoves in each hall no chance to protect the building from the freezing winter. Sanitation was also a problem. There was only one water tap, and the toilets were outdoors.

By the spring, the conditions had improved somewhat. The Hlinka Guard relaxed their oversight, and the Jews were allowed to venture into Bratislava, where they went shopping, read newspapers, made friends, and even found work. Some took walks in the nearby hills and woods, picking flowers. Others stayed inside, playing cards and chess or engaging in classes, discussion groups, and debates. One refugee later recalled a number of recitals in which Dr. Hans Neumann and another gentleman played the piano and violin. It is possible that the unnamed violinist was Erich.

Over the summer, the situation worsened yet again. As the Slovak Republic was increasingly consumed by Nazism, the Hlinka Guard reinstituted stricter security measures. The Slovak authorities grew frustrated that the Jews who had been issued temporary transit visas remained in their borders, and threatened to send them back. On June 17, 1940—the day that France announced that it would surrender—the Jews were ordered to pack their bags for deportation to Germany, where they would surely have been sent to concentration camps. The expulsion was averted with more bribes, but the need to leave Bratislava was becoming increasingly urgent.

Down the Danube and to the Mediterranean Sea

Back in Vienna, Storfer had been working hard to get the Jews out of Europe. He had secured a large amount

of funds from the American Jewish Joint Distribution
Committee to pay for the trip. He had also contracted the
same company that had owned the *Astrea* to charter larger
ships for the growing numbers of Jewish refugees gathering not only in Bratislava, but also in Berlin, Vienna,
Danzig, Prague, and Brno. The Greek shipping company
had started looking for new vessels as well as for a neutral
country that would allow them to sail under its maritime
flag. But delays in the funding and difficulties with securing passage to the Black Sea threatened to cancel the
voyage yet again.

It was not until the afternoon of August 28, 1940,
that the Jews finally began boarding the ships that
would take them to the Black Sea. The Nazi vessels were
already traveling down the Danube to pick up ethnic
Germans from Russian-occupied Bessarabia and bring
them back to the fatherland, so why not make some
money off Jews along the way? A group of around two
hundred refugees from the Patrónka joined five hundred
from Danzig aboard the *Helios*, a pleasure ship that was
designed to hold three hundred passengers. The *Helios*
was later packed even further with the addition of three
hundred Jews from the Slobodárni. Its sister ship the
Uranus, which was also built for three hundred, was just
as overcrowded, with four hundred refugees from Berlin
and six hundred from the Slobodárni and the Patrónka.
The *Helios* and the *Uranus* were joined a week later by
two tour boats from Vienna, both built for only 100–150
passengers: the *Melk*, carrying 220 Jews from Brno and

six hundred from Prague, and the *Schönbrunn*, carrying eight hundred Viennese refugees.

On the morning of September 4, the four Danube Steamboat Company boats left Bratislava, flying swastika flags and overloaded with more than 3,600 Jews. As the convoy departed, the Jews joined together to sing "Hatikvah."

On their slow and cramped voyage down the Danube, the Jews were constantly reminded of how precarious their situation was. On September 6, they passed several hundred Jewish refugees from Danzig and Austria who were stranded on the banks of the Danube in Yugoslavia. Unable to secure further passage to the Black Sea, the Jews were later imprisoned and ultimately massacred after the Nazis invaded Yugoslavia. On the very next day, the *Helios*, *Melk*, *Schönbrunn*, and *Uranus* encountered the *Pentcho*, a paddle-wheel steamship that had left Bratislava four months earlier with six hundred Jews. The *Pentcho* had been detained for seven weeks in Yugoslavia after being deemed unseaworthy, and was now quarantined in neutral waters between Romania and Bulgaria for lacking proper paperwork. After several other delays, the *Pentcho* would make it to the Black Sea before wrecking in the Greek islands. Its haggard and emaciated passengers would be interned in Italy, but would immigrate to Palestine after being liberated by the Allies. The *Helios*, *Melk*, *Schönbrunn*, and *Uranus* were also delayed for three days in Bulgaria. They were released only so the Nazi ships could continue on their official missions to Bessarabia.

On September 12, the transport reached the Romanian port of Tulcea, where the Jews discovered three decrepit tramp steamers undergoing renovations. On the next morning, the refugees were surprised to find that the ramshackle freighters would be their transport to Palestine. The listing ships now bore Panamanian flags and the newly painted names *Atlantic*, *Pacific*, and *Milos*. "It was like naming a Pekinese 'Nero' or a Chihuahua 'Caesar,'" one refugee later explained. "Except that these ships had never been thoroughbreds."[27]

The 820 passengers from the *Melk* boarded the *Milos* and the one thousand Jews from the *Uranus* boarded the *Pacific* on September 14. The largest and oldest of the ships, the *Atlantic*, had been retrofitted to accommodate 1,200 passengers, but ended up quartering all 1,800 refugees from the *Helios* and *Schönbrunn*. It was on this cramped behemoth that Erich would continue his odyssey.

Erich and the other passengers were shocked to find that the *Atlantic* was even more crowded than the *Helios* and *Schönbrunn* had been. There were five toilets inside the ship to serve 1,800 refugees, but they would not even flush unless one brought a bucket of seawater. Most of the passengers ended up using the six makeshift lavatories on the deck, which had been so hastily constructed that they hung over the side of the ship. Since the Panamanian flag was painted on the roof of those lavatories, making a visit there became known as taking "a trip to Panama."[28]

The tiny cabins and cramped bunks that had been constructed in the *Atlantic*'s holds were packed far beyond capacity, forcing many passengers to carve out whatever space they could in the hallways, decks, stairs, and the insufficient lifeboats. Even with these measures, the Jews had to take turns standing to ensure that others had enough space to sleep. They had to improvise makeshift kitchens in various corners of the ship. The quarrels that naturally ensued in such cramped quarters were policed by the Haganah (Defense), a band of refugees from Prague who took their name from the paramilitary organization that protected the Jews in Palestine.

After three weeks of frustrating bureaucratic delays, which were eventually resolved through more bribes, the *Atlantic* raised anchor at 10:45 a.m. on October 7 and started to follow the *Pacific* toward the Black Sea. The beginning of the journey was hardly auspicious. Lacking a radio and navigation instruments, the *Atlantic* traveled about two hundred yards before running aground on the muddy shore. The captain ordered the passengers to the back of the boat in an attempt to shift its weight from the front. After an hour of grinding its engines, the *Atlantic* freed itself of the mud, only to break down. The crew restarted the engines before once again running the *Atlantic* aground, damaging the rudder in the process. The *Atlantic* was slowly towed to the Black Sea port of Sulina for repairs, a process that delayed its departure for two days. The *Pacific* and the *Milos* sailed ahead.

The *Atlantic* finally got under way on October 9. As with everything else on the journey, the trip to Palestine took much longer than anyone could ever have anticipated. Rightfully worried that the *Atlantic* could be attacked by the German or Italian navy during its voyage through the Mediterranean Sea, the Greek captain would moor the *Atlantic* in various island coves during the day and sail only at night. When they were at sea, the captain would run the engines at full throttle to waste coal. The more often he could stop to refuel, the more often he could increase his profit margin by overcharging the desperate refugees.

The *Atlantic* anchored in Crete to refuel on October 16. Then another crisis presented itself: the captain would not continue the voyage.

From the beginning of the trip, the Jews had experienced problems with the captain and his crew. In addition to the initial troubles with running aground, the captain had continually extorted money from the refugees for the food, water, and coal for which they had already paid exorbitantly before their departure. Throughout the trip, the captain had acted erratically and had repeatedly tried to abandon ship. After the Greco-Italian War broke out on October 28, the Greek captain simply refused to sail into Italian waters.

The Jewish refugees would not allow the captain to delay them any further. They took command of the helm and the engine room and set sail on November 8, having wasted three weeks in Crete. They quickly discovered yet another setback: the captain and his crew had thrown much of the coal that had been purchased in Crete into the sea overnight. Lacking the fuel to make it to Palestine, the refugees had no choice but to point the *Atlantic* eastward toward British-occupied Cyprus, despite fears that they would be arrested as illegal immigrants.

After realizing that the *Atlantic* did not even have enough coal to make it to Cyprus, the Jews stripped the vessel of any wooden objects that could be burned for fuel. They removed planks, railings, partitions, bunks, floorboards, doors, and paneling. They tore down all but one of the masts and sawed them into pieces. They dismantled tables and even broke apart an old piano. When they were done, there was no wood left on the ship's bow.

By this time, the passengers were just as emaciated as the boat. Since they had boarded the *Atlantic* two months earlier, the refugees' food had been limited to a watery soup at noon and tea twice a day. They would sometimes receive a small ration of vegetables, cheese, and bread for dinner, but often had to make do with moldy biscuits. Many were already malnourished and weakened from the earlier legs of the journey, and lacked the strength to continue living. The cramped conditions and poor sanitation also led to outbreaks of diarrhea, dysentery, and typhus. Death became a part of daily life aboard the *Atlantic*.

On November 12, a stripped and powerless *Atlantic* drifted into the waters surrounding Cyprus. The immobile boat was intercepted by a British motor launch and towed to the port of Limassol, where it would stay until Great Britain could figure out what to do with its passengers. The British found themselves between a rock and a hard place. They were alarmed by the poor health of the refugees, who were suffering from exposure, exhaustion, and starvation, but could not allow them to disembark, because Cyprus lacked the infrastructure to care for them. At the same time, the British could not deport the Jews, because they had yet to break any laws. The British ultimately decided to escort the *Atlantic* toward Haifa. The refugees had no way of knowing that they were being taken to Palestine only so they could be arrested as illegal immigrants once they arrived.

Ten days after the *Atlantic* arrived in Cyprian waters, a British captain and an armed military guard boarded it to sail it to Palestine. The British were shocked by the condition of the overcrowded vessel, which was listing so much that forty portholes on one side were submerged underwater. To make matters even worse, there were only enough lifeboats for one hundred people, and about a third of the 1,800 passengers did not have life vests. The British loaded the *Atlantic* with food, coal, and other supplies—albeit at exorbitant prices that required many of the refugees to sacrifice the little jewelry that had survived the earlier extortions. The *Atlantic* got under way at five the next morning, escorted by a convoy of British warships and minesweepers.

On the next morning, November 24, 1940, the Jewish refugees finally set their eyes on the Promised Land. Almost a full year had passed since the first group of Jews aided by Storfer's committee had left Vienna. As the sunrise illuminated the bay of Haifa, the historic mountain range known collectively as Mount Carmel became visible in the background. "From the *Atlantic*'s ghostly deck, green Mount Carmel was like a glimpse of heaven," one passenger later recalled.[29]

The refugees shouted with joy. Just as when they had left Bratislava almost three months earlier, they joined together to tearfully sing "Hatikvah." This time, their joyful songs were accompanied by harmonicas and violins, perhaps including Erich Weininger's Violin.

The British anchored the *Atlantic* just outside the port of Haifa. The *Atlantic* was reunited with the *Pacific* and *Milos*, which had both arrived at the beginning of the month. Near the two empty ships was a large ocean liner named the *Patria*. Around noon, two British officers boarded the *Atlantic* and announced that all of the passengers would join their counterparts from the *Pacific* and *Milos* on the *Patria*. Later, civil servants boarded the *Atlantic* to question the passengers, search and seize their belongings, and give them forms to complete. The refugees naturally asked why they were not being allowed to come ashore. Were they being quarantined? Was the sequestration just a temporary measure until they could be accommodated on land? From the noncommittal answers they received, the Jews finally began to suspect that they would not be allowed to disembark in Haifa.

Palestine

The presence of the *Pacific*, *Milos*, and now the *Atlantic* in Palestinian waters presented a considerable problem for

Great Britain. The rise of anti-Semitism in Germany and Austria had led to a dramatic increase in Jewish immigration to Palestine, which in turn had instigated a violent three-year Arab revolt. To placate the Palestinian Arabs and their allies in the region, Great Britain in the White Paper of 1939 had drastically cut the number of Jews who could immigrate to Palestine in any given year. But these quotas had not provided the deterrence they had hoped for. Hundreds of Jewish refugees had continued to land in Palestine every month.

Great Britain had decided to put an end to illegal immigration once and for all. Beginning in January 1940, the naval Contraband Control Service had started to seize all ships carrying illegal immigrants before they reached Palestine. The captain, crew, and passengers of such vessels were brought to Palestine and placed in internment camps, but were ultimately released within a matter of months. The aggressive tactics seemed to have worked: by August 1940, the Mediterranean Sea was free of refugee ships.

The British authorities were therefore alarmed on September 17, 1940, when they received a telegram from their embassy in Bucharest, Romania, informing them that the *Atlantic*, *Pacific*, and *Milos* were preparing to leave the port of Tulcea with several thousand illegal immigrants. The British realized that their threats to impound the ships offered little deterrent. Immigrants would simply arrive on derelict vessels such as the *Atlantic*, *Pacific*, and *Milos* that were practically worthless. The warnings that refugees would be detained were also not working. The Jews were willing to risk being interned for a few months because they knew they would eventually be released into Palestine. Great Britain decided to send a strong message by immediately deporting all illegal immigrants elsewhere and making it known that they would never be permitted to return to Palestine.

To prevent the newest refugees from even setting foot in Palestine, it was decided that they would be transferred directly to the *Patria*. The 15,000-ton ocean liner was originally designed to carry 805 passengers, including a crew of 130. It was now being reclassified as a troop transport, which would allow it to hold 1,800 people without increasing the number of lifeboats.

When the *Pacific* arrived in Palestinian waters on November 1, it was intercepted by a naval patrol and escorted toward Haifa, where the 962 refugees who had survived the voyage were transferred to the *Patria*. The *Milos* received the same treatment two days later, at which time its 709 refugees were taken to the *Patria*. It was decided that when the *Atlantic* arrived, eight hundred of its passengers would be assigned to the *Patria*—bringing its total contingent to a whopping 2,500. The remaining one thousand Jews aboard the *Atlantic* would be transferred to another vessel, the *Verbena*.

But where would the refugees be taken? Jamaica, Africa, Cyprus, Australia, and even Great Britain were considered as possible internment locations for the illegal immigrants. All were ultimately rejected on logistical or political grounds. The British finally decided to take the 1,700 Jews from the *Pacific* and *Milos* to their colony on Mauritius, an island in the Indian Ocean five hundred miles east of Madagascar. The 1,800 refugees from the *Atlantic* would continue on to Trinidad.

On the morning of November 25, 1940, one day after the *Atlantic* arrived in Palestinian waters, the British authorities began to transfer its passengers to the *Patria*. They started with women and children. By 9 a.m., 134 refugees had been transferred and another transport was just shoving off. Erich was on that dinghy and was heading toward the *Patria*.

Suddenly, there was a violent explosion. Erich watched in horror as an intense flame shot out the side of the *Patria*. The enormous ship capsized immediately. It sank within fifteen minutes.

The explosion was caused by a bomb that had been planted by Haganah agents from Palestine who had secretly boarded after learning of the British plan to deport the Jewish refugees. They knew that the forced expatriation of 3,500 immigrants would discourage other imperiled Jews from leaving Nazi-occupied Europe. They were determined to not let his happen. The Haganah snuck a bomb into the engine room in the hopes of disabling the *Patria*. If the ship was immobilized, they hypothesized, the British would have no choice but to allow its passengers to disembark in Palestine.

But the Haganah underestimated the bomb's power and overestimated the integrity of the *Patria*'s hull. Instead of merely damaging the engine, the explosion tore a large hole in the side of the ship. The majority of the passengers found safety by clinging to the wreckage until they could be rescued, or by swimming to the long jetty that protected Haifa's harbor. But more than two hundred refugees died, along with fifty crew members and policemen. Some were trapped in their cabins. Some got stuck in the narrow portholes when they tried to escape. Others fell off the deck and were sucked underwater by the downdraft of the rapidly sinking ship.

The survivors of the *Patria* disaster were taken to the Atlit detainee camp, which Great Britain had established just a few years earlier to incarcerate illegal immigrants. Located twelve miles south of Haifa, Atlit was surrounded by barbed-wire fences and watchtowers. More barbed wire divided the camp into several sections that separated the survivors of the *Patria* from the former passengers of the *Atlantic*. The refugees were given blankets and cramped shelter inside the camp's hundred Nissen huts.

The British authorities now had an even bigger problem on their hands: what should they do with the 3,300 refugees who were now on Palestinian land? After several days of internal debates, Great Britain yielded to pressure from Jewish groups in Palestine and the United States and announced a compromise. Those who had been on board the *Patria* when it sank would be granted amnesty, released from Atlit, and allowed to stay in Palestine. The former passengers of the *Atlantic*, however, would be sent to Mauritius as quickly as possible.

On December 8, the British instructed the refugees from the *Atlantic* to deliver their packed bags by midnight and be prepared to wake at five the next morning for transport. Although the Jews were not told where they were going, they suspected that they were being expelled from Palestine. The Jewish auxiliary police who helped guard Atlit encouraged the refugees to resist, assuring them that they had the support of the entire Jewish community in Palestine. The refugees devised a plan of nonviolent protest in which they would leave their bags unpacked, lock themselves in their huts, sleep naked, and refuse to leave their beds in the morning.

Midnight came and went without any luggage appearing at the depot. The commandant announced that any missing luggage would be left behind. This, too, failed to produce any response.

The silence, combined with Jewish work strikes throughout Palestine protesting the impending deportations, convinced the British authorities that the refugees would not leave Atlit quietly. Overnight, police wagons and armored cars rolled into the camp. Armed British soldiers surrounded the barbed-wire perimeter and posted machine guns in the camp's corners. They replaced the Jewish auxiliary police with a special squad of Palestinian police officers who were known for their brutality. Finally, they entered the camp, fortified with clubs and metal helmets.

The order to wake for departure was given at 5 a.m. Nobody moved. The police waited fifteen minutes, and then started advancing from hut to hut. They broke open doors, overturned cots, and ripped blankets off the naked refugees. As soon as they moved on to the next hut, the protesters went back to bed.

An hour later, the police made a second round. This time they bludgeoned whoever refused to rise. Those who offered the most resistance were dragged outside and beaten unconscious. They were wrapped in blankets, dragged on the ground, and tossed into the backs of the trucks that had arrived throughout the night. Others were carried to cars and buses on stretchers with bleeding wounds and broken bones. Confusion reigned as the unarmed refugees tried to fight back, shouting, cursing, and crying in protest. Some courageous young men continued the protest by running around the camp naked. They were chased down and beaten until they collapsed into pools of their own blood. "Look at the bloody Jews!" the policemen taunted.[30] The abuse that the Jews were enduring in Palestine was not very different from the cruel treatment they had thought they had left behind in Europe.

Of all the injustices the Jews had suffered, this was the worst. For those who, like Erich, had suffered in Dachau and Buchenwald only to endure captivity in Bratislava before making the arduous trek to the Promised Land, the thought of being deported was too much to bear. Everyone was crying. "At least let me die here," pleaded one elderly refugee.[31]

As Erich was being corralled toward the military transport, British soldiers repeatedly tried to steal his violin.

Every time a soldier got close, Erich threw the instrument over a separation fence to detainees in the neighboring yard. Whenever a British soldier on the other side would try to seize the violin, it was thrown back to Erich. The British never got the instrument. Erich eventually disappeared into one of the trucks with the violin that had accompanied him from Vienna to Dachau, Buchenwald, Bratislava, and Atlit.

The Jews were taken back to Haifa, where they were put aboard two Dutch steamers that Great Britain had requisitioned to carry them to Mauritius.

Palestine to Mauritius

The *Johan de Witt* and *Nieuw Zeeland* left Haifa on December 9, 1940, with Erich and 1,600 other Jewish refugees on board. Escorted by two British warships that zigzagged along while sweeping for mines, they sailed toward Port Said, Egypt. The Jews had still not been told where they were going, and had no way of seeing for themselves. The portholes were shut, and although the holds' hatches had been removed to compensate for the closed windows, the refugees were not allowed on deck. Their only clue that they were even under way was the drone of the engines.

The Dutch steamers were former luxury liners that had been converted into troop carriers. Both had several hundred cabins. These were left mostly empty except for a few that were occupied by elderly refugees, women with children, and Palestinian police officers. While the open dormitories in which the majority of the Jews traveled would have hardly qualified as luxurious, they represented a significant upgrade from the accommodations aboard the *Atlantic*. The Jews had hammocks for sleeping, shelves for storing their belongings, and even benches and tables where they could sit and eat.

By the third day of the voyage, the *Johan de Witt* and *Nieuw Zeeland* had passed through the Suez Canal and had reached the Red Sea. The refugees were finally allowed on deck, but only for limited times. Eventually, as the temperatures in the hold grew stifling, the Jews were permitted to not only sleep on the deck but also use the ships' swimming pools. The portholes and the hatches were left open during the day, but were closed at night for blackouts.

The ships arrived in Port Louis, Mauritius, on December 26, 1940, after two and a half weeks at sea. The Jews were immediately struck by the island's tropical beauty. "Mauritius, rising in the distance out of the calm Indian Ocean, appeared more and more enchanting the closer we approached," one refugee later recalled. "The island, surrounded by lagoons of a blue I had never seen before, was fringed with thick green vegetation and tall, exotic coconut palms behind which rose hazy, purplish hills. Here was something new, something totally different from anything I'd ever known, so exciting I felt my pulse race; my eyes welled up with tears."[32]

The Jews were taken by bus to the town of Beau Bassin. Along the way, they continued to be struck by the beauty of the island and the friendly welcome they received from its residents, who threw flowers as they passed by. The reception was more befitting to war heroes returning from battle than to destitute refugees.

It was therefore quite a shock when the buses reached their destination. "There we had the biggest surprise of our entire voyage, which had contained quite a few during the past four months," one refugee recorded in his diary. "The bus stopped in front of a small one-story building. We crossed a porch and entered a large yard where we saw two enormous cellblocks, each 90 to 100 meters long, with barred windows—A PRISON!"[33] This prison was to be their home for the next four and a half years.

Mauritius

The island of Mauritius was first visited by Arab sailors in the Middle Ages, but was rediscovered by Portuguese en route to India in 1507. It was later settled by the Dutch, who named the island after Maurice of Nassau, Prince of Orange, and used as a naval base. It was the Dutch who discovered the now-extinct dodo bird on Mauritius. France took control of the island in the early eighteenth century, but lost it to England in the Napoleonic Wars. Great Britain had ruled the island and its valuable sugar-cane fields ever since.

Five miles south of the Mauritian capital of Port Louis is the Beau Bassin Prison. A maximum-security compound that dates back to the nineteenth century, the prison was once the home to thieves and murderers. The British had planned to intern fascist political prisoners there during World War II. Instead, the prison grounds became home to 1,600 Jewish refugees.

By the time the Jews arrived at the Beau Bassin Prison, many were suffering from a variety of physical and mental illnesses, ranging from malnutrition, dysentery, and diarrhea to psychological exhaustion and depression from their yearlong ordeal. Initially, the most critical of these maladies was the typhoid fever that had gone untreated throughout their flight from Europe. As soon as the typhoid epidemic came under control, an outbreak of malaria took its place. Lacking adequate medical facilities and medication, twenty-eight refugees died within the first five weeks.

The males were confined to the Beau Bassin Prison. The men from Prague and Danzig moved into Block A, while Erich and the other men from Vienna occupied Block B. In each block, endless rows of heavy doors led to inhospitable cells. Each cell was approximately twelve feet long and nine feet wide and contained only a hammock, a shelf, and a barred window. There was no electricity. The men were, however, free to wander around the cell blocks. The door locks had been removed. The men were even able to enjoy a large prison yard that included trees, grass, and flower beds.

On the other side of the fifteen-foot stone wall that surrounded the prison was a hastily constructed camp for the women and children. The camp was enclosed by a barbed-wire fence. When the refugees first arrived, the construction was still ongoing. The camp eventually included thirty wooden huts with corrugated iron roofs. Each hut could hold twenty-five to thirty women and children.

The refugees quickly fell into a predictable daily routine. They would rise at 7 a.m. to drink their morning tea and receive their daily ration of bread, margarine, and sugar. Lunch took place between 12:30 and 1 p.m., and often consisted of fresh meat, corned beef, or canned salmon, along with unfamiliar local ingredients such as sweet potatoes, dried beans, and breadfruit. At 7 p.m., the refugees would eat soup and jam for dinner. Between their meals, the Jews under the age of thirty-five would do light chores such as cooking, cleaning, gardening, and maintenance. It was not long before craftsmen opened workshops that provided their fellow refugees with essential items such as clothes, shoes, and custom-made furniture for their barracks. Eventually, the detainees even earned small allowances for their chores and wares, many of which were sold in Mauritius and abroad.

In their free time, the refugees engaged in a wide variety of educational, cultural, and social activities. They founded a school, where the children were taught English, German, Hebrew, religion, geography, history, mathematics, science, music, and art. The adults organized similar classes for themselves, and also studied Jewish history and Zionism. They read the local newspapers, as well as books and magazines that they received from the Mauritian police department and Jewish communities in Palestine and South Africa. They held literary and poetry competitions, as well as tournaments for cards and chess. For a while, they even published a daily newsletter, *Camp News*. Artists organized exhibitions, and playwrights and actors staged theatrical performances, puppet shows, children's plays, and musical revues. There were also dances, cabaret evenings, and Hanukkah parties. Such events helped to provide comfort and raise the morale of the detainees throughout their prolonged internment.

Not surprisingly, music played a major role in this vibrant cultural community. In February 1941, the residents of Mauritius donated pianos, violins, accordions, and other instruments to the refugees. Erich, of course, still had the violin that he had brought from Vienna. The musicians in the camp entertained themselves and their fellow detainees by transcribing Beethoven piano sonatas and performing them as string quartets. They repaid the generosity of their Mauritian benefactors by forming an orchestra that accompanied an amateur performance of Puccini's opera *La Bohème* in nearby Rose Hill that July. Twelve hundred detainees attended one of the performances. It was the first time many of them left the confines of the Beau Bassin Prison.

Erich and other refugee musicians regularly performed in the Beau Bassin Boys, a jazz orchestra formed by pianist and fellow detainee Fritz "Papa" Haas. In their first year in Mauritius, the Beau Bassin Boys provided the music for an English-language revue that consisted of songs, folk dances, and satirical poems about camp life. The vaudeville show was a big hit among those in attendance, which included the British commander of the camp and his wife, as well as members of the press. The Beau Bassin Boys were so popular in the prison camp that Papa Haas is often the first name that survivors recall when discussing their lives in Mauritius.

The popularity of the Beau Bassin Boys extended well beyond the prison walls. Their performances were broadcast over the radio and they were even allowed to leave the prison several times a week for performances. Dressed in matching white shirts and black pants, black bow ties with red cummerbunds, and white dinner jackets, the Beau Bassin Boys played at dances, weddings, and other official and festive events throughout Mauritius, including parties hosted by the island's governor. These performances gave the musicians their only moments of freedom. The frequent invitations to play elsewhere on the island provided precious opportunities to leave the Beau Bassin Prison.

When they first arrived in Mauritius, the Jews were not allowed to pass through the heavily guarded iron gate that separated the men from the women and children. These restrictions were gradually relaxed. Within the first year, married women were permitted to bring their children to visit their husbands during limited hours. Then all refugees were given the opportunity to intermingle for four hours a day in the recreation grounds that surrounded the prison. By the time the detainees finally left Mauritius in 1945, they were able to move freely between the men's prison and the women's camp.

Once the refugees were no longer separated by gender,

old relationships were rekindled and new ones began. The September 13, 1942, issue of *Camp News* teasingly reported that Erich had "succumbed to family life" by marrying Ruth Rosenthal,[34] whose family had left Danzig with financial assistance from relatives in the United States. The Beau Bassin Boys provided the music for Erich's wedding, which was one of thirty marriages that took place in the prison courtyard by the end of 1942. One year later, Erich's son Ze'ev became one of sixty Jewish children who were born in Mauritius.

Although Beau Bassin was nothing like a Nazi concentration camp, life within the prison was still dreary. Throughout their lengthy internment, the refugees yearned for freedom. They resented being sequestered behind prison walls, under the watchful eyes of a hundred members of the prison administration, staff, and guards. They felt oppressed by the limited opportunities to leave the camp. Worst of all was their frustration over having been stripped of their civil rights and incarcerated for an indefinite period of time with no opportunities to defend themselves or appeal their confinement through any legal system.

The refugees also continued to suffer from malaria. At some points during their detention, as many as 40 to 50 percent of them had the disease. While malaria was not the primary cause of many deaths, its chronic high fevers did fatally weaken the elderly and those with heart conditions. Lacking adequate medical care to deal with malaria and other illnesses such as malnutrition, dysentery, and cardiovascular diseases, 127 Jewish refugees died in Mauritius. This included Erich's father-in-law, who died of a heart attack at the age of fifty-five.

It was not until January 1945—four years after the refugees had been brought to Mauritius—that the British government finally changed its mind about their immigration to Palestine. Bowing at last to international pressure, Great Britain decided to include the Mauritian detainees in the 10,300 emigrants who would be admitted into Palestine that year.

Given the difficulties of traveling during the war—several ships had been torpedoed near Mauritius—the British could not pledge that the relocation would be swift. In the end, eight months would transpire between when the British decided to send the refugees back to Palestine and when they were actually able to fulfill that promise. One plan was to give the Jews passage aboard a convoy of warships that would be passing through Mauritius in May. This was abandoned when a polio epidemic broke out on the island. The refugees were quarantined and their departure was canceled.

They would not get under way until August 11, 1945. By this time, World War II had ended and the Jews had learned of the horrible genocide that had claimed the lives of countless relatives and friends they had left behind in Europe. Out of the 1,581 Jewish refugees who had been on board the *Atlantic*, 1,307 were still living on Mauritius in 1945. In addition to those who had died, several dozen emigrants had left to fight in the war. The remaining refugees joined several hundred British soldiers who were returning from India aboard the RMS *Franconia*.

Israel

On August 26, 1945, almost six years after leaving Vienna for Palestine, the refugees returned to Haifa. This time they would bypass Atlit and proceed directly to their predetermined housing arrangements. Some would stay with family members who were already in Palestine or would settle into one of the collective agricultural communities. About four hundred of them would move into houses that had been built for them in Haifa, Tel Aviv, and the northern coastal city of Nahariya. A few dozen who had opted to return to Europe were taken to a transit camp south of Gaza.

Erich was among the immigrants who settled in Nahariya. He renewed his career as a butcher, but still continued to play the violin that had accompanied him on his astonishing odyssey from Vienna to Dachau and Buchenwald, from Bratislava to Palestine and then Mauritius, and finally back to Palestine. He would often invite a pianist and a drummer he had met in Nahariya over to his home for intimate evenings of playing traditional Austrian folk music and waltzes.

Erich returned to Austria a few times for brief visits. He gave serious consideration to murdering the former friend who had informed on his father, but was talked out of it. "Don't do it," Erich's friends pleaded with him.

"They'll throw you in jail for the rest of your life. You've already spent enough time in prison."[35]

Erich died in 1988, at the age of seventy-six. His violin was passed down to his son Ze'ev, who lived in Germany, and his daughter Tova, who still lived in Israel. It stayed with Tova until 2012, when she started considering selling it. Her son took the violin to Tel Aviv to see how much the instrument was worth. He quickly learned that there was only one person who could appraise it: Amnon Weinstein. The violin was damaged from being played outside in Mauritius's tropical heat and had little monetary value, but Amnon immediately recognized the instrument's historical significance. He agreed to restore the violin for free. All he asked in return was permission to maintain Erich Weininger's Violin as one of the Violins of Hope.

3
—

THE
AUSCHWITZ
VIOLIN

An SS photograph of the Auschwitz Main Camp Orchestra in the spring of 1941. *(From the United States Holocaust Memorial Museum, courtesy of the Institute of National Remembrance, Poland.)*

Günther and Rosemarie Goldschmidt, the performers who founded the Palestine Orchestra, and Erich Weininger were among the last Jews to leave Nazi Germany. The country sealed its borders on October 23, 1941, prohibiting any other Jews from emigrating. Shortly thereafter, the Nazis began transporting Jews to camps designed not just to incarcerate and torment Jews, but to kill them by the thousands.

One of the musicians who suffered from this persecution was Henry Meyer. Henry was born in 1923 into an affluent and musical family of Jewish merchants in the culturally rich city of Dresden, Germany. He received his first violin at the age of five and began taking lessons with one of the best violin teachers in the city. He quickly established himself as a child prodigy by playing chamber music alongside his accomplished parents as well as professional musicians.

Henry's idyllic childhood ended when Hitler came to power in 1933. At the age of ten, Henry was expelled from his school and banned from social clubs, and was even stripped of his bicycle and pet dog. He was also forbidden to take lessons at the conservatory or the State Opera's orchestral school. He took a few private lessons from the concertmaster of the opera until the Gestapo forced his new instructor to stop teaching him.

Henry's parents wrote to family members in the United States asking for help with immigrating to America, but the relatives did not have the financial resources to vouch for a family of four. There was also the problem of America's immigration regulations. Henry, his younger brother, and their mother fell under the German quotas. Henry's father was subjected to the Polish quotas, since his hometown had been part of Poland when he was born. Securing permission to immigrate to the United States was difficult enough for Germans. For Poles, it was almost impossible.

When Henry was fifteen, he was invited to appear as a soloist with the small orchestra hosted by the Jewish Culture League in Dresden. Once again, fate intervened. The concert was scheduled for November 9, 1938—Kristallnacht. Instead of performing that night, Henry was arrested and sent to Buchenwald, where he was imprisoned alongside Erich Weininger. Henry was released a few weeks later when he was presented with the possibility of leaving the country. As with his family's attempt to emigrate in 1933, these plans never materialized.

In 1939, Henry moved to Berlin, where he was accepted into the culture league orchestra. In addition to quickly establishing himself as an exceptional performer, Henry became the self-proclaimed "Benjamin of the orchestra," as at the age of sixteen he was its youngest member. Henry also quickly grew close to fellow orchestra musicians Günther and Rosemarie Goldschmidt, often playing chamber music with the young couple.

When the Jewish Culture League was disbanded in August 1941, Henry was required to report to the employment office for labor service. Worried about his future as a violinist, he asked for work that would be easy on his hands.

"I have something for you," the bureaucrat responded. "A company that makes Sanitary Articles."[36]

Much to Henry's embarrassment, these "Sanitary Articles" were condoms for the German army. Henry was assigned to work in the Fromms Act factory, where Jewish entrepreneur Julius Fromm had invented the rubber condom before being forced to sell his lucrative business to Hermann Göring's godmother. Henry's job was to liquefy the rubber with a hazardous mixture of industrial chemicals. He worked for twelve hours a day without the benefit of the gas mask and extra milk rations that the Aryan workers received to combat the effects of the toxic fumes. To make matters worse, the pre-vulcanized rubber proved to be anything but easy on his hands.

In early 1942, Henry returned to Dresden to be with his family during the impending deportations. He and his brother were forced to work at the Zeiss Ikon factory, making devices that became parts of triggers for time bombs. Because they were providing useful labor, the brothers were not chosen to accompany their parents when the elderly Meyers were transported to the ghetto in Riga, Latvia, that March. Their mother died in Riga. Their father survived the ghetto and a death march to Dachau. He would die there in 1945, two months before it was liberated.

In March 1943, Henry and his brother were marched from Dresden's Hellerberg Ghetto to the Neustadt train station, where they were packed into cattle cars. Starving and cold, they rode for several days in a cramped and foul-smelling wagon. When the train stopped, they had no idea where they were. Voices from outside of the car commanded them to leave everything behind and get off the train. Through a hatch, Henry could see the steam of another locomotive. In the background was a sign for a place Henry had never heard of: Auschwitz.

Auschwitz

The largest and most notorious Nazi concentration camp, Auschwitz was a large complex in Poland that actually included several camps. The oldest was the Auschwitz Main Camp, which was built after Nazi Germany's defeat of Poland in 1939, by Jewish slave laborers from the eponymous town of Oświęcim. The Auschwitz Main Camp was a harsh penal complex where thousands of mostly Polish political prisoners were regularly tortured and executed. In 1941, the Nazis began constructing a camp that was much larger and even deadlier, a little less than two miles from the Auschwitz Main Camp. They named this second site Birkenau, after the German name for one of the Polish villages that had been razed to create the 15.5-square-mile camp. As the Birkenau extermination camp expanded, separate subcamps were developed for men, women, Roma, and Czechs. Gas chambers were erected to assist with the mass murders of the detainees. Crematoria were constructed to dispose of their remains. The Auschwitz III concentration camp was erected in 1942 to provide forced labor for the Buna chemical plant in nearby Monowitz. Over time, the Nazis built forty-five more satellite camps, mostly for forced labor.

Daily life in Auschwitz was so brutal that most of the prisoners died of exhaustion and starvation within weeks. After assembling for an early morning roll call, the detainees would march out of the camp for an entire day of torturous labor before dragging their fatigued bodies back to camp for an evening roll call. At the whim of the SS guards, additional roll calls could be held in the middle of the night, at which time the inmates were forced to stand at attention for hours in the rain and snow. Anyone who moved was sent to the gas chambers, as was anyone who appeared too sick or weak to continue working. Between those who were killed immediately upon arriving and those who perished in the camp, an estimated 1.6 million people, mostly Jews, died in Auschwitz.

Amateur violinist Jacques Stroumsa was deported to Auschwitz on April 30, 1943, as part of a transport of 2,500 Jews from Thessalonica, Greece. The Jews were herded into German cattle cars that were overcrowded with men, women, and children. Most of the deportees were forced to stand. They were given no food and just one bucket of drinking water for the entire car. They were also given a tub that was to serve as their communal toilet. From time to time, the locked doors would be opened from the outside, but only long enough to empty out the tub and refill the bucket. During a stop near Vienna, Jacques and another young man were chosen to help an SS officer unload some gold and jewelry the German had stolen in Greece. Other than that brief respite, all of the deportees remained in the packed and poorly ventilated cars for the entire eight-day journey to Auschwitz.

The transport arrived in Birkenau early in the morning of May 8. The doors were thrown open and the Jews were ordered out of the train. As the deportees frantically climbed down, they were blinded by a harsh spotlight and deafened by shouting voices and cracking whips. Disoriented, Jacques held on to his pregnant wife with one hand and his violin with the other, until the beatings forced him to let go of both. The Jews were lined up and quickly directed to a "selection," where an SS officer directed each of them to the left or to the right. The officer pointed 815 healthy men and women between the ages of fifteen and fifty to the left. Although they did not know it at the time, being steered to the left meant that they had been selected for work details. The remaining 1,685 sick and elderly Jews were sent to the right. They would be taken to the gas chambers and killed that day.

While his wife and parents were sent to the right, Jacques and his brother were directed to the left. They were taken to an SS officer who interrogated them about how old they were, what they did for a living, and what languages they spoke. The officer was gauging how useful each new arrival would be to camp operations.

After Jacques and his brother were marched into Birkenau, they were briefly reunited with a doctor they had known in Thessalonica. The doctor, who had arrived just a few days earlier, pulled Jacques aside to tell him the truth about what happened to those who were selected to go to the right. "By now, your wife, your parents, and her parents have already been gassed, and soon they will be burned in the ovens of the crematorium," he whispered. "The young people brought to the camp have a chance, a small chance to survive, but only provided that they never become ill."[37] Getting sick would result in no longer being useful. Being useless would result in being sent to the gas chambers.

The first stop in Birkenau was the "sauna," where the detainees were tattooed with their prisoner numbers. Jacques was given number 121097. The hair on their heads and bodies was shaved off. They were sent to a shower that fluctuated in temperature between freezing cold and boiling hot. Then they were given blue-and-white-striped prison uniforms with yellow and red Stars of David over their left breasts to mark them as being Jewish.

The shape and color of a detainee's badge indicated why that person was imprisoned and defined one's place in the Auschwitz hierarchy. Jews who wore Stars of David were at the bottom of the ladder, alongside the Roma, who wore brown triangles. Above them were the Poles and Russians, who wore red triangles as political prisoners. At the very top were German criminals, who wore green triangles. The higher a detainee was on the social scale, the more likely it was that he would be chosen for functionary positions within the camp administrative system. These positions included block elders who oversaw the prisoner barracks and capos who oversaw work details. In return for maintaining order by inflicting terror on their fellow detainees, the functionaries received better food and better living conditions, and therefore better chances of survival.

Jacques and the surviving members of his transport had just entered their new barracks and received their bunk assignments when their block elder ordered them to assemble at the doorway.

"Are there any prisoners here who play a musical instrument?" the menacing figure asked.

Jacques was stunned by the question. It seemed impossible to even think about playing an instrument in a place like this. Nobody spoke, but everyone looked at Jacques. They were all from Thessalonica and they all knew of his abilities.

"I play the violin, but that is not my profession," Jacques finally responded in German. "When I was admitted to the camp I indicated that I am an electrical engineer!"

"The fact that you did not reply to my question immediately, even though you are in fact a violinist, is the purest sabotage, and you could have gotten twenty-five lashes on your butt!" the block elder barked. "But because you say that you are an amateur, five lashes will be enough! First, though, I would like to hear you play!"

"My instrument was taken away from me as we climbed out of the wagon this morning!"

"That doesn't matter. I will find a violin for you at once."

Within minutes, Jacques had a violin and a bow in his hand. He tuned the instrument and began to play, performing for twenty minutes without interruption. His fellow prisoners listened blissfully as they were transported back to Thessalonica, back to freedom.

"You play very well!" praised the block elder, motioning for Jacques to stop playing. "And I know what I am talking about, for I am a pianist. Besides that, you are an engineer and speak good German!"

"I hope that you will not die on us here!" the block elder cruelly joked, placing his hand on Jacques's shoulder. "We will skip the punishment, for you will be brought right away to the audition in the conservatory."[38]

Jacques was taken to the "conservatory," a barracks that had been set aside for musicians in the camp. During an interview there, he revealed that he had studied the violin for six years in Thessalonica, then one year at the Lycée Musical in Marseilles, three years in Paris, and a year at the Bordeaux Conservatory. These credentials were so impressive that an audition was deemed unnecessary. Jacques was immediately invited to become the concertmaster of the camp orchestra.

Auschwitz Main Camp Orchestra

In addition to secret ensembles such as the one Herbert Zipper formed in Dachau in 1938, official orchestras had been performing in German concentration camps since 1933. Auschwitz was home to a number of ensembles, including a large orchestra in the Auschwitz Main Camp, orchestras in the men's and women's camps of Birkenau, and several other ensembles throughout the Auschwitz complex. These orchestras were composed of musicians who were recruited from the prisoner population.

The first orchestra was a small clandestine ensemble that initially played together in the Auschwitz Main Camp on January 6, 1941. It was composed of a handful of prisoners who had been allowed to have their instruments sent from home. After professional band leader Franciszek Nierychło received approval from the camp administration to form an official ensemble, the orchestra began to grow through the addition of current prisoners as well as new arrivals. For musicians like trombonist Tadeusz Jawor, having one's own instrument was a condition of being allowed to join the orchestra. Other instruments were confiscated by SS officials from the areas surrounding Auschwitz.

All detainees who were identified as musicians and who passed an audition were assigned to the gate orchestra. By May 1942, that ensemble included more than one hundred musicians. Most of the performers were Polish prisoners, but some were Czech or Russian. Jews were not admitted.

Several of the musicians were former members of military bands and professional orchestras, while others were accomplished amateurs. The orchestra's main responsibility was to play marches at the camp gate, to provide a cheerful façade and rhythmic orderliness as the work details marched out of camp and returned every day. The ensemble also performed during executions, roll calls, and official visits by luminaries ranging from SS commander Heinrich Himmler to a delegation of the Red Cross.

The gate orchestra's repertoire consisted primarily of German marches such as the popular military march "Old Comrades." On special occasions the ensemble would play fanfares and popular compositions such as *Light Cavalry Overture.* As an apparently unnoticed form of defiance, the musicians would sometimes perform marches by American composer John Philip Sousa to celebrate rumors of Allied victories. Since the orchestra did not own any sheet music at first, the musicians would collect slips of paper from the administration office, draw lines for music staves, and add the musical notation. Some wrote down tunes they remembered, while others notated the harmony. Later, the members of the orchestra gave bread to a descendant of a famous Polish bookseller, who in return gave them access to his personal bank account to purchase an entire library of music.

The top eighty musicians from the gate orchestra also played in a symphony orchestra that gave concerts on Sunday afternoons and holidays for the SS officers and guards, as well as for their fellow prisoners. In addition to dance tunes and selections from popular operas and operettas, the symphony orchestra performed classical masterworks such as Mozart's *Eine kleine Nachtmusik* and Beethoven's piano concertos. For camp commandant Rudolf Höss, the performances provided regular opportunities to present himself to his visitors and family members as a cultured patron of the arts. For Höss's SS subordinates, the concerts lent a sense of normalcy, decency, and even nobility to working in the camp. For the members of the orchestra, the events offered opportunities to earn food and cigarettes from their captors. And for the detainees who attended the symphony orchestra's performances, the music provided a mental escape from the harsh realities of life in Auschwitz. "The Germans put barbed wire all around the camp so that no one will escape, but I just close my eyes and I'm on the other side of the wires," one of the prisoners would say. "They have no idea that we're all fugitives."[39]

In addition to the official gate orchestra and symphony orchestra, impromptu ensembles often performed at private parties. Some musicians even played at an SS wedding outside of the camp. Although jazz and swing music had been forbidden by the Third Reich because of their "degenerate" African-American and Jewish influences, a jazz combo led by Dutch trumpeter Lex van Weren was one of the most popular ensembles in Auschwitz.

As a reward for their contributions to camp life, the orchestral musicians sometimes received preferential treatment. This included special uniforms and lighter work details such as copying music and repairing musical instruments. Many of the performers were assigned to work in the kitchen, giving them access to extra food while also allowing them to work inside.

But membership in the orchestra did not by any means spare the musicians from reassignment, deportation, or death. One violinist was selected for execution during a rehearsal. He was allowed to finish the piece before being taken away and killed. The turnover in personnel was so great that a total of eight hundred musicians performed during the orchestra's four-year existence, even though the ensemble never included more than 120 musicians at any given time.

On October 27, 1944, the Polish musicians were transferred to concentration camps in Germany, along with most of the other Polish prisoners in Auschwitz. The only Polish member of the orchestra who stayed behind was Adam Kopyciński, who had taken over the orchestra after Nierychło had volunteered for the German army. The symphony orchestra was disbanded and Kopyciński had to put together a new gate orchestra. To replace the Poles who had constituted the majority of the previous ensemble, Jews were allowed to participate in the Auschwitz Main Camp Orchestra for the first time. They quickly replaced Poles in the majority. By late November, all but ten of the seventy-seven musicians in the orchestra were Jewish.

The Auschwitz Main Camp Orchestra was dissolved when Auschwitz was evacuated on January 18, 1945. By that time, it had become a model for orchestras in other camps, including the ensembles elsewhere in the Auschwitz complex.

Birkenau Men's Camp Orchestra

In August 1942, Johann Schwarzhuber, the camp commander of Birkenau, decided to form his own ensemble. Unlike the Auschwitz Main Camp Orchestra, the Birkenau Men's Camp Orchestra included Jews from its very beginning.

One of the most influential Jewish musicians was the Polish violinist and composer Szymon Laks, who had been arrested in Paris in 1941. In the summer of 1942, Szymon was deported to Auschwitz, where he was assigned prisoner number 49543. At first, he had been assigned to a grueling work detail. After twenty days of growing increasingly emaciated and depressed, fortune had smiled on him. Like Jacques Stroumsa, Szymon was saved by his block elder.

"Is there someone here who speaks Polish and plays bridge?" asked the Polish block elder one evening. He and two other block elders needed a fourth for their nightly game. Since the prisoners in that barracks had all been transported from France, Szymon was the only one who qualified.

While playing bridge with the three block elders, Szymon happened to mention that he was a violinist and a composer.

"Why didn't you tell me this sooner?" his block elder asked. "Tomorrow you'll stay in the barracks and I'll take you over to the orchestra."

"And if you're accepted, maybe you'll live a little longer," one of the other block elders added, laughing.[40]

At dawn the next morning, Szymon's block elder took him to the music barracks, where conductor Jan Zaborski handed Szymon a violin and asked him to play. Szymon's fingers were stiff and bruised from three weeks of labor duty. His arms were so sore he could barely hold the bow. But he somehow found the strength to launch into Mendelssohn's difficult violin concerto—forgetting that the Jewish composer had been banned by the Nazis.

Zaborski stopped him after just a few measures. "Good. Technique not bad, not bad," the conductor said. "Tell your barracks chief that you have been accepted and for him to transfer you to this barracks. Also tell him to take you to the clothing storeroom, where they'll exchange those rags you're wearing for decent stripes."[41] And so Szymon was accepted into the orchestra.

Like Szymon, Henry Meyer did not join the orchestra immediately upon arriving in Auschwitz. Instead, he and his brother were put to work in Auschwitz III, building a factory for the Buna chemical plant. Henry's job was to sit atop scaffolding high in the freezing air and hold a hammer for a riveter. It was extremely dangerous work that few survived for very long.

Henry's brother died within a month of arriving at Auschwitz III. He developed a severe case of diarrhea one morning and was unable to go out to work. By the time Henry returned that evening, his brother had simply disappeared. Henry never knew whether his brother died of a disease or was selected for the gas chambers because he was no longer fit for work.

Shortly after his brother's death, Henry himself fell ill. He was taken to the infirmary, where he was scheduled for a selection the very next day. His musical background ended up saving his life when a Jewish doctor paid him a visit.

"What did you do before?" the doctor asked.

"I have not done very much, since I am very young," Henry replied. "But I was a child prodigy on the violin and played in several cities."

"And where are you from?" Henry asked the doctor.

"Breslau."

"Ah, Breslau, I know it. I performed there. I played with the culture league orchestra."

"The Tartini Concerto?" the doctor asked, referring to a fiendishly difficult work for solo violin and orchestra by Giuseppe Tartini.

"Yes."

"I was at that concert," the doctor marveled. The performance had left such an impression on the doctor that he had recalled every moment of it.

"I'll be right back," the doctor promised Henry. He returned a few minutes later with a corpse slung over his shoulder. He plopped the body next to Henry on the bed. Then he picked up Henry and carried him to the dead man's former bed. "Everything has to be in order," he explained, exchanging Henry's file card and prisoner number for the corpse's.[42]

The doctor gave Henry extra medication and nursed him back to health. He then arranged for Henry to be assigned an undemanding job cleaning and making beds for SS doctors in the Auschwitz Main Camp, including Josef Mengele, the infamous "Angel of Death."

Henry's privileged job came to an abrupt end one day. "You! Number 104944!" an SS guard shouted at him. "Report for instructions!"[43] Henry had been transferred to Birkenau, where he would join the orchestra.

As with the Auschwitz Main Camp Orchestra, the main task of the Birkenau Men's Camp Orchestra was to perform for the parades of work details leaving camp every morning and returning every night. At dawn, the musicians would line up outside the music barracks in rows of five, just like every other work detachment. The trumpets would stand in the first row, followed by the horns, accordions, clarinets, and the saxophone. Bringing up the rear would be the tuba, the snare drum, the bass drum, and the cymbals. At the front of the ensemble, proudly holding his baton, would be Franz Kopka, a drummer who in addition to being the capo of the orchestra managed to have himself named its conductor after Jan Zaborski died in November 1942.

"Forward, march!" Kopka would shout,[44] followed by the title of the march the band was to play. The snare drum would establish the tempo with a brief cadence, accompanied by the boom of the bass drum and the crash of the cymbals. The band would join in as the ensemble marched toward the stage that had been erected next to the camp gate. On their way, they would pass the capos who were busily lining up their detachments for an orderly march out of the camp.

When the band reached the stage, Kopka would cut off the music and bring the formation to a halt. The musicians would scamper to their places on the stage, spread out the music on their stands, and await their next command. Instead of launching immediately into another march, Kopka would often indulge himself by calling for a tango. This would allow him to emulate what he thought a great conductor should look like, waving the first two fingers of each hand in the air while contorting his entire body in ridiculous gestures. The musicians would simply play on, ignoring the antics of their pretentious conductor. Sometimes, the SS guards would interrupt Kopka's selection to make a request of their own, with which Kopka would readily comply.

"Come on! Music!" the guards would shout once the detachments were in formation and once their requests had been performed.[45] Both sides of the gate would swing open while the orchestra performed "Old Comrades." The detachments would march out of the camp for their work details while a functionary counted each row of five to make sure every prisoner was accounted for. The process of marching all the detainees out of the camp could last two or more hours, during which time the orchestra would play without interruption.

After the last detachments had passed through the gate, the orchestra would reassemble in its parade formation and march back to the music barracks. The performers would stow away their instruments and begin their daily work. Privileged musicians like Szymon Laks would remain behind every day to arrange and copy out music for the orchestra to perform. Everyone else would line up again and march out of the gate. Although they were not exempt from forced labor, they did have the advantage of working slightly less, since they were the last ones to leave camp every morning. They were also the first to return in the evening, at which time they would perform marches for the exhausted workers hobbling back into the camp.

While the woodwind, brass, and percussion players would form a marching band during the procession to and from the stage, the violinists would follow behind them with their instruments still in their cases. It did not take long for the SS guards to notice that Henry Meyer and the other violinists did not have anything to do during those parades. "Why don't you play?" they would ask. "What are you needed for?"[46]

Knowing that being seen as "useless" would result in a transfer to a more difficult work command or in a trip to the gas chambers, Henry decided to give himself a task. When the cymbal player fell ill and disappeared, Henry convinced Kopka that he was a virtuoso cymbalist, even though he had never held a pair of cymbals before in his life. The first time he crashed the cymbals, he slammed them together with such force that he almost broke his wrists. Nevertheless, he quickly mastered the proper technique and became the marching band's permanent cymbal player. From that point on, instead of being an object of derision for the SS guards, Henry was a source of entertainment. The guards made a game out of throwing pebbles in Henry's direction. He would deflect the pebbles with his cymbals, often to the beat of the music.

By October 1942, Szymon Laks had become the chief arranger for the Birkenau Men's Camp Orchestra. Since commander Schwarzhuber insisted that his orchestra continually expand its repertoire, Szymon would re-create existing marches from memory and compose new marches in the German style. From time to time, Schwarzhuber and his subordinates would pass along the melodies of popular marches such as "Fatherland, Your Stars," a march that served as the leitmotiv for a popular propaganda film. Szymon would harmonize these songs and orchestrate them for the ensemble.

As Schwarzhuber and his subordinates continued to request more and more music, the orchestra members struggled to learn so many pieces. At Szymon's suggestion, Kopka successfully petitioned Schwarzhuber to excuse the entire orchestra from their labor details for two rehearsals per week. This gave all of the musicians brief reprieves from the grueling work detachments, if only for three hours at a time twice a week.

One day, the orchestra received an order from Schwarzhuber to start performing the popular march "Berlin Air" as soon as possible. Szymon completed the arrangement and the creation of the parts in a matter of days. When the orchestra played the arrangement for the first time, it just so happened that the Sonderkommando (special detachment) was marching by. Because the Sonderkommando was in charge of carrying decomposing corpses to the crematorium, the unit gave off a terrible odor that took several minutes to dissipate. The members of the orchestra were accustomed to the smell and did not think twice about it. The SS guards, on the other hand, immediately noticed the concurrence of the stench of death and the performance of "Berlin Air." A shrill whistle and a shout from the watchtower brought an abrupt end to the performance. Kopka was summoned to the guardhouse, where he received twenty-five blows to his backside for mocking the German capital.

Szymon's arranging responsibilities were complicated by the fact that the ensemble kept changing. Its members continued to fall victim to disease or grow so weak from exhaustion and starvation that they were sent to the gas chambers. Others committed suicide.

Among those who decided to take his own life was Leon Bloorman, a former violin professor at the Jewish Conservatory of Music in Rotterdam. Just a few days after arriving in Birkenau, Bloorman approached his old violin student Louis Bannet, who had since become a virtuoso trumpeter.

"Louis, do you know what they made me do today?" he asked. "They made me play my violin while they hanged a man. He was a Frenchman. Other than being a Jew, I don't know what crime he committed.

"They pulled him on a cart to the gallows. I had to stand behind him and play *La Marseillaise*," Bloorman continued, referring to the French national anthem that he was forced to perform to mock the executed Frenchman. "Can you explain such a thing to me?"

"I don't have an answer," Louis simply responded. "There are no answers here."

"Louis, you are stronger than me," the elder violinist tearfully admitted. "I don't think I can go on like this much longer."

"Try to think of this," Louis suggested. "The man they hanged today, the last sound he heard was your beautiful playing."

This was not enough to console the violinist. A few nights later, Bloorman tried to kill himself by running into the electric fence. Before he got that far, he was gunned down by SS guards who were sparing themselves the trouble of scraping his body off the fence. The next morning, when the orchestral musicians took their seats, they found Bloorman's dead body tied to his chair. Around his neck hung a sign that explained why he had been shot and why his body had been positioned there as an example. The sign read, "I tried to escape."[47]

Szymon Laks eventually succeeded Kopka as the capo of the orchestra. In his new position, he was able to offer more protection to the orchestra members. He convinced the camp administration to assign them the easiest work details, arguing that they would be able to perform better if the nimbleness of their hands and fingers were not compromised by difficult manual labor. During a snowstorm, Szymon successfully argued that the camp instruments would be damaged if they were not taken inside immediately. From that point on, the orchestra was exempt from playing during bad weather.

As the orchestra grew in size, quality, and repertoire, its responsibilities expanded beyond just performing at the gate to playing at various camp functions. On Sunday afternoons, the orchestra would perform concerts of light classical music for SS officers and guards. The orchestra would occasionally perform as transports arrived. Seeing an orchestra playing in front of a manicured lawn landscaped with flowers tricked the new arrivals into believing that Auschwitz was a welcoming place. In perhaps its most gruesome performance, the orchestra once played next to a building in which women prisoners were being gassed, to drown out their screams.

From time to time, small groups of musicians would cheer up their sick comrades in the infirmary by playing classical music for them on Sunday afternoons. One patient was so grateful for Jacques Stroumsa's performance of a Mozart violin concerto that he wept openly when he bumped into Jacques thirty-six years later at a café in Israel. "Jacques, it is really you!" he exclaimed. "Jacques Stroumsa, the violinist from Auschwitz who came to us on Sundays in the hospital to play Mozart!"[48]

Various ensembles also played at birthdays and other holidays celebrated by camp functionaries and SS men. Three or four musicians would rise early to wake up the celebrant with a serenade or triumphant march. After the honored party feigned surprise and thanked his serenaders with gifts, the musicians would perform a sentimental tune and convey their best wishes in whatever language was appropriate to the celebrant. That evening, a larger ensemble would perform a private concert, while the hero of the day ate and drank himself silly.

On the evening of March 16, 1943, Louis Bannet was rousted out of his bed along with a clarinetist, a drummer, and a violinist. They were loaded into a car and told that they would be providing entertainment for a birthday party. They were driven to a large country house, dropped off in the back, and taken to a second-floor loft. The balcony overlooking the first floor was screened off with large plants so the prisoners would be heard but not seen. After a German soldier told them to begin playing, Louis snuck a peek at the guest of honor as he jubilantly entered the room. The birthday boy was none other than Josef Mengele.

The celebration of Schwarzhuber's birthday on August 29, 1943, was an even bigger affair. The musicians were released from work detail for the three days prior to the celebration to prepare. To honor the camp commander, four trumpets played a regal fanfare that had been composed specifically for the occasion, just as Schwarzhuber stepped out of his car with his wife and two small children. The commander saluted smartly as the orchestra launched into "Fatherland, Your Stars." Szymon later recalled that Schwarzhuber and his family barely noticed the proces-

sion of thousands of recent camp arrivals marching to the
gas chambers.

Through their performances, the musicians of the orchestra were able to curry favor with camp functionaries.
Albert Haemmerle, an otherwise particularly monstrous
block elder, called on the orchestra to relieve his heart-
break after a charming young Polish boy broke up with
him in favor of another camp functionary. Haemmerle
would take every opportunity to visit the orchestra and
ask them to play romances and sentimental melodies for
him while he drowned his sorrows in alcohol. In return,
he spared the musicians from his fury and even brought
them gifts.

More important to the orchestra members than their
relationships with camp functionaries was the way in
which music forged personal connections with their SS
captors, whom they called "esmen." "When an esman listened to music, especially of the kind he really liked, he
somehow became strangely similar to a human being. His
voice lost its typical harshness, he suddenly acquired an
easy manner, and one could talk with him almost as an
equal to another," Szymon wrote in his memoirs. "Sometimes one got the impression that some melody stirred in
him the memory of his dear ones, a girlfriend whom he
had not seen for a long time, and then his eyes got misty
with something that gave the illusion of human tears. At
such moments the hope stirred in us that maybe everything was not lost after all." The irony of such barbarians

having so much appreciation for beauty was not lost on Szymon: "Could people who love music to this extent, people who can cry when they hear it, be at the same time capable of committing so many atrocities on the rest of humanity?"[49]

The orchestra continued to comply with demands for specific repertoire, including medleys of tunes from popular German operettas, a medley of Schubert songs, and a medley of Russian Gypsy music titled after the famous tune "Dark Eyes." In creating the latter, Szymon was assisted by Leon Weintraub, a Russian Jew from France and a brilliant violinist who specialized in both Russian folk music and Gypsy romances. The collaboration was a big hit. It was said that whenever the orchestra played the "Dark Eyes" medley, Schwarzhuber would stop whatever he was doing and walk over to his office window to lose himself in the music.

Some of the pieces that the Germans requested ended up being poor choices from a political standpoint. One music-loving officer brought the orchestra two military marches to which he was sentimentally attached. The first, "Argonne Forest," commemorated the Battle of the Argonne Forest, in which the officer had fought in World War I. The second, "Greetings to Upper Salzburg," referred to the region in which the officer had grown up. Szymon worked late into the night to finish the orchestrations for the next day, but the orchestra never played either arrangement in its entirety. Schwarzhuber, who apparently paid great attention to the orchestra's daily repertoire, had "Argonne Forest" stopped halfway through because he objected to celebrating a battle that was part of a lost war. The commander also interrupted the performance of "Greetings to Upper Salzburg" because he felt it was inappropriate for an ensemble of mostly Jewish prisoners to salute the region that was home to one of Hitler's most famous residences.

Despite its status as a forbidden genre, jazz music was popular among the SS officers and guards in the Birkenau Men's Camp, just as it was in the Auschwitz Main Camp. SS section leader Pery Broad regularly visited the music barracks to jam with a jazz combo that included virtuoso trumpeter Louis Bannet. A world-class accordionist, Broad knew many jazz standards by heart and could hold his own with the orchestra's most skilled improvisers. Broad would even smuggle into the camp the sheet music to popular tunes written by Jewish-American songwriters like Irving Berlin.

Other performances were even more subversive. SS junior squad leader Heinrich Bischop would sneak into the music barracks during odd hours and ask a few of the musicians to play popular Jewish songs. During these visits, the musicians would play as quietly as possible and would post a guard at the door to make sure that nobody walked in on the prohibited music. Despite their best efforts to keep Bischop's love for Jewish music a secret, their clandestine performances were discovered and Bischop was redeployed from Auschwitz to the front lines of the war.

The irony that the German officers and guards were

brutal bigots by day and sentimental lovers of forbidden music by night was not lost on the musicians. "The SS were quite crazy for this music. In the evenings we played this music for these people, who, to put it mildly, had been plaguing us all day long," explained Henry Meyer. "What did we play for them? American melodies. The Americans were their biggest enemies. Who were the composers? Gershwin and Irving Berlin: Jews. Who played? Jews. And who listened and sang along with these schmaltzy songs until tears rolled down their faces? The members of the SS, our tormentors. What a grotesque situation."[50]

While the members of the SS seem to have enjoyed the musicians' performances, the same could not always be said for their fellow prisoners. On Christmas Eve 1943, commander Schwarzhuber ordered a small group of musicians to play Christmas carols at the infirmary of the Birkenau Women's Camp. The musicians brought with them an arrangement of "Silent Night" as well as a selection of Polish carols. They started with "Silent Night" and had just started playing the first Polish carol before quiet weeping grew into deafening sobbing. "Enough of this! Stop! Be gone! Clear out!" the female patients cried shrilly in Polish, offended by the clumsy attempt to bring them comfort. "Let us die in peace!"[51]

In October 1944, several orchestra members were taken to the crematorium camp, where they gave a two-hour concert for the members of the Sonderkommando. This squad had aided in the disposal of captives who had died in the gas chambers. Its members' reward was a little music before they were sent to the gas chambers themselves. As a tribute to their fellow Jewish prisoners, the orchestra played some of the Jewish melodies of which Bischop had been so fond. Between the pieces, the musicians tried to talk with the members of the Sonderkommando, who responded with curses and profanities.

Sometimes, the musicians would simply perform for their own enjoyment. After picking up a piece of trash on the ground that turned out to be the sheet music to "Three Warsaw Polonaises of the Eighteenth Century," Szymon Laks arranged the melodies for three instruments. Since Polish music had been forbidden by the Nazi regime, Szymon and two of his friends would play the polonaises in secret while the other orchestra members were out on their work details. If an outsider suddenly appeared in the music barracks, they would quickly switch to another piece that had been agreed on in advance. For Szymon and his friends, playing the polonaises was not just a way of remembering their homeland. It was a way to show that they would not completely bend to Nazi prejudices.

As the Red Army worked its way toward Poland, the ranks of the SS became smaller and less disciplined. Schwarzhuber himself once appeared in front of the orchestra reeling drunk. He yanked the baton from Szymon's hand, pushed him aside, and took his place in front of the ensemble.

"Now play 'Fatherland, Your Stars,'" he commanded, raising the baton. The orchestra responded professionally, ignoring the clumsy gestures of the intoxicated commander.

Schwarzhuber was still conducting when the march ended. Clearly confused, he asked, "Can you play for me the 'Internationale'?"

The musicians were shocked. Was the camp commander of Birkenau really asking them to play the Soviet national anthem?

"Unfortunately, we cannot play the 'Internationale' because we do not have the music," violinist Leon Weintraub wisely responded.

"And why don't you have the music yet?"

The orchestra just stared at him in silence.

"It doesn't matter," Schwarzhuber finally conceded. "You'll soon have it."[52]

Schwarzhuber was indeed rather sentimental about his orchestra. In November 1944, when the musicians were being transported to the Sachsenhausen concentration camp in preparation for the complete evacuation of Auschwitz, the camp commander pointed to them and sighed with both pride and regret, "My beautiful orchestra!"[53]

Birkenau Women's Camp Orchestra

The orchestra in the Birkenau Men's Camp had a counterpart in the Women's Camp. Like the ensembles elsewhere in Auschwitz, the Birkenau Women's Camp Orchestra provided marching music for the work details as they marched out of camp every morning and back in every evening. The musicians also played at camp inspections, at the arrivals of transports, at the infirmary, and during Sunday concerts.

The women's orchestra was founded in April 1943 by Maria Mandel, who was the commandant of the women's camp. In its first month of existence, only female Aryans were allowed to participate. Jews were soon added to complete the ensemble. The orchestra started with just a bass drum and cymbals, but gradually grew to include mandolins, guitars, a few violins, a cello, a piano, and a few singers.

The absence of winds, specifically brass instruments, gave the women's orchestra a more intimate sound than the orchestra in the Birkenau Men's Camp. Despite the rivalry that emerged between the two ensembles and their Nazi patrons, the members of the orchestras regularly interacted with each other. Heinz Lewin, a Jewish violinmaker from Germany who was equally proficient on clarinet, saxophone, and double bass, would go into the women's camp twice a week to give bass lessons. The orchestras eventually adopted a practice of performing in each other's camp on alternating Sundays.

No examination of the Birkenau Women's Camp Orchestra would be complete without discussing its most famous member, Alma Rosé. Rosé came from one of the most distinguished families in Austro-German music. Her father was Arnold Rosé, the concertmaster of the Vienna Philharmonic Orchestra and the leader of the famed Rosé String Quartet. Her uncle was the composer Gustav

Mahler. Alma was herself a virtuoso violinist of great renown, for her solo playing as well as for her leadership of the Viennese Waltz Girls, a popular all-female ensemble that she had founded.

Rosé fled to London with her father after the German annexation of Austria in 1938, but naively left for Holland to resume her career as a performer. After Germany invaded the Netherlands in May 1940, she found herself trapped in Nazi-occupied Europe. On December 14, 1942, after being ordered to report to the Westerbork Transit Camp, Rosé tried to escape to Switzerland by slipping through Belgium and France. She was arrested in Dijon four days later and was sent to the Drancy Internment Camp, where she was imprisoned for several months before being deported to Auschwitz in July 1943.

After reaching Birkenau, Rosé was appointed conductor of the Women's Camp Orchestra. Because of her stature within the classical music world, she was held in high esteem by the SS guards, who reverentially called her "Frau Alma." Rosé was able to exploit her exalted status by recruiting Jewish musicians into the orchestra and by making sure that all of her musicians enjoyed special privileges such as permission to shower daily and new uniforms weekly. They also received more food and better accommodations, as well as lenient work assignments. As did Szymon Laks in the men's camp, Rosé was able to convince the administration of the women's camp to exempt the orchestral musicians from performing outside during inclement weather.

Rosé was even able to convince the Nazis to spare her musicians from selections. When mandolin player Rachela Zelmanowicz was in the infirmary with typhus—a death sentence for any other prisoner—Josef Mengele was prepared to send her to the gas chambers.

"What's with this one?" he asked during his rounds.

"She's from the orchestra."[54]

Mengele continued on his way without any further discussion. As a member of Rosé's orchestra, Zelmanowicz was untouchable even by him. Her life was spared.

Given the low percentage of female orchestral musicians in the early twentieth century, it is not surprising that there were fewer professional musicians in the women's orchestra than in the men's orchestras of Auschwitz. To compensate for the relatively low levels of ability, Rosé rehearsed her ensemble tirelessly to improve the quality of both their performances and their repertoire. In addition to performing at the camp gate for two or three hours a day, the orchestra rehearsed eight hours a day, six days a week. Rosé knew that the fate of the musicians rested in the reputation of the ensemble.

Rosé died of mysterious causes on April 4, 1944. After ten months of dedicating herself to protecting all of the women in her orchestra, in the end she was unable to save herself. It is suspected that her death was caused by alcohol poisoning, but it is not clear whether the poisoning was accidental or intentional.

After Rosé's death, the orchestra's repertoire and duties were scaled back and its members were put back to work.

The orchestra was dissolved in November 1944, when the non-Jewish members of the orchestra were transferred to the former men's camp. The Jewish performers were deported to the Bergen-Belsen concentration camp.

Other Auschwitz Ensembles

There were a number of ensembles in Auschwitz in addition to the Main Camp Orchestra and the orchestras of the Birkenau Men's and Women's Camps. One was a small ensemble in the subcamp of Birkenau that was established in September 1943 to house transports of Czech Jews from the Theresienstadt concentration camp. This subcamp became known as the "Czech Family Camp," because the prisoners were allowed to remain with their spouses and children instead of having their family members separated and sent to the Men's Camp, the Women's Camp, and the gas chambers.

As with their counterparts throughout Auschwitz, the men who made up the Czech Family Camp orchestra performed for marches and camp inspections. From time to time, they were also ordered to play during the public beatings of prisoners who had broken minor camp rules or who had been sadistically chosen at random. While the other detainees were forced to watch, the guards would make their victim take off his pants and stick his head into an access hatch on the side of the barracks. The guards would command the orchestra to start playing while they savagely whipped the victim's bare backside twenty-five to fifty times. On some nights, drunken guards would roar into the camp on their motorcycles. They would make the orchestra play while they drank, sang songs, and dragged young Jewish women off to rape.

The Czech Family Camp orchestra was disbanded in May 1944, when almost four thousand healthy men and women were sent to other camps. The seven thousand who remained behind were all killed in the gas chambers over two nights in June. After the camp was liquidated, twelve music stands that had been used by its orchestra were reappropriated to the Birkenau Men's Camp Orchestra, along with a few violins, a trumpet, and a cello. This was the first time that the ensemble in the men's camp had possessed a cello. They took full advantage of it by forming a string quartet.

The subcamp of Birkenau that was occupied by Roma in February 1943 had its own ensembles, including a jazz quintet and a band that played popular German songs. The "Gypsy Family Camp" was also home to the notorious laboratory of Josef Mengele, who decided to establish a Gypsy orchestra there after the success of his birthday party. Mengele assigned the task of convening the ensemble to Pery Broad, the SS section leader who regularly played jazz accordion with trumpeter Louis Bannet and other members of the Birkenau Men's Camp Orchestra. It had been Broad who had brought Louis to Mengele's birthday party in March 1943. Now Broad assigned Louis to train the Gypsy orchestra, which was composed of thirty Roma playing violins, accordions, mandolins, and guitars.

"Why should we play for the people who are going to murder us?" a suspicious Romani woman asked Louis at the beginning of the first rehearsal.

"I do not play for them," Louis responded. "I play for me."[55]

For the next few weeks, Broad escorted Louis to the Gypsy Family Camp almost every evening to rehearse the ensemble. On the day the orchestra had its debut, Louis found the Roma dressed in colorful costumes. Men swung from high bars and rings, children performed acrobatic tricks, and a woman walked a tightrope that was strung between two gasoline drums. As Louis led the orchestra in a rhapsody, Mengele stood on his laboratory steps watching the Roma sway and spin to the music.

At the conclusion of the performance, Louis asked Broad whether he would be returning the next day. "That won't be necessary," Broad replied.[56] The entire camp was sent to the gas chambers that evening.

After the Gypsy Family Camp was liquidated in August 1944, the Roma were replaced by more transports from Theresienstadt. Just days after the Gypsy orchestra had played for the first and last time, jazz guitarist Heinz "Coco" Schumann and a fellow prisoner picked up the leftover instruments and performed cabaret songs and operetta melodies for their new block elder. Schumann quickly formed a new orchestra with several other arrivals, including the surviving members of the "Ghetto Swingers" big band, which had been popular in Theresienstadt. If they could not find an appropriate instrument for someone, they would give him an instrument he could not play and have him fake his way through the performances. Sometimes a musician's life depended on his ability to fool the SS officers and guards. "We played music for sheer survival," explained Schumann. "We made music in hell."[57]

The orchestra in Auschwitz III was established in August 1943. It originally consisted mostly of Polish cavalry musicians, a few Russians, and two Jews. The ensemble was later expanded with the arrival of professional musicians from the Netherlands, Poland, and Greece. As was customary for camp orchestras, the musicians played at the camp gate for the departures and returns of the work details. They also gave concerts for the entertainment of SS officers and guards, especially on holidays like Christmas and Hitler's birthday. On Sunday afternoons or in the evenings, they would play peppy marches during the executions of prisoners who had tried to escape.

During the first few months of the orchestra's existence, the musicians spent eight hours a day copying out music and practicing instead of leaving the camp for work details. Once the ensemble and its repertoire were firmly established, the performers were put back to work. By summer 1944, the musicians were working twelve hours a day in the Buna chemical plant. Even then, they were the last ones to leave in the mornings and the first ones to return at night so they could provide the marching music for the other detainees.

One morning, the musicians were joined in their work

detail by a group of young men from the formerly Romanian town of Sighet.

"We work in a warehouse of electrical materials, not far from here," a Jewish violinist from Warsaw named Juliek explained to one of the new arrivals. "The work is neither difficult nor dangerous."

"You are lucky, little fellow," another musician chimed in. "You fell into a good work detail."[58]

The "lucky" arrival was a sixteen-year-old boy named Elie Wiesel, who would later become a revered Holocaust memoirist and a winner of the Nobel Peace Prize.

On January 19, 1945, after the survivors of Auschwitz III had been taken on a two-day death march to the Auschwitz subcamp of Gleiwitz, Wiesel found himself on top of Juliek in a packed barrack. Later that night, Juliek extricated himself from the pile of living and dead bodies long enough to play a Beethoven concerto on the instrument he had brought with him from Auschwitz III.

"Never before had I heard such a beautiful sound. In such silence," Wiesel later recorded. "All I could hear was the violin, and it was as if Juliek's soul had become his bow. He was playing his life. His whole being was gliding over the strings. His unfulfilled hopes. His charred past, his extinguished future. He played that which he would never play again."[59]

When Wiesel woke the next morning, he saw Juliek's lifeless face staring back at him. Next to Juliek was his crushed violin—a fitting symbol of the hundreds of thousands of Jewish lives that had been destroyed in Auschwitz.

Legacies of the Auschwitz Orchestras

The legacies of the Auschwitz orchestras are complicated. Some survivors have asserted that the sounds of the orchestra inspired them to stay alive. "When exhausted in concentration camp Auschwitz by a full day's work, the prisoners came staggering in marching columns, and from afar heard the orchestra playing by the gate—this put them back on their feet. It gave them the courage and the additional strength to survive," recalled one survivor. "We could clearly hear how our colleague musicians spoke to us in masterly fashion on their instruments . . . 'Don't give up, brothers! Not all of us will perish!' "[60]

But many prisoners resented the orchestras. The members of the Birkenau Men's Camp Orchestra saw this when they played in the women's hospital and in the crematorium. Holocaust memoirist Primo Levi wrote of similar reactions he experienced while convalescing in the Auschwitz III infirmary. "One cannot hear the music well from the infirmary. The beating of the big drums and the cymbals reach us continuously and monotonously, but on this weft the musical phrases weave a pattern only intermittently, according to the caprices of the wind. We all look at each other from our beds, because we all feel that this music is infernal," he wrote. "The tunes are few, a dozen, the same ones every day, morning and evening: marches and popular songs dear to every German. They lie engraven on our minds and will be the last thing in camp that we shall forget: they are the voice of the camp, the perceptible expression of its geometrical madness, of the resolution of others to annihilate us first as men in order to kill us more slowly afterwards."[61]

For the musicians who played in the orchestras, music often provided a welcome escape from thoughts that were otherwise filled with despair and death. "For all of us in the orchestra it was our music making that served as our most important life preserver and stimulant during this period," documented a former member of the Auschwitz III orchestra. "We derived so much satisfaction and joy from performing in concert that we found ourselves forgetting for a moment that we were condemned souls living in a hell that the uninitiated could never even imagine."[62]

Music offered the performers opportunities to live a little longer, if only for one more day. While participation in an orchestra did not guarantee survival, it did protect musicians from the harshest of labor assignments and sometimes offered warmer uniforms and slightly better food. In many cases, these advantages offered just enough benefits to allow musicians to outlive the Nazi regime. "Music has kept me alive," Henry Meyer later confirmed. "There is no doubt about it."[63]

Some of the musicians who played in the Auschwitz orchestras continued to make music after the Holocaust. Henry moved to the United States and became a founding

member of the world-famous LaSalle Quartet. Szymon
returned to Paris and resumed his career as a composer.
Jacques also went back to France, but he later immigrated
to Israel, where he ultimately passed his violin down to his
granddaughter.

But many of the musicians never played again. Survivor's guilt, combined with deep regret over having been
forced to exploit their art to save their lives, rendered making music too painful.

One former Auschwitz musician sold his instrument
to Holocaust survivor Abraham Davidovitz. Abraham
was from Tiraspol, in the Romanian region of Bessarabia
(now in Moldova). In 1939 he became one of the million
Eastern European Jews who escaped Nazi oppression by
fleeing to Central Asia. He was imprisoned in Uzbekistan for more than three years, during which time his
wife Manya fed herself and their young son Freddy by
working in a bakery. After the war, a bureaucrat who
mistakenly thought that Tiraspol was in Poland allowed
Abraham and his family to return to Europe with repa-
triated Polish Jews.

In 1946, Abraham was working near Munich with the
American Jewish Joint Distribution Committee to assist
other Holocaust refugees. An impoverished Auschwitz
survivor approached him holding a violin. The survivor
told Abraham that he had played in an orchestra in the
concentration camp and that the violin had saved his life.
Now he wanted to sell the violin. He needed the money,
and had no interest in ever playing the instrument again.

Abraham, who had already been thinking about encouraging Freddy to play, purchased the violin for fifty dollars, a respectable amount of money at the time. Abraham gave the violin to his son, but unfortunately never told him the name of its original owner.

Abraham immigrated to Israel in 1949 with Manya, Freddy, and his new twins, Devorah and Shmuel. They brought with them the violin, which Freddy had already stopped playing.

By 2009, it was time to do something with the instrument, which had been neglected for sixty-five years. They refused to sell it, insisting, "For us, this is a memory of our parents, and a memory of all the Holocaust." The Davidovitz brothers considered donating the instrument to Yad Vashem—Israel's Holocaust Martyrs' and Heroes' Remembrance Authority. They ultimately decided that it belonged not in a museum but on the stage. They brought the instrument to Amnon for restoration and donated it to the virtuoso Shlomo Mintz so that he could play the violin all over the world in the memory of everyone who suffered during the Holocaust. As Freddy explained, "It will go on playing after me and, I hope, for many generations."[64]

4

———

OLE
BULL'S
VIOLIN

The Oslo Philharmonic Orchestra, ca. 1928. Ernst Glaser is sitting
in the concertmaster's chair, a position he would occupy for an
astounding thirty years. *(Courtesy of Ernst Simon Glaser.)*

During the 1940–41 concert season, the Norwegian city of Bergen was celebrating the 175th anniversary of the founding of its orchestra. The Bergen Philharmonic Orchestra was instituted in 1765—a date that establishes the city as the home to one of the oldest orchestras in the world. During one point in its proud heritage, the ensemble's music director was none other than the renowned Norwegian composer Edvard Grieg, one of Bergen's most famous native sons.

The highlight of the Bergen Philharmonic's 175th season was to be an appearance by Ernst Glaser, the concertmaster of the Oslo Philharmonic Orchestra and the country's most prominent musician. Anticipation was especially high because Ernst was going to be performing on a valuable Guarneri del Gesù violin that had once been owned by the celebrated nineteenth-century Norwegian virtuoso Ole Bull—another international figure from Bergen.

But after Nazi youth staged a riot to protest Ernst's plans to perform on the national treasure, his appearance in German-occupied Bergen was canceled in the middle of the concert.

The Nazi Occupation of Norway

Norway declared its neutrality on May 27, 1938, and re-affirmed this position on September 1, 1939. But by April 1940, it was clear that the country would soon be occupied by either Germany or Great Britain. Germany wanted access to Norway's naval and air bases, as well as to the northern port of Narvik for the continued transport of crucial iron ore from neutral Sweden. England wanted to block Germany from having that very same access.

Germany struck first and won a decisive victory. Moving swiftly by air and sea, German forces invaded Norway early in the morning on April 9, 1940. Norwegian cities from the southern coast to the Arctic Circle—including Bergen and Narvik—were occupied within hours. By that afternoon, German troops were marching unchallenged down Oslo's main thoroughfare. Although fighting continued elsewhere in the country for two months, the Norwegian forces were poorly equipped, badly outnumbered, and grossly underprepared. They had no choice but to surrender and did so on June 10, 1940. The German conquest had taken longer than it had in other countries, but it was now complete.

In their mission to Nazify Norway, German leaders found a ready collaborator in Vidkun Quisling, a Norwegian politician whose last name has since become synonymous with opportunistic traitors. In 1933, Quisling had founded the National Union, Norway's Nazi Party. Within two years, Quisling had started accusing Jews of engendering world communism by controlling monetary systems and presses. There were only around 1,600 Jews living in Norway at the time. Although this was less than 0.1 percent of the population, Quisling had asserted that they had secured influential positions as part of an international conspiracy to destroy the country.

Bolstered by the rise of Nazism in Germany, Quisling had ramped up his vitriolic anti-Semitism with each passing year. His goal was to create a "New Norway" in the mold of Hitler's Third Reich, using any means necessary to preserve what he saw as the purity of the Nordic race. To assist him with propagating anti-Semitism and persecuting Jews, Quisling had even created his own paramilitary force. Modeled after Nazi Germany's infamous Brownshirts, the "Hird" took its name from legendary Norse warriors.

After the German invasion, Quisling was named acting prime minister and ultimately minister-president of Norway. With the blessings of the occupying German authorities with whom he shared power, Quisling and the Norwegian state police quickly introduced a number of measures intended to ostracize and eventually eliminate Norway's already small Jewish population. In May 1940, the police confiscated radios belonging to Jewish families. In addition to preventing Jews from listening to foreign broadcasts, this measure marked the first efforts to identify Norwegian Jews and rob them of the legal rights afforded to other Norwegians. The process of registering Jews was expanded that fall, when the Nazis demanded and received lists of the Jewish residents of Oslo and Trondheim, which were the two largest Jewish communities in Norway.

The Norwegian Nazis instigated a campaign of harassment against the newly identified Jews. They smashed the windows of stores that were owned by Jews, or painted over them with anti-Semitic slogans such as "Jewish Parasites!" and "Jews not tolerated in Norway."[65] A number of Jewish doctors were deprived of their medical licenses and therefore of their right to work.

There was also an attempt to dismiss Jewish musicians from their positions. Edvard Sylou-Creutz, who was named a co-director of the Norwegian Broadcasting Corporation after the Nazis took power, announced that all music by Jewish composers should be banned and that all performers should be required to be members of the National Union Party. Shortly thereafter, composer and prominent music critic Per Reidarson proposed a Union of Norwegian Artists and Journalists. Modeled after the Reich Culture Chamber, Reidarson's Union would have excluded all Jewish artists from their professions.

It was this same movement to blacklist Jews that blocked Ernst Glaser from performing in Bergen.

Ernst Glaser

Ernst Glaser was born in Germany, but had identified himself as a Norwegian ever since he moved to Norway on August 28, 1928. In return, he became one of the country's most beloved cultural figures. Known for his virtuosic performances as much as for his devilish sense of humor and good looks, he was a national celebrity.

Ernst was born in Hamburg on February 24, 1904, to Jewish umbrella manufacturer Felix Glaser and his wife, Jenny Rosenbaum. It was Jenny, a pianist herself, who decided that Ernst would play the violin, while his older sister Lizzie would play the piano. From 1921 to 1925 Ernst was a student of the legendary violin pedagogue Carl Flesch in Berlin. Ernst subsequently earned a position as the associate concertmaster of the Bremen State Orchestra, a position he held from 1926 to 1928.

In 1928, Ernst became the concertmaster of the Oslo Philharmonic Orchestra at the recommendation of Max Rostal, a fellow student of Flesch's. Rostal had been the concertmaster in Oslo, but was leaving to move back to Berlin, where he had been offered a teaching position at the prestigious music conservatory. Issay Dobrowen, the conductor of the Oslo Philharmonic who would later serve as one of the principal conductors of the Palestine Orchestra during its first three seasons, selected Ernst from seven finalists. Ernst immigrated to Norway and was immediately smitten with both the country and the Norwegian pianist Kari Marie Aarvold, whom he married in 1929.

Shortly after arriving in Norway, Ernst dedicated himself to raising the level of music in his newly adopted homeland. One way he accomplished this was by teaching two generations of Norwegian violinists. Indeed, most of the important Norwegian violinists of the latter twentieth century—including Ernst's successor as the concertmaster of the Oslo Philharmonic and a number of other members of the orchestra—were his students.

Ernst made his most significant contributions as a performer, serving both as the concertmaster of the Oslo Philharmonic and as the leader of the orchestra's string quartet. A devoted advocate for contemporary music—especially new music from Norway—he initiated a tradition of performing a violin concerto with the orchestra every year. These were often the world premieres of concertos by contemporary Norwegian composers who otherwise would have been relegated to obscurity. He also performed abroad, in Sweden, Denmark, and Germany, bringing distinction back to the country he now called his home.

Ernst applied for citizenship in 1933, the same year that his daughter Berit was born. He sensed the mounting anti-Semitism in Germany, and was eager to become naturalized in Norway. He became a Norwegian citizen in 1934. He welcomed his second daughter Liv into the world one year later. Ernst begged his parents to join his new family in Norway, but his father was among the many German Jews who did not foresee the danger and insisted on staying. He maintained that he had no reason to live in fear in the country that had always been his home.

Ernst's sister Lizzie also remained in Germany. She was more concerned about the future of German Jews than her father was, but she still refused to leave. Lizzie changed her mind after her husband was arrested on Kristallnacht.

Having served Germany honorably in World War I, Ernst's brother-in-law was fortunate enough to be released within three weeks. After being warned that he would be arrested for a second time, he and Lizzie drove straight across the border to Holland.

The Kristallnacht riots also convinced Ernst's father to finally emigrate. With the help of the board of directors of the Oslo Philharmonic and members of the Norwegian government who had grown fond of his playing, Ernst was able to overcome discriminatory immigration policies and secure entry visas for his Jewish parents. They moved in with Ernst and his family with just their suitcases, their umbrellas, and two German reichsmarks in their pockets.

Ernst's favorite aunt did not make it out of Germany. She perished in a concentration camp.

Ole Bull's Violin

For his January 16, 1941, appearance with the Bergen Philharmonic Orchestra, Ernst was going to play a violin concerto by Christian Sinding to commemorate the venerable Norwegian composer's eighty-fifth birthday. As a special treat for the Bergen audience, Ernst planned to perform the concerto on a violin that had been recently donated to the Oslo Philharmonic by the descendants of Ole Bull.

In addition to being hailed as one of the greatest violinists of all time, Ole Bornemann Bull (1810–80) was—and still is—a source of immense national pride in Norway. While teaching himself to play the violin, he developed new techniques for replicating sounds from Norwegian nature and for performing folksongs and country dances. When the king of Denmark asked Bull who had taught him to play, he replied, "The Mountains of Norway, your majesty."[66]

The result was a ruggedly individualistic style of playing. Bull preferred long, heavy bows that are more appropriate to the traditional Norwegian Hardanger fiddle than to the classical violin. His own experience playing the Hardanger fiddle also convinced him to flatten the bridges and fingerboards of his violins to allow him to draw the bow across several strings at the same time. Even his repertoire was unique. He had a penchant for performing his own flamboyant compositions—often based on Norwegian melodies—instead of the established warhorses.

Bull did much more than bring prestige to his homeland. He seemed to personify it. Born and raised in Bergen, he grew up mingling with Norwegian peasants at the local market and in the country. From them he developed a deep respect for the Norwegian folk character that had been subjugated during the country's four-hundred-year union with Denmark. Bull became a patriotic leader in the Norwegian National Revival, spearheading the establishment of the Norwegian National Theatre in Bergen and later attempting to found a National Academy of Music in Christiana (now Oslo) with Grieg. Bull felt that his countrymen held "a wonderfully deep and characteristic sound-board" vibrating in their breasts,[67] and his mission was to endow them with the strings that would resonate the unique Norwegian sound throughout the world. He spent most of his life touring the world's greatest capitals, but never grew tired of returning to his homeland to share his talent with his compatriots. Charismatic and patriotic, he was Norway's most famous and most loyal son.

In May 1940, Bull's granddaughter presented the Oslo Philharmonic with a violin that was made in 1742. The instrument was already valuable because it was a Guarneri del Gesù, and such instruments are generally considered to be equal to—if not better than—the finest Stradivariuses. But this instrument was also a historic treasure because it was once owned and played by Ole Bull himself.

Ernst was the first person to play the violin after several decades of neglect. Taking the valuable instrument out of the elongated case that was custom-built to carry Ole Bull's extralong bows, Ernst played Ole Bull's song "The Herd Girl's Sunday." "I have never heard such applause," Ernst later recalled, adding with his typical lighthearted humor, "although *that* had nothing to do with me."[68]

The instrument was not in great shape and required some restoration. Despite a slight defect in the construction of the scroll—a common problem among late Guarneris—the experts in Oslo nevertheless claimed that the violin was among the best instruments that Bartolomeo Giuseppe Guarneri ever made. Ernst found the violin to have a relatively small sound, but he did note that it had a lovely, shining tone. He played the violin in Oslo in the fall of 1940, and spent the next several months continuing to acclimate the instrument back into playing condition. Now he was bringing the instrument to Ole Bull's hometown for one of its first appearances in the twentieth century.

The citizens of Bergen were quite eager to hear Ole Bull's Violin. None of them had even dreamed that they would ever get to witness the magical sound with which the revered Norwegian virtuoso had enchanted audiences all over the world a century earlier. To reinforce the connection to Ole Bull, Harald Heide—who had been the philharmonic's artistic director since 1908—had prepared something special. The grand finale would be Heide's arrangement of Ole Bull's *Polacca Guerriera* for violin and orchestra, with Ernst once again playing the solo part on Ole Bull's Violin.

Bergen

The philharmonic concert began innocently enough, with a performance of Haydn's *Military* Symphony. About fifteen minutes into the Haydn, a large group of teenage boys entered the concert hall and occupied the empty seats. Some audience members found it nice that the young people were taking an interest in classical music, even if they did arrive late. Others immediately suspected that the teenagers' motives were much more sinister: the boys were members of the National Youth—Norway's version of the Hitler Youth—who were planning a demonstration if the Jewish concertmaster from Oslo set foot on the stage.

The Nazis had already called for a partial boycott of

the performance. Although Quisling's National Union Party had allowed the philharmonic to hold the concert, it had forbidden the newspapers from reviewing it. The German authorities had approved the program, but had prohibited their people from attending the concert. They saw the appearance of a Jewish soloist as a slap in the face of the occupying forces.

Up to that point, the Nazi censorship of the Bergen Philharmonic had been limited to their repertoire, much like Germany's suppression of compositions by Jews. Music by composers who were obviously Jewish had been banned, but the censors had been oblivious to the Jewish heritages of figures like the Czech composer Jaromír Weinberger. Later that year, after Nazi Germany invaded the Soviet Union, the works of Russians were also prohibited, robbing the audience of their favorite composer, Tchaikovsky. But a Nazi demonstration in the middle of a concert was unthinkable, especially since Ernst had played the same concerto on the same violin three days earlier in Oslo.

The violin concerto was supposed to follow the Haydn symphony, but Ernst did not appear. The lengthy gap between pieces and the presence of the National Youth created a foreboding silence throughout the audience. Backstage, Nazi officials were telling maestro Heide that Ernst must not be allowed to perform. Heide was instructed to stop the concert. He refused. He did, however, buy himself some time by postponing Ernst's appearance to later in the concert.

Heide returned to the stage and announced a change: the orchestra would now play *The Flute of Sanssouci*, an orchestral suite by German composer Paul Graener that came after the concerto on the printed program. The appearance of *The Flute of Sanssouci* on the program must have placated the German censors who had originally signed off on Ernst's performance. The work, which pays homage to the flute-playing eighteenth-century Prussian king Frederick the Great, was composed by an ardent Nazi who was also the vice president of the Reich Chamber of Music.

The orchestra played all four movements of Graener's suite. Then there was another long pause. Instead of returning to the podium, Heide could be seen pacing back and forth behind the orchestra, looking distraught. The members of the orchestra looked at him and at each other in confusion. Finally, Heide resigned himself to the fact that he would be putting Ernst at too much of a risk if he allowed him to perform. Heide stepped to the front of the stage and announced that he was very sorry, but that due to unforeseen circumstances the remainder of the concert would have to be canceled.

"What the hell!" yelled one of the National Youth from the balcony. "Why doesn't he come?" They had been waiting to protest Ernst through half of the Haydn and all of the Graener. They had grown impatient for the protest to begin.

"Is it because Glaser is a Jew?" someone else shouted.[69]
Then all hell broke loose.

The demonstrators started booing and chanting "Down with the Jews! Down with the Jews! Away with the Jew Moses Salomon,"[70] referring to the object of their scorn not by his true German name "Ernst Glaser" but by "Moses Salomon," a very Jewish-sounding name that they invented for him. The National Youth dropped flyers from the balcony that read, in poorly spelled Norwegian:

OLE BULL'S VIOLIN.
is a Norwegian national treasure.

His works are the founding pillars of *Norwegian* music

THE NORWEGIAN YOUTH will not allow our Germanic honor to be soiled by

THE JEW MOSES SALOMON
(alias Ernst Glaser)

This Jewish peddler has misappropriated Ole Bull's fiddle, our national treasure, and is traveling by land and sea making money off of it.

WE DEMAND THAT MOSES SALOMON'S PED-DLING TOUR BE STOPPED HERE IN BERGEN:
                                    National Youth

The lights in the concert hall came on, allowing the audience to finally see the uniforms of the National Youth. In what is surely one of the most heroic moments in the history of music, the music lovers in attendance became enraged and attacked the demonstrators.

After Germany had occupied Bergen, the audience had

resolved to keep the philharmonic concerts as free from Nazi politics as possible. They had accepted the presence of German soldiers and civilians in the concert hall, but these new audience members had not interfered with the performances. This protest was something completely different. It was an unwelcome intrusion into their artistic sanctuary. They decided to fight back.

In response to the chants of "Down with the Jews," the Norwegian actor Hans Stormoen called out, "Down with the rioters."[71]

Fights broke out throughout the concert hall. One member of the audience struck a Nazi hooligan with the handle of her umbrella. A violinist from the orchestra tore off his tuxedo jacket and jumped from the stage to join the bloody fistfight against the National Youth.

Before things could get too far out of hand, Heide leapt to the podium and quickly instructed the orchestra to strike up the Norwegian national anthem.

The entire orchestra rose. As soon as the audience and the National Youth heard the opening chords, their patriotism obliged them to stop what they were doing and sing along. The fighting ceased, with the exception of a few minor skirmishes at the back of the hall that were caused by the state police's removing Hans Stormoen and other counterprotesters. The ejected audience members were released later that evening with the flimsy explanation that they had been detained for their own protection during the angry demonstration. The members of the National Youth were never even questioned for their role in the fracas. Instead, they were praised by the German authorities for their passion.

When the orchestra finished the national anthem, the audience spontaneously launched into the Norwegian royal anthem, which begins "God save our gracious King." (It is sung to the same melody as Britain's "God Save the King/Queen" and America's "My Country 'Tis of Thee.") By singing the royal anthem, the audience was thumbing their noses at the Nazis by brazenly displaying their allegiance to King Haakon VII.

Norway's first king after the country gained independence from Sweden in 1905, Haakon had fled Oslo during the German invasion on April 9, 1940. He and his government had retreated to the town of Elverum, where they had laid the legal groundwork to continue the war against Germany from outside the country. Since fleeing to England on June 7, 1940, the king-in-exile had become an international symbol of Norway's resistance to the Nazi occupation. Despite several attempts both before and after Haakon's escape to pressure him to use his constitutional authority to legitimize the Nazi regime, the defiant king had steadfastly maintained that he would abdicate rather than support the appointment of the Quisling government. In an inspirational address over the BBC on July 8, 1940, King Haakon had announced that he would maintain Norway's sovereignty until the country was liberated.

Throughout the national anthem, the National Youth had been compelled to stand at attention, extending their right arms in the Nazi salute. While the rioters had stood motionless, Heide had made sure that Ernst and Ole Bull's Violin were safely escorted out of the hall. Members of the Nazi Party had been waiting for him outside the main doors to the concert hall, but were fortunately too naive to realize that an artist would leave by the backstage door.

By the time the royal anthem started, the National Youth realized they had been tricked. "Close the doors!" they shouted as they ran to block the exits. "Get the Hird here!" they cried.[72]

The National Youth were no match for the determined audience, which simply laughed loudly and booed them. One man forced himself through the blockade, slapping one of the youths in the face as he passed by. The rest of the defiant audience simply marched out the door.

The courage of the Bergen citizens did not stop at the performance. Despite being warned against printing anything about the concert, Bergen's *Morning Paper* and *Evening Gazette* both published editorials blasting the riot, the latter categorizing the demonstration as "regrettable" and "exceedingly unfortunate." The actions of the National Youth, the *Evening Gazette* maintained, were "an assault against the music-loving public in our city."[73] The philharmonic board sent a letter to city leaders and the Norwegian Department of Public Information and Culture to protest the behavior of the National Youth. The department responded by praising the rioters for the successful demonstration and by punishing those who spoke out against it. From that point on, the members of the philharmonic board were forbidden from serving on the city council.

Oslo

Ernst returned to Oslo, where he continued to face anti-Semitism. In February 1941, the German occupation authorities ordered his removal from the Oslo Philharmonic. Philharmonic leaders protested, insisting that Ernst was so important to the orchestra, they would put their jobs on the line to protect him from being fired. At first, the Germans refused to relent, insisting, "A Jew cannot have an official position in Norway."[74] They ultimately yielded to pressure and announced that the question of whether Ernst could keep his job would be put off until later.

The pressure came from philharmonic leaders as well as from Dr. Gulbrand Lunde. As the minister of the Department of Public Information and Culture, Lunde was in charge of propaganda for the Nazi regime and second in command only to Quisling himself. He was, simply put, the Norwegian equivalent of Nazi Germany's Joseph Goebbels. Although Lunde was an ardent devotee of Nazism, he also maintained a deep respect for Ernst's artistry and wanted him to continue performing. Like the German Nazis who oversaw the orchestras in Auschwitz, Lunde's personal pride in supporting an outstanding ensemble overshadowed his aversion to the Jews who played in it.

Across Norway, the oppression of Jews continued to worsen. In July 1941, all Norwegian Jews in civil service were dismissed, and Jewish lawyers and other professionals were permanently stripped of their licenses. That fall, all

Jewish stores were confiscated. In February 1942, Quisling amended Norway's constitution to reinstate a prohibition against admitting Jews into the country. This restored the exact language that had been part of the original constitution in 1814 but which had been rescinded in 1851.

The Jews in central and northern Norway became the victims of increasingly vicious campaigns of terror. In April 1941, the Germans seized the synagogue in Trondheim, removing all of the Hebrew inscriptions and replacing the Stars of David in the stained-glass windows with swastikas. In June, the Nazis arrested Norwegian and stateless Jews in Harstad, Narvik, and Tromsø, sending them to the Sydspissen concentration camp in Tromsø. The Jews arrested in Trøndelag, Møre, and Romsdal were sent to the concentration camp that had been established in the Vollan prison in Trondheim and later to the one at Grini, near Oslo.

In southern Norway, especially in Oslo, the Jewish community was living in relative calm. When the Germans had declared on September 25, 1940, that all religious denominations would be protected, the Jews had believed them. Some of the Jews who had fled to Sweden during the German invasion had even returned to Norway after assuming that there would be no danger. Yes, some of their apartments and homes had been commandeered by the Germans, but this had also happened to gentiles. The Jews had no reason to believe that they would be singled out for persecution.

The period that allowed Oslo's eight hundred Jews to live in peace came to an end on September 24, 1942, when the German security police ordered the Norwegian state police to begin making plans to arrest all of Norway's Jews and their families for deportation.

Ernst's Nazi defenders immediately understood that they would not be able to protect him any longer. Jim Johannesen, a high-ranking member of the Hird, told Ernst that plans were being made for a large-scale campaign against the Jews, but that senior officials in the Quisling government did not want anything to happen to him. In his efforts to save Ernst from being arrested, Johannesen volunteered to drive him across the Swedish border in a car owned by Captain Oliver Møystad, the commander of the Hird and the acting head of the state police. Ernst refused.

Johannesen was an accomplished violinist who had even been the concertmaster in Bergen for a while. He was also known for inventing fantastical stories. Like other Jews living in Oslo, Ernst was blissfully ignorant of the full extent of the Nazis' evil plans for the Jews. He decided not to take Johannesen's warnings seriously. He did not even bother to tell his family, as he felt that there was no reason to worry them.

To convince Ernst of the severity of the situation, Johannesen took him to see Minister Lunde, who welcomed Ernst warmly. Lunde confirmed that the Jews were in jeopardy. He encouraged Ernst to find refuge in Sweden, promising that this would only be a temporary measure. Ernst would be welcome to return home once the war was over and the Norwegian government regained its autonomy from Nazi Germany.

Ernst appreciated the sentiment, but insisted that he could not leave his children and parents.

"Yes, we can fix that," Lunde replied. "We could put the children in Telemark. Isn't that where Quisling is from?"

The very thought came as a terrible shock to Ernst. "And what about my parents?" he asked.

Lunde assured him that arrangements could be made for them, as well. Ernst remained unconvinced. As with his father four years earlier in Germany, Ernst simply could not believe that he and his family would really be in danger in their own country.

Within one month, all of that changed. At nine o'clock on the evening of Friday, October 23, the state police started planning a massive operation that would result in the arrests of all Jewish men in Norway between the ages of fifteen and sixty-five in one day. They scheduled the campaign for Monday, October 26, and spent the weekend hastily compiling a list of male Jews.

The plot was supposed to be a secret, but there was a mole in the office of Nikolaus von Falkenhorst, the German general who had led the invasion of Norway and who had remained in the country to command the occupying troops. That secret agent was Theodor Steltzer, an officer in the German army who had never been sympathetic to Nazism. Near the end of the war, Steltzer would be called back to Berlin, arrested by the Gestapo, and sentenced to death for his role in the failed attempt to assassinate Hitler on July 20, 1944.

In 1942, Steltzer was secretly working with the Norwegian resistance movement. He often met with his underground contacts in the home of Wolfgang Geldmacher, a German businessman who was married to a Norwegian. When Steltzer notified Geldmacher of the impending arrests, Geldmacher quickly mobilized his contacts in the resistance movement and urged them to help their Jewish compatriots escape to Sweden. Their campaign was a remarkable success. By the beginning of 1943, the heroes of the Norwegian resistance movement would help 850 Jews—more than half of all of the Jews living in Norway before the Holocaust—flee to safety in Sweden. Yad Vashem would later declare the members of the movement "Righteous among the Nations" for risking their lives to save the Jews.

Sweden was an ideal destination for Norway's Jewish refugees. It shares a thousand-mile border with Norway, allowing for numerous passages through the Scandinavian mountain range. Sweden was also politically convenient as one of only five European countries that managed to remain neutral during World War II. Most important, the country welcomed Jewish immigrants. By receiving thousands of Jewish refugees from twenty-seven countries, Sweden became the only European country to double its Jewish population during the Holocaust.

Geldmacher's associates in the Norwegian resistance

included pianists Robert Riefling and Amalie Christie, who both paid Ernst a visit on October 25, 1942—the day before the arrests were to take place.

"We're not leaving this apartment until you agree to leave," they told him. They had already made plans to hide Ernst and his family.

Ernst and Kari remained in Oslo, secreted in the apartment of the famous Norwegian architect Magnus Poulsson. The children stayed with family friends in the coastal town of Moss. Ernst's parents were sent to a guesthouse owned by a sister of the Norwegian pianist Mary Barratt Due, but were later relocated several times.

The next morning, Ernst and Kari called the couple who lived in the apartment below the one they had abandoned. The neighbors confirmed that Ernst and Kari's apartment had been raided. Once the Norwegian police officers had established that nobody was home, they had moved on. The two policemen who had visited the Glaser apartment were one of sixty-two pairs of state policemen, Oslo policemen, and members of the German SS who had gathered that morning at five thirty. Each set of partners had been given an envelope with the names of ten Jews whom they were to hunt down and arrest.

Meanwhile, Geldmacher and Riefling were trying to figure out what they could do with Ernst. While all of the Jews in Norway were in danger, they knew that Ernst would be under particular scrutiny. He had been in the spotlight ever since the incident with Ole Bull's Violin in Bergen. It was quite possible that he would be singled out for persecution.

Still not fully comprehending the magnitude of his danger, Ernst continued about his business by attending a philharmonic rehearsal that morning. Then he did something reckless. He went to visit Lunde to ask whether the minister would keep his word about protecting his family. He was unable to get in. Ernst learned that Lunde and his wife had died earlier that day when their car had fallen off a ferry dock. It was—and still is—suspected that the bizarre accident was really an assassination by Germans who wanted a minister whose views were more closely aligned with their own.

Ernst finally realized that his life was in jeopardy. He also understood that with Lunde gone there was no longer anyone who would protect him. He had no choice but to disappear quickly. But he was still determined to play the concert that evening, which was also to be broadcast over the radio. The Norwegian painter Henrik Sørensen got on his knees and begged Ernst not to show up to the concert, but Ernst remained resolute. He would perform, even if it meant appearing in a very public venue where the Nazis could be waiting for him.

Ernst played the concert. He was on pins and needles the whole time. The program featured a modern work by a Finnish composer. There were several violin solos, but Ernst found it difficult to focus on the music. Preoccupied with the dangers he faced, he came in late on one of his solo entrances.

"Too late, too late," the Finnish conductor Georg Schnéevoigt admonished him in their shared language of German.

"That doesn't sound good," Ernst thought to himself, nervously wondering if the same could be said for his delay in leaving the country.

Fortunately, it was not too late. After the concert, Ernst escaped into a car that was waiting for him by city hall and vanished. He was taken to meet Søren Christian Sommerfelt, who worked in the Ministry of Foreign Affairs. Sommerfelt gave Ernst some money and told him to hide with an accomplice in Oslo and await further instructions. He would be taken out of the country as soon as possible.

Other Jewish men were not as fortunate. On October 26 and 27, 260 of them were arrested and taken to the Bredtveit Prison, just outside Oslo. From there they were transported by train to the Berg concentration camp, where they were joined on October 28 by 350 other Jewish men. The prisoners spent the next month suffering from starvation, inadequate medical care, and an absence of clothing and bedding in a facility that lacked water and sanitation.

The first Jews to arrive in the Berg concentration camp were trumpeter Herman Sachnowitz, his four brothers, and their father. The Sachnowitz family had been contemplating leaving Norway ever since the German invasion, but the four oldest males were continually arrested by the Nazis. Knowing that whichever Sachnowitz was being held captive at any given time would be shot if any of the others fled the country, the family had no choice but to stay. All five male members of the Sachnowitz family were arrested at four thirty in the morning on October 26 and taken to Berg.

On November 26, 1942, the Sachnowitz men and around 275 other prisoners from the Berg concentration camp were transported on a special train back to Oslo, where they were reunited with 562 Jews, including women, children, and elderly people. Among them was one of Herman's sisters. They had all been arrested the night before as the final stage of a campaign to round up not just the males but every Jew who remained in Norway.

Jews who held citizenships in England, America, Central and South America, neutral countries, and countries allied with Germany were spared from deportation. The remaining 532 were put on the German troop ship *Donau*, sailed to Stettin—the same Polish seaport from which Germany had embarked for its invasion of Norway in 1940—and loaded into cattle cars bound for Auschwitz. There 186 able-bodied men were put to work in Birkenau and Auschwitz III, while 346 women, children, and elderly people were sent directly to the gas chambers.

On March 3, 1943, 158 Jews who had been interned in the Bredtveit Prison after missing the first deportation arrived in Auschwitz. From this second transport, thirty-eight were put to work while 120 Jews of ages ranging from fourteen months to eighty years were sent to their deaths.

Herman Sachnowitz's father and sister were selected for death immediately upon disembarking at Auschwitz in November 1942, as were both of Herman's remaining sisters when they arrived in March 1943. Herman and his four brothers were among those from the first transport who were sent to work at Auschwitz III. Herman's three older brothers would die in Auschwitz III within four months. Herman's little brother would later die in Josef Mengele's infamous experimental block.

Herman's own life was spared in August 1943. That was when he was accepted as a trumpeter into the newly formed orchestra at Auschwitz III, an ensemble with which he performed until the camp was evacuated on January 18, 1945. He was transferred to Buchenwald and then to Bergen-Belsen, where he was liberated on April 15. He traveled back to Norway as quickly as possible and returned to his home. It was empty. Herman was the only member of his entire family who had survived.

The Sachnowitz family was certainly not the only Norwegian family to be completely erased during the Holocaust. Of the 762 Jews deported from Norway, all but twenty-three died in German concentration camps.

Flight to Sweden

On October 27, 1942, while Herman and more than six hundred other Jewish men were being taken to the Berg concentration camp, Ernst was secretly taken to see Lise Børsum, a key figure in Geldmacher's circle who was later arrested for her role in the Norwegian resistance. It was in Børsum's house that Geldmacher had met with and mobilized forty members of the Norwegian resistance movement two days earlier. And it was Børsum herself who would arrange Ernst's escape to Sweden. Børsum informed Ernst that he would have to leave Kari and their daughters behind in Norway. At the time, nobody guessed that the Nazis would come for the Jewish women and children one month later.

Ernst was given shelter by a man named Hasselberg, whose wife was out of town. While he hid at Hasselberg's house, Ernst had two tasks: to cook dinner and to avoid being seen through the windows. On his second day at Hasselberg's house, Ernst received a visit from Kari. She informed him that he would be leaving that day. She gave him a series of complex instructions from Børsum. The cloak-and-dagger plot to get Ernst out of Norway sounded like something out of a spy novel.

Ernst would be picked up by Berit Poulsson, who was disabled and who was therefore allowed to drive wherever she wanted. Poulsson would drive him to the train station, where he was to wait for Amalie Christie. When Christie arrived, Ernst would pretend to ignore her, as if she were a total stranger. He would follow her as she boarded the train. Through a secret signal, she would draw his attention to a luggage compartment that would contain a backpack full of items he would need for his journey.

Ernst did as he was instructed. He even had Kari cut off all of his hair in the hopes that nobody would recognize him. It was raining, so he was able to shield himself from view underneath a large umbrella. Since holding a violin case would ruin his disguise, Ernst left behind his personal violin—an excellent instrument made by the eighteen-century violinmaker Giovanni Battista Guadagnini that his father had bought for him. While Ernst was waiting for Christie at the crowded train station, Børsum showed up. She brought with her a letter that she explained was a coded message. She instructed Ernst to take the document with him to Sweden. "Of the group with which you are going, you seem to be the most sensible," she said. "So please keep this with you and deliver it to the Norwegian legation in Stockholm."

Ernst boarded a train that would take him toward Hamar, seventy-five miles north of Oslo. His disguise seemed sufficient until he heard someone calling his name. A young man whom Ernst did not recognize told him to get off the train.

Ernst was relieved to see that the young man was accompanied by Christie. The young man pushed something into Ernst's hand. It was Swedish kroner, to give Ernst a little extra money. Then he gave Ernst his final instructions from the Norwegian resistance movement in Oslo. Until then, Ernst had not been informed of his destination, out of fear that he would be arrested and tortured into betraying details about the escape routes being cultivated by the resistance movement. Now that he was safely on board the train, Ernst was told to disembark at Romedal, the last station before Hamar, and find a taxi driver named Thorleif Bronken.

Once the train was finally under way, Ernst hid his face behind a newspaper. Despite his efforts to travel incognito, a young woman on the train recognized Norway's most famous living musician.

"Aren't you Mr. Glaser?" she asked.

"No, I'm afraid you're mistaken," he audaciously replied.

When Ernst disembarked at Romedal, he and four other escapees were whisked away in Thorleif Bronken's taxi. They were driven to a small schoolhouse in Åsbygda, where a teacher named Kjellaug Herset lived. The escapees hid in the schoolhouse attic for two nights, maintaining complete silence during the days. If Herset's Nazi colleague heard something fall on the floor, a bed squeak, or any other noise overhead, it could have meant their deaths. On the second night, Kjellaug's fiancé Lars Sagberg informed the escapees that he would take them by truck to the Glomma River, which runs near the Swedish border. They would cross the river on a barge. Another guide would help them finish the journey over the mountainous terrain on foot.

A few weeks before helping Ernst and the other four refugees get to the Glomma, Sagberg had met with another group of escapees in the schoolhouse. The nine refugees had gathered around a radio listening to the BBC, whose broadcasts had been forbidden. After Sagberg changed the channel to the Nazi-controlled station in Oslo, they all heard a declaration that anyone who helped Jews escape the country would receive the death penalty. The escapees bristled and looked at Sagberg nervously.

"Oh, that makes no difference," he assured them.

"Doesn't it frighten you to hear that there is a death penalty for helping a Jew, when there are nine of us?" one refugee asked Herset.

"That makes nine death penalties," she responded defiantly.

"This is something we have heard several times before, so we're not worried," Sagberg confirmed.[75]

After crossing the Glomma, Ernst and the other escapees in his convoy were taken to a log cabin. During their second night at the cabin, they started their journey on foot. A farmer followed behind the group on a horse and sled to cover their tracks. After several hours of walking through the snowy night, they arrived at another log cabin, where they were given food and coffee. Cold, wet, and tired, they were hoping to find a warm place to rest, but the log cabin was unheated. So they continued their journey. They did not find another log cabin until 1 a.m. the next day.

Ernst was exhausted. He was in no shape for this type of physical activity. One of his knees had become so stiff from overuse that it would no longer move. He fashioned a cane to assist him the rest of the way. He was also freezing. Other than the long coat he had brought with him, he was not properly dressed for hiking in the snow. He was given a raincoat, but he was so short that the coat dragged on the ground when he walked. To make matters worse, when he placed his soaked ski boots next to the fire to dry them, they shrank so much that he could not put them back on.

On the next day, a third guide rowed the refugees across a lake to Sweden. Ernst made his way to Stockholm, where he knew he would have the best chance of earning a living through playing the violin. He also intended to take the letter from Christie to the Norwegian legation. It was only later that Ernst opened the letter to find that it contained not a coded message but money. It was the same amount that Ernst had held in his bank account in Norway. It was his to spend.

Ernst's wife Kari and their daughters fled to Sweden a few weeks after him. Warned of impending danger by the girls' schoolteachers, they escaped Oslo just as the Nazis started rounding up women and children. Although Kari would have been considered an Aryan by Germany's Nuremberg Laws, Quisling's severe interpretations of Jewishness would have included her for being married to a Jew. She and her daughters—who despite having been christened would be considered Jewish by virtue of having a Jewish father—would have been arrested, deported to Auschwitz, and sent directly to the gas chambers.

At first, Kari and the girls traveled north, just as Ernst had done. They hid on a farm in Hamar for three weeks before being sent back to Oslo. After returning to the capital city, they continued traveling south. When they reached the southeastern Norwegian border town of Ørje, they walked in the rain toward the Swedish border with twelve other women and children.

After becoming separated from their guide and getting lost in the forest, they arrived at a farm the next morning. Approaching the farmhouse could have meant walking right into the arms of Nazi sympathizers, but Kari had no choice. By this time, seven-year-old Liv and nine-year-old Berit were too cold and exhausted to continue any farther.

Kari knocked on the door. When an old woman answered, Kari blurted out that they were refugees on their way to Sweden who had gotten lost. The old woman proved to be friendly. She informed them that they were still in Norway, and had been heading in the wrong direction. She invited them in for coffee and told them, "You must not stay here for longer than an hour, because there are inspections here every morning.

"But you are not far from the border," she assured Kari. "My husband will guide you across."

After struggling to wake the exhausted children, Kari and the girls continued their journey. She and her daughters joined Ernst in Stockholm on December 19.

Ernst's parents had an even more difficult odyssey. They had escaped Nazi Germany just a few years earlier and were now fleeing a second country. Exhausted and freezing in the Norwegian winter, the elderly couple could not keep up with their transport. There were Germans in the same forest that night with dogs and guns searching for two deserters, but the elder Glasers simply could not run anymore. They found a stump in the forest and sat down. Their guide did not realize that they had fallen behind until much later. He brought the rest of the group to the border and went back to Norway for the Glasers.

When he found them later that night, they were sitting by themselves in the woods, holding hands, expecting to die together. Instead, he brought them safely to Sweden.

Sweden

In Stockholm, Ernst used his contacts to establish a new life. He and his family stayed with old friends who owned an antiquarian bookstore. He borrowed a violin from the son-in-law of the late concertmaster of the Royal Stockholm Philharmonic Orchestra. It was not until several months later that Ernst would be reunited with his Guadagnini violin, which Geldmacher smuggled into Sweden hidden in a suitcase full of clothes.

When Ernst visited the Swedish Music Society, he was told that he was free to give concerts, but that as a refugee he was ineligible for steady employment. In the spring of 1943 he was nevertheless hired by Georg Schnéevoigt, the Finnish conductor who had led Ernst's last concert in Oslo. Schnéevoigt was the principal conductor of the symphony in Malmö, Sweden's third-largest city after Stockholm and Gothenburg. Despite strict regulations that only Swedes could be hired for paid positions, Schnéevoigt was able to use his considerable influence to not only appoint Ernst as the orchestra's substitute concertmaster, but also to get Ernst a job teaching at the music conservatory in Malmö.

While Ernst was playing with the Malmö Symphony Orchestra, the ensemble brought in the famous Norwegian soprano Kirsten Flagstad as a soloist. Flagstad was one of the greatest opera singers of the twentieth century, but was also suspected of being a Nazi sympathizer. At issue was her decision to ignore an unspoken boycott by returning to Nazi-occupied Norway to be with her husband. This in itself might have been forgivable were it not for her husband's ties to Quisling's National Union Party.

"You must know our concertmaster," Schnéevoigt told Flagstad when she arrived in Malmö. "He was the first violinist of your orchestra in Oslo. He fled your country a short time ago."

"Of course, I know who he is. He played several times for me in the orchestra. I'm so happy to hear he's all right. Isn't he a splendid musician?"

"An excellent one," Schnéevoigt concurred, adding that Ernst was still a little shaken by his stressful escape from Norway.

"I can well understand that. I'd very much like to say hello to him. Could you let him know?"

"Gladly."

Flagstad waited and waited for Ernst to appear, but he never showed up.

During the concert, she was pleased to find that Ernst's playing was still in top form. At the end, she shook his hand and thanked him for playing. "I want to talk to you," she whispered.

Ernst nodded politely, but he did not go to see her after the concert.

Later, when Ernst finally visited Flagstad, he was rather distant.

"How are you?" she asked. "I'm so happy to see you here and all right."

Ernst did not respond.

"Your friends have been worried about you in Norway," Flagstad continued. "And now I can tell them that you are happy and well in Sweden. Is there anything I can do for you in Norway?"

"No," he quietly replied. "Nothing."

"There must be some relatives I can call up for you," Flagstad volunteered.[76] It was only after she confided in Ernst that her brother had been helping a desperate Jewish colleague in Norway that Ernst finally smiled and asked her to make some inquiries on his behalf.

Playing the violin provided Ernst with the opportunity to support his family throughout their exile. He was even able to send his children to an excellent boarding school near Stockholm. With his daughters tucked safely away, Ernst was free to tour throughout Sweden, often collaborating with Kari. In their performances in Sweden, Ernst and Kari promoted Norwegian music, specifically compositions by Grieg. In a concert in Stockholm on October 17, 1943, Kari played Grieg's beloved piano concerto. Less than two weeks later in Gothenburg, Ernst and Kari gave an all-Grieg recital that included a sonata for violin and piano, some songs, and Ernst's transcription of the quintessentially Norwegian "Solveig's Song" from *Peer Gynt*. The Glasers also toured schools, playing Norwegian folksongs and teaching the Swedish children about Norwegian history and culture.

Ernst and Kari would often perform alongside other well-known Norwegian artists at benefit concerts to raise money for Swedish Aid for Norway. A local aid committee somewhere in Sweden would call the Norwegian legation in Stockholm seeking entertainment for a fund-raising event. The educational office would see who was available, and dispatch performers accordingly. The performers were each given a modest allowance of twenty kroner per day for their food, travel, and lodging.

Over time, the refugees started performing more and more for the "Boys in the Woods." These brave young men were Norwegian freedom fighters who had gathered in camps along the Swedish border. Under the pretext of undergoing instruction as a reserve police force, the Boys in the Woods were actually receiving military training from the Norwegian resistance movement in preparation for their country's liberation from the Nazis. The performances by Ernst and the other Norwegian artists provided comfort to the Boys in the Woods while also reminding the homesick young men of what they were training to protect. Ernst took great pride in contributing to the Norwegian cause and giving back to his fellow countrymen. "It was good to be able to do something for our boys," he later explained.[77]

The performance environments in the camps could hardly be considered ideal. Cabaret musician Robert Levin later recalled performing on a piano that was strapped to the back of a truck for easy transport from camp to camp. One outdoor performance was so cold that his fingers froze stiff, causing him to make all kinds of mistakes. In that particular performance, he was accompanying Norwegian soprano Randi Heide Steen. When a gust of wind blew snow into Steen's mouth, she nearly choked to death. At a different camp, Levin encountered a piano that was missing its sustain pedal. Throughout the entire performance, Levin worked the piano keys while journalist and author Leif Borthen played the role of the missing pedal. Crouched underneath the piano, Borthen would release the damper mechanism every time Levin would put his right foot down and return it whenever Levin would lift his foot. This time it was not the cold weather but his own laughing that made it difficult for Levin to play.

The willingness of Norway's greatest artists to travel up and down Sweden performing in such wretched conditions astounded and inspired the Boys in the Woods. One freedom fighter later recalled trudging through the camp in Öreryd one drizzly, cold evening in May 1944 and stopping dead in his tracks upon hearing the sound of a violin playing. After weeks of training in the rough forest terrain, the young soldier had completely forgotten what great music sounded like.

He followed the sound to an officers' barracks, where he immediately recognized Ernst. The Norwegian legend was warming up by playing "Zapateado," from Pablo de Sarasate's extraordinarily difficult *Spanish Dances*, op. 23. Kari was sitting peacefully beside him darning socks.

When the soldier learned that Ernst would be playing in the camp that night, he immediately assumed that the virtuoso violinist would be playing repertoire as advanced as "Zapateado."

"Surely you're not going to serve that one up tonight!" he cautioned. "You'll be booed off!" He suggested that Ernst would be more successful playing Norwegian folksongs for the unsophisticated soldiers.

"Snob!" Ernst retorted. "Silly fool! I know these guys. I've been playing in Norwegian barracks and camps throughout Sweden since I came here in 1942, and I know what they want. They want good stuff, my friend! There's no point in cheating." Ernst admitted that the most complex works might not be appropriate for an audience of Boys in the Woods, but he promised to compensate for that by limiting his repertoire to the works of their countrymen. "Let's take our pick of Norwegians and there are plenty of great works they would be happy with," he continued. "Right, Kari?"[78]

Kari simply nodded, and continued her darning.

Ernst and Kari had long since figured out how to entertain the Boys in the Woods, including those who had never been exposed to classical music before. To appeal to their new audience, they did indeed make sure to include some popular compositions in their repertoire. But they also felt an obligation to avoid watering down their programs too much. They wanted to not only inspire the soldiers, but also educate them. They underscored this approach by prefacing the classical works by Grieg and other Norwegian composers with spoken introductions and with poems read by Norwegian writers. They called these presentations "Journeys Through Norway in Poetry and Sound."

The air was filled with excitement for the Glasers' performance in the Öreryd camp. The Boys in the Woods always looked forward to their weekly entertainment. This time, the gray monotony of camp life would be lifted by none other than the concertmaster of the Oslo Philharmonic and his piano-playing wife. Although the soldiers may have been a little baffled by Johan Svendsen's complex *Romance for Violin*, they showed their appreciation at the end of the concert with a rousing ovation. Unlike the reserved, genteel applause preferred by Oslo's concertgoing elite, the Boys in the Woods responded to the performance by clapping their hands, stamping their feet, hitting the walls, and shouting "hurrah!"[79]

The Norwegian performers became very close friends while traveling all over Sweden performing for Swedish Aid for Norway and for the Boys in the Woods. Ernst, Levin, and two other artists formed an especially intimate circle that they called the Philosophy Club. After each benefit concert, they would be invited to extravagant parties that they suspected cost more than the proceeds from the performance. Whoever had the largest hotel room would host the rest of the club after the party so they could recap that evening's escapades. They talked and laughed for hours.

It was during this time that Ernst began to rediscover

his Jewish heritage. Like many German Jews of the early twentieth century, he and his parents had always thought of themselves exclusively as German and had given little thought to Judaism. But Ernst became compelled to explore the language and traditions of his ancestors by his experiences during the Holocaust, as well as through the deep connection that he forged with Levin, who had been a devout Jew his entire life. Ernst started studying Hebrew with Levin. He would bring a Hebrew-language copy of the Old Testament with him on tours so he and Levin could read it together on the train. Ernst's proficiency in the language became so strong that Levin later started referring translation questions to him.

On October 25, 1944, the northeastern town of Kirkenes became the first Norwegian locality to be liberated by the Russians. At the request of the Norwegian legation, Levin composed a *Kirkenes March* to celebrate the historic event, set to a new text by Norwegian playwright Arild Feldborg. A few days later, Levin conducted the march's premiere in Järvsö, Sweden, where Norwegian military commander Olaf Helset had just completed a major maneuver with five thousand armed and uniformed Norwegian soldiers. It was a momentous occasion that signaled that the Boys in the Woods had evolved from a motley collection of refugees into a full-fledged military operation that would soon be ready to cross back into Norway. Ernst played the violin and also helped Levin arrange several Norwegian folksongs for the celebration.

Return to Norway

Ernst and Kari returned to Oslo immediately after the end of the war. Unlike half of Norway's prewar Jewish population, their family had survived the Holocaust. Most of their personal belongings had also been miraculously safeguarded. The arrest orders of October 26, 1942, had come with instructions to confiscate all Jewish property, especially valuables, jewelry, and cash. But when Ernst and Kari returned to their apartment, they found only their grand piano and three chairs missing. These items were quickly returned, thanks to a decree the Norwegian government-in-exile had issued from London in 1942 guaranteeing that all belongings appropriated during the war would be returned to their original owners.

Ernst also resumed his post as concertmaster of the Oslo Philharmonic. On December 6, 1945, he even returned to Bergen to perform Jean Sibelius's First Violin Concerto—on Ole Bull's Violin. It was the first time he had touched the instrument since his canceled appearance in Bergen almost five years earlier. The entire affair had robbed him of his interest in playing that particular instrument, but the opportunity to finally play Ole Bull's Violin in Bergen allowed him to put the circumstances of his previous trip to Bergen behind him.

He also continued to perform with Kari, including a live studio recording they made together for the Norwegian Broadcasting Corporation on January 10, 1946. A recent rerelease of this recording on the first volume of the series *Great Norwegian Performers 1945–2000* has renewed interest in Ernst's playing.

In the 1950s, Ernst was forced to back away from his most visible positions after developing a nervous tremor in his right hand that some say was a lingering aftereffect of his experiences during the Holocaust. He left the string quartet in 1956 and accepted a demotion to associate concertmaster in 1958. He was replaced by one of his students—one of many protégés who would represent the next generation of great Norwegian violinists. In that same year, Ernst founded the Oslo Philharmonic's popular chamber orchestra, an ensemble that he led until 1963. In 1965, he stepped down as associate concertmaster of the philharmonic but remained in the first violin section. A man of extraordinary intellect, Ernst spoke several languages and continued to serve as the orchestra's interpreter whenever foreign soloists and ensembles were visiting.

Ernst retired from the Oslo Philharmonic in 1969. He moved to Bergen to become the director of the city's music conservatory, which is now known as the Grieg Academy. Kari stayed behind in Oslo, and the two drifted apart. In 1971, Ernst caused a minor scandal by falling in love with violinist Christine Torgersen, who was principal second violin in the Bergen Philharmonic. In addition to being thirty-six years younger than Ernst, Christine had two children with her current husband, who sat close to her in the Bergen Philharmonic as the orchestra's principal violist.

In 1972, after divorcing Kari and marrying Christine, Ernst left the disapprovingly conservative atmosphere of Bergen in favor of the small town of Ålesund, Norway. Ernst directed a new music school and conducted the local orchestra, while Christine taught in the conservatory and served as a concertmaster of the orchestra. In addition to adopting her young son and daughter, Ernst fathered two more children with Christine: Ernst Simon and Susanna.

In 1976 Ernst returned to Oslo, where his friend Robert Levin had become the first director of the Norwegian Academy of Music three years earlier. Ernst immediately began making new contributions to Oslo by teaching violin and chamber music at the new academy. He also served on the board and program council of the Oslo Philharmonic, as well as on the board of the New Music Association. He died in Oslo on April 3, 1979.

Today, Ernst's musical legacy lives on through three of his children: his daughter Liv, who grew up to become a piano professor at the Norwegian Academy of Music; his stepson Torleif Torgersen, a piano professor at the Grieg Academy in Bergen; and his son Ernst Simon Glaser, who is rapidly establishing a career as one of the finest cellists of his generation.

Ole Bull's Violin remains in the possession of the Oslo Philharmonic, where it is played by their current concertmaster. In 2007, the orchestra loaned the instrument to

the Violins of Hope project for a performance by Shlomo
Mintz. Amnon outfitted the violin with a new bridge and
a new sound post while adjusting the entire instrument
to suit Mintz's discerning tastes. The virtuoso played the
renewed violin in a sold-out concert in Paris that marked
the debut of the Violins of Hope.

5

FEIVEL
WININGER'S
VIOLIN

Feivel Wininger (far right) with his five-piece band Freedom to
the Homeland, ca. 1945. His daughter Helen is sitting in front of
the bass drum looking up at her father. *(Courtesy of Helen Wininger
Livnat.)*

On October 10, 1941, all of the Jews in the Romanian town of Gura Humorului, in the region of southern Bukovina, were ordered to appear in the town center. They were instructed to report to the train station by 2 p.m. that day, at which time they would surrender their valuables, money, and house keys. They would be permitted to bring with them only what they could carry, including bread and water.

The mandate could not have been more ominous. Romania's Jewish population—the third largest in Europe after Russia and Poland—had been maligned for centuries. Beginning in the late 1930s, the rise of Romanian fascism led to a renewed campaign of anti-Semitic regulations that robbed Jews of their citizenships, professions, property, and civil rights. The enactment of the Romanian equivalent of Nazi Germany's Nuremberg Laws was accompanied by a series of increasingly vicious attacks on the Jews.

The most notorious of these massacres took place in the eastern border town of Iaşi on June 28 and 29, 1941. In their attempts to rid Iaşi of its fifty thousand Jews, Romanian soldiers, policemen, and citizens joined German soldiers in hunting, robbing, and killing thousands of Jews. Those who survived were taken to the train station and packed into windowless freight cars. Although the railcars

could only accommodate forty people, Romanian policemen and German soldiers used rifle butts and bayonets
to force between eighty and two hundred Jews into each
car. They nailed wooden boards over the small ventilation
slots, depriving those trapped inside of much-needed fresh
air as the stench of blood, urine, feces, and death grew
increasingly unbearable with every passing hour.

The first of two death trains left Iaşi early in the morning of June 30, but did not reach its ultimate destination of
Călăraşi—a mere 250 miles away—until July 6. Throughout their weeklong ordeal, the captives were given neither
food nor water. Some of them grew so desperate for hy-
dration that they drank their own urine or the blood from
their injuries. Others tore their shirts into shreds, tied the
strips together, and tossed the makeshift ropes into the
mud puddles alongside the train tracks to sop up water.
They were also not given the opportunity to leave the railcars to relieve themselves. On the few occasions when the
freight car doors were opened, the survivors were only allowed to toss out the dead bodies. And there were many
dead bodies. By the time the train reached Călăraşi, only
1,011 of the 2,530 Jews who had departed from Iaşi had
survived. Most of the victims had died of dehydration, exhaustion, or suffocation as the train cars had baked in the
summer heat. Others had been murdered by the guards or
had committed suicide.

The second death train set out just a few hours after
the first one, traveling so slowly that a guard was able to
walk alongside it. Although it traveled for only one day,

1,194 of its 1,902 passengers had died by the time it reached its destination. Their deaths, combined with those who died on the first train and those who were murdered in the streets of Iaşi, made for a total of 14,850 Jewish casualties over a matter of days.

In the weeks that followed the Iaşi massacre, Romanian soldiers were joined by Romanian and Ukrainian peasants in a ruthless campaign to "cleanse the land" of its Jewish population. Jews throughout the country were robbed, brutalized, raped, and murdered by the thousands. By the end of 1941, between 45,000 and 60,000 Jewish men, women, and children would fall victim to the mass killings in the regions of Bessarabia and Bukovina. In Bukovina's capital of Czernowitz, two thousand Jews were murdered in just one day.

Romanian fascists were determined to kill or expel every Jew in the country. In addition to the mass murders, at least 155,000 Romanian Jews were marched toward the Dniester River, which formed Romania's eastern border. Across the river was a territory that Romania had recently annexed from the Soviet Union that was inhabited by a large number of Ukrainians. The Romanian government had dubbed the land on the other side of the Dniester "Transnistria," because it was across from the river they called the Nistru. The Romanians had designated Transnistria as the ethnic dumping ground for their remaining Jews. The Jews would be marched into Transnistria and either subjected to more mass killings or simply left to die with no food, nor water, nor means to support themselves.

By 1943, at least 105,000 of the Jews who were expelled to Transnistria would be dead. Another 115,000 to 180,000 Jews who had already been living in Transnistria would also die.

They did not know it at the time, but when the Jews of Gura Humorului were ordered to the train station on October 10, 1941, it was to begin their horrific journey to Transnistria. The first train from southern Bukovina had left the day before. By October 14, a total of 21,229 Jews from southern Bukovina would be deported, leaving behind only 179 Jews whose professional and medical knowledge was deemed essential.

Deportation to Transnistria

When he heard the order to report to the train station, Feivel Wininger was gripped with fear. He and his elderly parents had already been forced to sell their home and land in nearby Vama for a pittance. They had moved into the home of Feivel's grandparents in Gura Humorului, where Feivel had gotten a job in a sawmill before this too had been taken away because he was Jewish. Since then, Feivel and the other Jews of southern Bukovina had been subjected to forced labor, incarcerations, curfews, and other restrictions on their movements. They had heard the terrible news from throughout Romania, not only of the massacres but also of the trains that had resulted in the deaths of thousands of Jews. The directive to appear at the train station signaled that the brutal anti-Semitic campaign had reached Gura Humorului.

Feivel hurried home to his wife Tzici and their sixteen-month-old daughter Helen. "There is no time for crying," he quickly explained. "We have to leave in four hours." He and Tzici frantically started packing, a task made difficult not only by their state of shock, but also by the fact that they did not know where they were going, how long the journey would last, or what was going to happen to them once they got there. They wrapped up a few days' worth of bread, sugar, and water, hoping that this would be enough to sustain them until they reached their unknown destination. They packed warm clothes to ward off the coming winter, smartly stitching some of their most expensive jewelry into the linings so they would not have to hand it over to the police.

After he was done packing, Feivel quickly gathered his family. With his mother, his uncle, and his daughter riding in a carriage they borrowed from a sympathetic neighbor, Feivel and his family walked to the train station, leaving everything else behind. There were still plates with food on them on the kitchen table. In his haste, Feivel even forgot his cherished violin.

On their way to the station, Feivel's family met up with many of the four thousand Jews who had been concentrated in Gura Humorului. Uncertain of their fates, everyone was struck with terror and struggling to carry their hastily packed suitcases. Little children were crying in the streets, following their parents with small bags in their hands. The elderly were leaning on canes and family members. The sick and injured had been brought from the hospital on stretchers. Everyone had been told that any Jew who failed to show up or who tried to escape would be shot.

The entrance to the train station was crowded and chaotic. While gentiles stood around celebrating the Jews' mistreatment and waiting to collect belongings that got left behind, Romanian soldiers herded the Jews toward cattle cars. There were desperate screams as the soldiers clubbed and beat the Jews, forcing them to quickly climb aboard. Feivel avoided being struck by the butt of a rifle by swiftly lifting his uncle and his mother into the car, handing Helen to Tzici, and then jumping in himself. They found a corner and sat on their suitcases.

The car quickly became overcrowded. "There is no more room in here!" Feivel shouted. "We'll all suffocate!" The soldiers just laughed and continued to shove people in with their belongings.

The doors were slammed shut and locked from the outside. Since all of the ventilation slots had been covered with boards, the captives were left in the dark. Just a little light peered in through the tiny gaps between the boards and the side of the car. Suddenly, they heard the roar of the engine and the squeal of the wheels as the train started moving. They were under way. The moans and cries of the cramped passengers were soon accompanied by the monotonous pounding of the train's wheels on the tracks.

The unwilling travelers knew what had happened on the trains from Iași. They could not help but suspect that they would fall victim to the exact same fate.

The train crisscrossed Romania for three days. The passengers kept track of nightfall by the absence of light coming in through the slits in the wall, and daybreak by the return of the slim streams of sunlight. It was not long before the passengers exhausted their supplies of food and water. Many died of hunger, thirst, and suffocation. Although a bucket had been placed in one of the corners as a toilet, the car was too cramped for the passengers to access it. They had no choice but to urinate and defecate where they stood, filling the already stifling car with the stench of human waste.

Every twelve hours or so, the train would stop in the middle of nowhere and the doors would be opened loudly. The terrified passengers would be ordered to abandon all modesty and relieve themselves in open fields. Meanwhile, the bodies of those who had died would be thrown out of the cars. Local peasants would arrive to quickly strip the cadavers of expensive clothing. After only the briefest of reprieves, the soldiers would drive the deportees back into the cars. Those who were too weakened to climb back on board would be shot, as would anyone who tried to help them.

On the evening of October 13, the train stopped and the cattle car doors were flung open one last time. Romanian soldiers ordered the Jews out of the train and onto a swampy field that was littered with the corpses of previous deportees. The captives were told to line up and prepare for a long walk in the freezing wind and rain.

A large group of Ukrainian peasants appeared, offering to help the Jews carry their bags. Several gratefully handed over their luggage, only to watch as the Ukrainians walked away with them a few minutes later. Other belongings were abandoned on the train or on the landing after the Romanian soldiers announced that the deportees would be allowed to carry only a few bags with them. Feivel tossed aside all but three of his family's suitcases. He carried two of them while his ailing mother leaned against him for support. Feivel's seventy-year-old father carried the third suitcase, while Tzici carried Helen in her arms.

The Jews were taken on a difficult two-mile march to Ataki, a town on the banks of the Dniester River. It was raining and the road was slippery with mud and rocks. The Romanian soldiers continually pushed the exhausted and starving deportees to move faster and to take bigger steps, a task made especially difficult by the swampy conditions. Each step required a great amount of energy just to lift a foot out of the thick mud. Meanwhile, the soldiers kept driving the Jews forward with clubs, rifle butts, and the threats of bullets. Feivel's legs shook as he dragged his body forward, but he was determined to not stumble.

Ataki, once home to thousands of Jews, was a gutted shadow of its former self. The Jewish Quarter had been liquidated and then bombed into oblivion. All of the houses were burned down or in ruins. Only a few gutted walls and crumbling chimneys remained. Decomposing corpses were scattered in the muddy streets and in the cellars, or simply tossed into the trash. Thousands of dazed deportees wandered the streets, desperately looking for food. When they entered the abandoned homes, the refugees found broken furniture and blood everywhere—on the beds, on the walls, and on the floors. On the walls and doors they found messages written in blood. "Say Kaddish for us!" the haunting messages read in Yiddish, referring to the traditional Jewish prayer for the dead. "Do not forget us! Tell the world what happened here!"[80]

As night descended, the Jews searched for shelter. Some spent the night in roofless houses. Most simply lay on whatever dry spots they could find on the ground outside. Still others wandered around searching for food, shouting and crying as they became separated from their family members in the dark. Starving and scared, very few of them were able to sleep.

Feivel and his family settled in a room inside an empty house that could at least protect them from the wind. They lit a fire and heated up some water. They drank the warm water with sugar cubes and used the remaining water to wash themselves. Despite the horrible conditions, they considered themselves lucky to be able to change their clothes and stretch their legs a bit. "Don't look around," Feivel told his family. "Just try to get some sleep. I'll try to get us a little food in the morning."

The next morning, Ukrainian peasants arrived to sell bread and milk to the deportees. Feivel exchanged some of the money and jewelry his family had smuggled from Gura Humorului for a little food. At the exorbitant prices the peasants were charging, the small amounts of gold and money Feivel's family had brought would not last long.

Suddenly, the streets were filled with even more people—thousands of Jews from the town of Edineṭ, Bessarabia. They had been on a death march for three weeks. Having exchanged all of their clothing and belongings for food over the course of their march, they were now emaciated skeletons barely covered in filthy rags. The nightmarish figures scarcely looked human as they dragged themselves along, shivering and crying. Feivel and the other deportees surrounded the convoy, sneaking a few men away and giving precious food and clothing to the others. The Romanian soldiers kept driving the death march forward with whips and bullets, shouting, "Whoever lags behind will be shot dead!"[81]

After a few restless days in Ataki, the deportees were told that they would be marched across the Dniester River. Terrifying rumors circulated about the Jews who had died during earlier crossings. Some had been pushed into the water and then machine-gunned in the back. Others had simply drowned in the river. Still others had successfully crossed the river only to be shot by cruel Romanian soldiers on the other side. The river had been filled with bodies of Jewish men, women, and children.

Before crossing the Dniester, the deportees were ordered to exchange their Romanian lei for Ukrainian rubles at overly inflated exchange rates that ensured that their money would lose 80 percent of its value. The Jews were also told to hand over all gold and jewelry or face immediate execution. Feivel and his family decided to defy these commands. They held on to what remained of the currency and the jewelry they had sewn into their clothes. They did, however, hand over the gold necklace that had been the first present that Feivel had given Tzici. They had briefly considered trying to hide the necklace, but Tzici's parents had convinced them that it was not worth the risk. Little Helen needed her parents now more than ever.

By the time the convoy reached the Dniester River, the rain that had been falling nonstop since they had reached Ataki was causing the river to overflow. The Romanian soldiers decided to postpone the river crossing until the next day. Feivel and his family lit a fire that once again allowed them to enjoy warm sugar water. They slept as a group, with the men forming a perimeter to protect the women from the marauding Romanian soldiers. They covered themselves as best as they could, but it was impossible to ward off the wind and rain. They spent yet another restless night, frozen, hungry, exhausted, and terrified.

The next morning, wooden rafts arrived to ferry the Jews across the river. The deportees crowded onto the decrepit rafts, which were barely able to support their weight. Some overturned, leaving dozens of bodies floating in the freezing river. Shouting and cursing, the Romanian soldiers continued to shove the Jews onto the rafts with their rifle butts. Before long, they started pushing deportees into the water, mockingly wondering aloud whether the

Dniester River would part for the Jews like the Red Sea
had for their ancestors. The first people to be thrown in
the water were the rabbi from Gura Humorului and his
six children. Unable to swim, they screamed and flailed
in the river for a few seconds before they all disappeared
into the current. Feivel watched as the soldiers stood there,
clapping their hands and laughing.

The Winingers made it across the river, but a Romanian soldier stole one of their last suitcases along the way.
They were herded down yet another muddy road to the
town of Mogilev-Podolski, the first stop on what would
become a lengthy death march deeper into Transnistria
for forty thousand Jews.

Harry Löbel

One family that was allowed to stay in Mogilev-Podolski
was that of a young violinist named Harry Löbel. Harry
started playing the violin at the age of five and was already performing with the local symphony orchestra in
Czernowitz when he was nine. By the time the Löbels
reached Transnistria, they had lost all of their possessions except for the small violin that young Harry carried on his back. Knowing that his family would die of
starvation and exhaustion if they were forced to march
farther into Transnistria, Harry's father convinced the
commandant of the Mogilev-Podolski transit camp to
allow the family to stay there.

Harry's violin playing saved him and his family from

starvation during their three-year detainment in Mogilev-Podolski. When the commandant, who was an amateur pianist, heard that Harry played the violin, he summoned the boy to perform. The commandant was moved to tears by Harry's playing. He decided that the boy and his family deserved special treatment. He ordered that they be given extra food and that Harry be allowed to take lessons from a teacher from another camp. The commandant followed Harry's progress, summoning the boy to play for him once a month.

In March 1944, Harry was again rescued by the violin. A member of a Romanian delegation charged with caring for war orphans visited Mogilev-Podolski. She heard Harry play and was so captivated by his talent that she issued him a special permit to leave Transnistria, even though she knew his parents were alive. Harry traveled to Bucharest and was then sent to Palestine, where his parents joined him one year later. Harry's child-sized violin also survived the Holocaust. It was later sold to purchase a new instrument that was more suitable for a professional adult.

After the Holocaust, Harry Löbel changed his name from German to Hebrew, choosing the Hebrew form of Abraham for his given name and Melamed, a word for a yeshiva teacher, as his surname. Avraham Melamed joined the Israel Philharmonic Orchestra as a member of the first violin section, and was with the ensemble when they traveled to Auschwitz in 1988. En route to the death camp, Melamed was so overcome with emotion that he was unable to say a word. So he let his violin speak for him. He took it out of its case and played the "Kaddish" movement from Maurice Ravel's *Two Hebrew Melodies*. As he played, tears came to his eyes, as well as to those of his fellow orchestra members. During the same tour, the ensemble performed a historic concert in Berlin, ending with "Hatikvah." It was one of the most emotional performances of Melamed's distinguished career.

Death March to Obukhov

Unlike the Löbels, the Wininger family did not stop in Mogilev-Podolski. Instead, they were forced to continue walking seven miles eastward to an abandoned military school in Scazinetz. The thousands of Jews who greeted them looked like walking corpses. Their feet were bare, their clothes were in tatters, and their bodies were covered with flea bites. Feivel spotted an old friend from Czernowitz. He, too, was emaciated, filthy, and flea-ridden.

The soldiers shoved the convoy into a large garrison that was already crowded with thousands of people. The looks of despair on people's faces and the stench of human waste were overwhelming, as was the earsplitting din of cries and screams. Some of the deportees had gone insane during their journey from Romania. Feivel watched in horror as a mother cradled an empty blanket, singing, laughing, and crying as if her dead baby were still there.

For the first time, Feivel started to fully process the gravity of his situation. In Gura Humorului, on the train, and in Ataki, he had been too shocked to truly grasp what was happening. At the Dniester River, he had been too focused on mere survival to give any thought to the future. Now that he was finally at a standstill, reality started to sink in. He pressed his fingernails into the palms of his hands and quietly braced himself for the challenges ahead.

A group of Romanian soldiers entered the hall and ordered some of the younger deportees to remove the gray corpses that littered the barracks floor. When the soldiers returned early the next morning, more bodies of men, women, and children lay lifelessly on the cold floor. Another crew of young men was conscripted to dig a large trench near the camp fence, load the bodies into a cart, and dump the corpses into the mass grave.

The Jews were once again jostled, cursed at, and struck with rifle butts as they were ordered to line up in rows. Miserable and confused, with tattered and foul-smelling clothes, they formed their lines and renewed their death march.

The soft mud continued to make walking very difficult. Several deportees got their shoes stuck in the mud. They had no choice but to leave their shoes in the slime to avoid being beaten or shot for slowing down. This only prolonged their deaths, as they were now even more exposed to the harsh elements of the nonstop rain and snow. Before too long, the soldiers started to push the soaked and exhausted Jews along. With increasing frequency, Feivel heard shots ring out as the soldiers opened fire on the deportees who were moving too slowly. The bodies of those who were killed were simply left on the roadside.

Early into the first day, Feivel could see that Tzici was losing her strength. She kept changing the arm with which she was carrying Helen. She needed Feivel's brother-in-law to push her from behind to keep moving forward. Feivel could not help her because he was too busy propping up his mother, who would have collapsed into the mud without his assistance. Feivel opened his last remaining suitcase and gave more of his rapidly dwindling possessions to a soldier in exchange for allowing his ailing mother and baby Helen to ride in one of the two horse-drawn carriages that followed the procession. On the second day, Feivel exchanged more of his belongings for a ride for his mother, but received a whip to the face for asking if Helen could also sit in the wagon. Instead, Feivel created a sling for Helen by cutting a slit across the back of Tzici's jacket and adding a rope to support the baby's weight. Helen had continued to grow thinner and weaker. Hungry and freezing, she had even lost the strength to cry.

Feivel watched as others were forced to abandon their parents, spouses, and children who were too weak to walk any further. One morning, Feivel overheard a daughter arguing with her elderly mother over the impossible decision of whether to remain in the barn and die with her or leave her behind when the death march continued. The sadistic soldiers ended the debate by shooting both of them. Another mother abandoned her young daughter on the side of the road when she was no longer able to carry her.

A few hours later, the remorseful mother simply stopped walking. She offered no resistance when a soldier beat and shot her for not keeping up with the rest of the convoy.

At night, the Jews were locked in barns. Feivel would look around and see how their numbers had dwindled during the day. When he woke the next morning, Feivel would count the numbers of deportees who had died overnight. This included his uncle, who died during the first night of the death march from Scazinetz. The soldiers would add to the numbers by shooting the children and sick people who were too weak to continue walking.

After three days of a brutal death march through the rain and snow, the convoy arrived at an abandoned train station in Obukhov. By this time, only half of the Jews who had left Scazinetz remained. The soldiers warned them to not leave the train station. They turned around their wagons and drove off, leaving the deportees with neither food nor any other supplies. Although the Jews had been strictly forbidden from traveling to the nearby village, many went there to beg, to exchange their belongings for food, or to find jobs. More often than not, the Ukrainians welcomed them by throwing rocks or siccing dogs on them.

Feivel's mother had grown very sick. She had suffered from heart problems before the deportation, and had contracted pneumonia during the death march. A doctor from Gura Humorului visited her in the train station and told her that she would not last much longer. She died in her sleep that night.

The Shargorod Ghetto

Feivel decided to take his remaining family members to Shargorod, a larger city where there was already an established Jewish ghetto. Because the large Jewish community had been able to organize itself, Shargorod promised better prospects for food and employment. Shargorod was also in the district of Mogilev, a region that saw less German involvement and Romanian cruelty than other parts of Transnistria.

Since they could have been sentenced to death for trying to relocate themselves, Feivel's family hired a carriage driver to take them overnight to avoid detection. The trip cost the Winingers a gold earring—their last valuable item.

The Shargorod Ghetto was packed with seven thousand deportees who were squeezed into 337 schools, community buildings, homes, cellars, and attics. Feivel was able to rent a single room from a Ukrainian peasant that became home to his family and another family—seventeen people in all. Feivel found a job cutting down trees, for which he was paid a quarter of a loaf of stale and moldy bread daily. This was not nearly enough to feed his family. Feivel gave the bread he earned to his father, Tzici, and Helen. He sustained himself by eating snow and leftovers that he foraged from the garbage.

If they were to have any chance of procuring enough food and firewood to stay alive in the freezing ghetto,

Feivel and his family knew they would have to risk their lives by engaging in illegal activities. Tzici earned food from their Ukrainian landlord by disguising herself in his wife's clothes and traveling by train throughout Transnistria selling his sausages. Had she been caught smuggling food or simply roaming around without a permit, she would have been tortured and killed as a warning to other Jews. Feivel stole wood from his job to keep his family warm and to heat drinking water during the deadly Romanian winter. He, too, would have been shot on the spot had he been discovered.

Thousands of Jews died during that first winter in Transnistria from starvation and exposure, as well as from dysentery and other illnesses. An untreated typhus epidemic ran rampant throughout the cramped, unsanitary, and lice-infested Transnistrian ghettos, claiming 1,449 lives in Shargorod alone in just a few months. The bodies of the dead were simply left in the street, where other ghetto residents would strip them of whatever precious clothing they had left. Once or twice a day, a group of deportees would roam the streets on a horse-drawn carriage, picking up the cadavers and taking them to the cemetery. Sometimes the makeshift undertakers would light bonfires to thaw the icy ground enough to dig mass graves. Other times, the corpses would simply be added to piles of other frozen bodies. When the spring came, the deportees hacked the frozen bodies apart with axes to separate them from each other for burial.

The Amati

It did not take long for Feivel to find a way to protect his family from starvation and exposure—one that did not put their lives at risk but involved playing the violin.

Ten days after Feivel arrived in Shargorod, a man paid him a visit. Feivel barely recognized him as Judge Robinson. As the chief justice of Gura Humorului, Judge Robinson had once been a tall, elegantly dressed man of great distinction in both the Jewish and gentile communities. Now the judge was stooped, emaciated, and wearing a dirty, shabby suit. He approached Feivel extending a trembling hand that was dried and blistered. In his other hand, he carried a violin case.

"Please be seated, Mr. Robinson," Feivel said, quickly adding, "Your Honor."

The judge sheepishly smiled a toothless grin and sat down.

"I live nearby with my two sisters," the judge started. "I am too weak and too old for the jobs here. We have no food, nor wood." Then he stopped. "Could I please have some warm water?" he asked.

Feivel gave him warm sugar water.

The judge took just a few sips and said, "I will bring the glass back later. The rest is for my sisters." He rose to leave.

"Drink the whole glass," Feivel urged him. "We will give you more water and sugar for your sisters."

The judge sat back down and relaxed. He closed his

eyes and drank very slowly. When he had gathered his strength, he finally got to the point of his unexpected visit.

"I know that you are a musician," he said. "I also played once, when my hands still worked. You are young and will be able to play for many years."

The judge opened the case and took out an Amati—an instrument crafted by one of the most respected names in violinmaking. It was Nicolò Amati who had taught Andrea Guarneri, the patriarch of the Guarneri dynasty and the grandfather of the man who made Ole Bull's Violin. Nicolò may have also been Antonio Stradivari's teacher.

Feivel's hands shook as the judge handed him the expensive instrument. He could not even remember how long it had been since he had played a violin.

"Take it," the judge insisted. "What good is a violin if I have no food? If you're able to earn a little something from making music, then don't forget me."

The judge left as quickly as he had appeared. Feivel had not even had the time to react. He was too stunned by the gift to do anything but put the violin back in its case and set it aside.

Music had played a large role in Feivel's life for as long as he could remember. As a little boy, he heard a violin being played at a wedding and decided then and there that he wanted to play the instrument. In the absence of a violin, he would escape to the forest as often as possible to listen to the birdcalls that he thought sounded like one. Once, while bringing his father his lunch, Feivel heard a violin playing through an open window. He sat underneath that window, listening intently until the violinist chased him away.

When Feivel was nine years old, his mother brought home a violin for him. His first lessons were with an elderly teacher who had a habit of falling asleep during his sessions, so Feivel taught himself to play by practicing for hours. When Feivel was ten, he proudly earned his first salary by playing principal violin in an orchestra that accompanied silent films. As a teenager, he bicycled to Hungary with a mandolin-playing friend for six weeks, playing concerts along the way to earn money. He also learned to play viola and cello, and enjoyed many happy evenings making music with his friends. For a short while, he even formed a jazz band consisting of a piano, guitar, saxophone, and violin that played in the spa and ski resort town of Vatra Dornei—until his mother found out and dragged him home.

When Feivel was drafted into the Romanian army, the violin shielded him from basic training. Upon learning that Feivel was a musician, an officer summoned him for an impromptu performance. The officer was so impressed that he invited Feivel to sleep at his house instead of in the barracks with the other recruits. While his comrades were training on the rifle range, Feivel enjoyed easy duty entertaining the officers. Even during his yearlong military service in Bucharest, Feivel was adopted by a lieutenant who would invite him to his house on the weekends to play duets with his pianist daughter.

Although music continued to play an integral role in

Feivel's daily life, he never dreamed of attending a conservatory and launching a musical career. Instead, he worked as an accountant and then as the cafeteria manager for a large silk factory in Bucharest. After he and his family were forced to move to Gura Humorului, he managed the nearby sawmill before he was fired for being Jewish. Now, in Transnistria, music would become not just a profession for Feivel, but a means to spare his family and friends from almost certain death.

The day after the judge's visit, Feivel returned home from his job chopping wood and decided that it was time to try out the violin. He nervously removed the instrument from its case, placed it against his neck, and drew the bow lightly across the strings. He was instantly enchanted by the sound. He had never heard such a beautiful instrument.

He closed his eyes and started playing. The music transported him to a different place, to a different time. He was no longer in the ghetto. He was not hungry, he was not soaking wet, and he was not wearing shabby rags. He was the richest man in the world.

When Feivel stopped playing, he opened his eyes. Everyone in the room was staring at him in amazement. Several fellow deportees from the street had entered the room to hear him play. People who were hungry, sick, and infested with lice simply stood there with smiles on their faces. They, too, had been carried away by his violin playing.

Feivel's Ukrainian landlord appeared and shooed away

all of the strangers. "You really play nicely," he said. "Do you know how to play Ukrainian music? I could recommend you to play at a wedding."

"I play everything." Feivel stretched the truth, eager to secure employment.

"Find another musician who plays another instrument," the landlord instructed. "I'll let you know when the wedding takes place."

Feivel had a friend in the Shargorod Ghetto who had played accordion with him prior to their exile. When the accordionist had been forced out of his home, he had stuck a small harmonica in his pocket.

Two days later, the landlord brought Feivel and his harmonica-playing friend to a wedding in a nearby village, where they saw two large tables that were filled with food. When Feivel and his friend were given permission to eat whatever they wanted, they devoured chicken cutlets, dough with milk, and lots of bread. Stuffing their empty stomachs with such rich food made them both sick for four weeks. A doctor in the ghetto told them that it could have killed them.

The wedding was a traditional Ukrainian celebration that lasted three days and three nights. Feivel and his friend played nonstop, one waking the other if he dozed off. They had never heard the Ukrainian folksongs that the partygoers requested, but they had good ears and quickly learned the tunes as they were sung to them. In exchange for delighting the wedding guests, they each received a five-pound loaf of bread to take home.

When Feivel returned to Shargorod, he immediately went to see Judge Robinson to give him a quarter of the loaf. He was determined to honor the judge's request that he share everything he made playing the Amati. Feivel arrived at the judge's house only to learn that Justice Robinson and his two sisters had been taken to the cemetery the day before. They had poisoned themselves. They simply could not bear another day of starving and freezing in the ghetto. Feivel could not help but wonder if they were better off dead than he was alive. He brought the violin to his chin and accompanied himself while singing "El Malei Rachamim," the traditional Jewish prayer of remembrance.

Feivel and his friend quickly became popular among Romanian officers and Ukrainian peasants looking for entertainment. The musicians were happy to play in exchange for food that they could bring home to their families. At one party, Feivel and his friend met a music-loving Ukrainian farmer who continually complimented their abilities. He asked them to accompany him while he sang. Once again, Feivel and his friend listened to the melody for just a few seconds and then started playing along, as if they had been performing the tune their whole lives. When the party ended two days later, the farmer tipped the musicians generously.

Feivel would also play the violin in the ghetto, bringing comfort to himself as well as to his friends and family members by performing Jewish melodies that they all remembered from their childhoods. Among these was "My

Yiddishe Momme," which had been a favorite of Feivel's own mother.

The local celebrity that Feivel earned by playing the violin convinced a Romanian gentleman to hire Feivel as a servant when he fell ill. Feivel held cold compresses to the Romanian's head and stoked the fire to keep his bedroom warm. He picked up the Romanian's medicine from the pharmacist and made sure that his new master took it as prescribed. After the Romanian recovered, he arranged for Feivel to receive two kilograms each of sugar, rice, cornmeal, and yeast, as well as two liters of milk. It was enough to feed Feivel's family for a long time.

As with many ghettos, Shargorod was controlled by a Jewish Council, which governed the ghetto, and a Jewish Police force, which maintained order. The Shargorod Jewish Police also prevented marauding Ukrainian militiamen from entering the ghetto at night to rob and torture its residents. Although the council and the police both were composed of fellow ghetto residents, membership in either organization came with preferential treatment that was often abused. In Feivel's case, the abuse came at the hands of a Jewish policeman who was jealous of the special favors Feivel was receiving from Romanians and Ukrainians.

One day, a well-dressed young man entered Feivel's room. "Who has a violin here?" he asked.

"I do," Feivel replied quickly, hoping that his guest was looking to hire him. A second later, he recognized the young man as a member of the Jewish Police and realized that this would not be a friendly visit.

"We know that Judge Robinson left his violin at your place—an Amati violin," the policeman stated. "You are to bring it to the police station immediately."

Feivel was shocked. Without the violin, he and his family would starve. "The judge gave me the violin because he was an old family friend," he protested. "The violin is mine now."

"If you love your family, you will bring the violin to us today," the policeman sneered. "It will not be of any use to you in the cemetery outside of town."

The policeman was not done intimidating Feivel. "Have you heard what the Germans like to do with Jews?" he asked, turning to Tzici. "If your husband chooses the violin over his family, be ready to travel to a German death camp tonight. Only then will you understand that here you are living in paradise.

"Of course, do not forget the girl," the policeman continued, walking toward Helen and taking her hand. "You are coming with me," he threatened Feivel's daughter. "We have a special place for orphaned children.

"The girl or the violin," the policeman said, turning back to Feivel. "A tough choice for someone like you."

The choice was not difficult at all. Feivel took the Amati out of its case and played it one last time. A farewell melody to a dear friend. Then he took the precious violin down to the police station and walked away with tears in his eyes.

The Cello

Feivel's performing days were not over. One day, he was stacking firewood for a Romanian officer when he heard the sound of a cello. He could not resist knocking on the door.

"You have already received the flour that I owe you," the officer growled, not understanding why a Jew would be standing on his doorstep.

"The cello," Feivel responded.

"What about the cello?" the officer asked, eager to end the conversation.

"I play the cello."

"A Jew with a cello?"

Feivel did not reply.

"Clean yourself up a bit," the officer finally capitulated. "Wash your hands, take off your stinking shoes, and come on in."

Feivel quickly complied.

"Show me your hands," the officer commanded. When he was satisfied that Feivel was sufficiently clean, he issued one more order: "Play."

Feivel took the cello and began playing. He was a violinist first and foremost, but he played the cello with the same amount of passion. Back in Romania, when his mother had recovered from a lengthy illness, he had celebrated by playing "Kol Nidrei"—the Jewish annulment of vows that begins the Yom Kippur evening service. Then, as now, Feivel had poured his heart and soul into

his performance, sweating profusely with every movement of the bow.

The Romanian officer listened for a long time. "You
play very well," he finally said. "Whenever you bring me
wood, you can come in and play for a bit."

"I would be glad to," Feivel replied. He had formed
another unlikely alliance through his playing, one that
would again save his life.

One morning, Feivel was arrested by German soldiers
who were working with the Jewish Police to apprehend
ninety men who could provide slave labor in Germany.
Tzici visited the cello's owner and asked for his help. The
Romanian officer marched over to the German camp in
the middle of the night and demanded to see Feivel. He
kicked Feivel in the ribs to wake him up and held a gun
to Feivel's head.

"You stole money from my home, you dirty Jew!" the
officer screamed, striking Feivel with his fists and with the
butt of his gun. "I'm going to kill you! I'm going to shoot
you like a dog! You're not going anywhere! I'm going to
destroy you! You thought you would go to Germany and
I would not be able to catch you?"

"You're not going to take him with you," the Romanian
officer instructed the German soldiers, who were watching the beating unfold with great amusement. "I will not
allow you to save this lowlife thief. I will kill him after I
torture him in every possible way."

The ruse worked. The Germans stepped aside as the
Romanian pushed Feivel forward. When they were out-

side the prison, the officer told Feivel to run home to his wife. Feivel had two broken ribs, but he was free.

The Placht Brothers Violin

One day, Feivel received a visit from the Ukrainian farmer who had tipped him at a party. The farmer remembered Feivel's playing fondly, and now wanted to hire Feivel to play at his daughter's wedding.

"They took away my violin," Feivel explained.

"I'll find you a violin."

"I'm willing to pay for it," Feivel insisted. "I want to keep it so I can practice."

"If I find a violin for you, will you play at my daughter's wedding? I treated you well last time."

"For you, I will try my hardest to play well. I noticed that you know a lot about music."

"We'll find a violin tomorrow," the farmer promised, flattered by Feivel's compliment.

The next day, the farmer took Feivel to a Ukrainian who had a cheap violin for sale. The farmer helped with the haggling, and Feivel left with a violin that he could finally call his own.

Feivel's new violin was made around the turn of the twentieth century at the Placht Brothers' Musical Instrument and String Factory. The Placht Brothers were descendants of a proud dynasty of instrument makers from Schönbach, Bohemia (now Luby, in the Czech Republic), a town with a rich tradition of violinmaking that dates back to the sixteenth century. The violin was a decent instrument, but was nowhere near as good as the Amati. Today a Placht Brothers violin might sell for a few hundred dollars, while an Amati could command several hundred thousand.

Although the Placht Brothers violin was of considerably lesser quality than the Amati, it was more than suitable for performing at weddings and other parties. The Ukrainian farmer was so pleased with Feivel's playing that he tipped him half the price of the violin, in addition to the leftovers that Feivel customarily received as payment for performing. Feivel continued to play the Placht Brothers violin for the next three years, earning enough food, water, and precious firewood to sustain himself and the sixteen family members and friends with whom he shared a room throughout the remainder of the Holocaust.

Return to Romania

One evening in early 1944, there was a knock at the door. Two German soldiers walked in. "You will come with us immediately," they instructed Feivel.

Tzici started crying. "Don't take him away from us," she begged. "We have suffered enough."

The soldiers replied that they merely wanted Feivel to entertain them. "Nothing is going to happen to your husband," one of them promised. "I'll bring him back to you."

On the way to the engagement, a soldier confided in Feivel that the German army would soon be passing through Transnistria as it retreated westward. He knew that the soldiers would be taking their frustrations out on any Jews they met along the way. He suggested that Feivel go into hiding.

The soldiers brought Feivel to a large hall full of members of the German army and prostitutes. There was plenty of food and alcohol everywhere. A stage had been constructed out of upside-down crates, and it was there that Feivel played for more than twenty-four hours straight. Whenever he would try to take a break, a chorus of protests would cry out, "Music! Where is the music?" Feivel played every song he knew, including a few Hasidic melodies. He considered the fact that the soldiers did not know that they were dancing to Jewish music to be his own private revenge on the soon-to-be-defeated Nazis.

The Nazis withdrew from Shargorod on March 16, 1944. As the German soldiers had predicted, the retreating Germans and Romanians were massacring Jews throughout their westward retreat. The Jews of the Shargorod Ghetto even learned that a special Romanian "execution unit" was working its way toward them, slaughtering Jews along the way. As the Germans for whom Feivel had played suggested, they hid in secret caves they had dug until it was safe to come out. Finally, on March 20, the Red Army arrived to arrest the execution unit and occupy Shargorod.

Sadly, the Russian occupation initiated a new wave of anti-Semitism. The Russians stole money and belongings and conscripted the Jews into military service and forced labor. Knowing that they were too physically and mentally weak for work battalions, a number of ghetto residents fled back to Romania.

Feivel and his family were just crossing into Romania when they were intercepted by a Russian border patrol. They were arrested and imprisoned for espionage, but Tzici and Helen were released the next day and sent back to Czernowitz. Confined to his jail cell, Feivel knew that he would receive a death sentence within days. He was convinced that he would never see his wife and daughter again.

Looking out the prison window, Feivel spotted a young woman he recognized. She was a Russian officer who had taught him some Russian folksongs at a Ukrainian wedding in Transnistria. He banged on the iron bars with all of his strength to get her attention.

"What are you doing here?" she asked.

"We tried to cross the border into Romania and got caught. Please, try to get me out of here. I'm accused of spying. You know exactly what will happen to me if you don't."

The woman promised to see what she could do.

She returned that evening with some food. "The situation isn't good," she whispered. "The commanding officer here is very strict. He was angry that I meddled, but I didn't give up. I got him to promise to come and speak with you tomorrow. You can tell him the whole story. I can't tell you what your odds are."

The next morning, Feivel was summoned by the commanding officer, to whom he presented his case. "I know that your decision will be just," he concluded. Before he left, Feivel tried one more tactic. Knowing how much the Russians loved food and music, he offered to host a dinner party that evening at a small tavern in a nearby village, using money that he had received from one of his sisters in Czernowitz. The officer would be the guest of honor, and Feivel would entertain him by playing Russian music on his violin.

The officer was pleased with the suggestion, and agreed to the dinner. That night Feivel played all of the Russian songs he knew—ones that he had learned in Transnistria. He played his heart out, because he knew that he was once again playing for his life.

The officer visited Feivel in his cell the next morning. His mood was just as good as it had been during the celebration the night before.

"Stay here," the officer joyfully suggested. "We'll assemble an orchestra, and you'll direct it."

A chill ran down Feivel's spine. "I would be delighted to," he lied. "But my parents are very old, and they are all alone in Romania. I have to get back to them."

"Fine. I will issue you a passport so that you can return to Czernowitz." On his way out the door, the officer added, "You're a very talented musician. I will remember last night for a long time." Yet again, Feivel's playing had earned him an unlikely ally.

On his way out of the prison, Feivel ran into the female officer who had saved his life and thanked her. She informed him that in two weeks, eight Russian carriages would be heading into Romania for supplies. She helped Feivel bribe the Russian drivers to smuggle him and his family as far as Dorohoi.

After the war, the Winingers quickly settled into a new life in Dorohoi. They secured an apartment and Feivel found work, first at a storage facility and then as an officer in the police department. He supplemented his income by forming a successful five-piece band that called itself "Freedom to the Homeland."

By "homeland," Feivel was not referring to Romania, the land that had once offered both employment and a last name to his Russian grandfather. He was instead referring to the Land of Israel. Ever since his student days, he had wanted to immigrate to the land of his biblical ancestors. After completing his graduation examinations, he had spent six months at a Zionist school near Czernowitz, where he worked as a farmer and a teacher during the day. At night, the forty young men and four young women would sing songs about the land that their ancestors had been dreaming about for two millennia. Feivel had even raised money to support his immigration. He had postponed his plans when his mother had started developing heart problems. Since she had never fully recovered, he had never seriously considered immigrating.

In Dorohoi, Feivel became active in the Zionist Party. He once again started making plans to immigrate to the Holy Land. In 1947, when it became obvious that the Soviets had no intention of withdrawing from their occupation of Eastern Europe and that Zionist activists would not be welcome in communist Romania, Feivel fled the country illegally, bringing Tzici and Helen with him.

Israel

The Winingers sailed to Palestine aboard the *Medinat Israel* (State of Israel), a retrofitted icebreaker that was designed to carry two thousand passengers but which was now packed with four thousand illegal immigrants. Just a few days into their voyage, a convoy of British warships began to track them. Once the *Medinat Israel* approached Palestine, the warships moved into formation to surround the unlawful vessel. As the British sailors boarded and took control of their ship, the four thousand Jews threw tin cans and sticks at them, singing "Hatikvah."

The British announced that they would be deporting the refugees to Cyprus, where they had established a detention camp for Holocaust survivors who were trying to enter Palestine illegally. The sick, however, would be treated at the Atlit detainee camp, where Erich Weininger had been briefly incarcerated seven years earlier. That is where Feivel and his family were taken, as well, after Tzici claimed to be pregnant and Helen pretended to be sick. The Winingers spent several months at Atlit. It was during this time that the United Nations General Assembly endorsed the creation of the State of Israel.

Finally, on February 2, 1948, Feivel moved his family into a one-room apartment just outside Tel Aviv. They shared a kitchen with two other families, but it nevertheless seemed like a five-star hotel compared to the conditions they had endured in Transnistria. They worked hard to create a new life. Tzici got a job at an orange plantation, while Feivel worked on a road construction crew during the day and went out on patrol with the Israel Defense Forces at night. After a year, they had saved up enough money to open a small Laundromat. They expanded their family with the birth of a son and purchased a two-bedroom apartment. After Feivel got a job at a bank in Tel Aviv, the family moved into an even larger apartment.

Feivel continued to treasure the Placht Brothers violin that had saved him and his family, an instrument that he called "Friend." He took Friend everywhere and played him every Saturday. As Helen grew up, Feivel told her the stories over and over again about how Friend had saved her and her family during the Holocaust.

As Feivel aged, he developed arthritis that made it difficult to play Friend. After a few years of not even touching the violin, he told Helen, "I want to play again." He was approaching the age of ninety.

"Okay. What can I do?"

"Please repair my violin."

Helen took the instrument to Amnon—a logical choice given Amnon's status as the finest maker and repairer of violins in Israel.

"Can you please repair this violin?" she asked. She did not tell him about the instrument's astonishing history.

"Leave it here. I will look at it and I will call you."

A little while later, Amnon telephoned Helen to tell

her that the instrument was in serious disrepair. He explained that it would be rather expensive to fix the violin, because he would have to take it apart for extensive restoration. "Why don't you buy him a new violin?" Amnon suggested, pointing out that it would be much cheaper.

When Helen told her father that she would buy him a new instrument, he started to cry. "The violin is something that I cannot let go," he said tearfully. "It is my best friend."

Helen returned to Amnon and finally told him about the role the instrument had played during the Holocaust. This changed everything. "Okay," he told her. "I will do whatever I can to just make it playable."

"Don't tell me how much it will cost," Helen said. "Whatever it will cost will be okay."

The cost was indeed no problem. As a tribute to Feivel, Amnon brought the instrument back to life for free.

Feivel was delighted to be reunited with Friend. He tried to play the instrument, but his advanced arthritis made it impossible. This did not matter. Feivel was elated just to once again hold his friend in his arms. He cherished the instrument to his last day, hugging it as his eyes welled with tears of gratitude for saving his family.

6

MOTELE
SCHLEIN'S
VIOLIN

Moshe Gildenman was the commander of "Uncle Misha's Jewish Group," a partisan brigade that operated in the Polish-Ukrainian region of Volhynia and the Ukrainian province of Zhytomyr. *(Courtesy of Yad Vashem.)*

The twelve-year-old boy was fast asleep when the six armed men discovered him. He was lying by himself near a smoldering fire in the woods of the Polish-Ukrainian region of Volhynia. His head was resting on a violin case. It was just after midnight on January 4, 1943.

"Where did this little boy come from?" asked one of the men.

"He probably got lost in the forest," responded their leader. "He's probably also hungry. Let him sleep for now. When the soup is ready, we'll wake him up so he can tell us who he is."

The men lit a new fire. They melted snow in the aluminum boxes that they carried on their belts. When the water started boiling, they added some wheat and frozen meat.

"Wake up, young man!" the leader yelled, shaking the boy when the soup started to cook. "You shouldn't sleep so soundly in the forest."

The boy's eyes cracked open and quickly closed. He rolled over and went back to sleep.

The leader grabbed him by the arms and sat him upright. The boy opened his eyes again. Seeing the strange men with their weapons, he jumped up. He tried to run away, but the leader gripped his hand.

"Don't be scared, little boy," the leader said. "We

won't harm you. We're partisans. Do you know what partisans are?"

The boy knew exactly who they were. They were members of a Jewish guerrilla force. Freedom fighters who had escaped into the woods when the Germans and Ukrainians had come to liquidate their hometowns. From their hideouts in the forest, they launched paramilitary attacks and performed acts of sabotage on the Nazis and their collaborators.

"I know, I know!" the boy exclaimed, recognizing the patches of red fabric they wore on their caps. "I've been looking for you for the past three days."

"What's your name, boy?" the detachment leader asked.

"They call me Mitka," the boy lied. He had learned to disguise his Jewish identity around strangers, even fellow Jews. He had adopted a name that implied that he was Ukrainian. His real name was Mordechai "Motele" Schlein, but he would not share this with the partisans for several months.

He did, however, tell them the partial truth about how he had ended up in the woods. Motele was from the Volhynian village of Krasnovka and had escaped into the forest in the previous spring, right after his family had been shot. He told the partisans that his parents had been killed along with other townspeople in retaliation for the burning of a German warehouse. The truth was that his parents and little sister had been murdered simply for being Jewish. As Motele explained to the partisans, he had lived in the forest by himself for the entire summer. When winter had arrived, he had gone into a nearby village and gotten a job as a shepherd for a rich peasant. After suffering months of physical abuse from the peasant's wife, the boy had slipped back into the forest on New Year's Day in the hopes of joining the Nazi-fighting partisans.

"I like you! We'll take you with us," declared the detachment leader, impressed with the boy's resourcefulness. "You'll be in Uncle Misha's Jewish Group." The detachment leader just happened to be Simcha "Lionka" Gildenman, the son of the "Uncle Misha" after whom the partisan brigade was named.

"Aren't you afraid of being around Jews? Here in Volhynia, the Ukrainian children are afraid of being called 'zhid,'" Lionka continued, invoking a Russian epithet for a person of Jewish descent.

"I'm not afraid of Jews," the boy responded, turning his head and wiping away a tear with his sleeve. "They're just like everyone else."

Krasnovka

Motele was born in 1930 in Krasnovka, a small village near the border between Poland and the Soviet Union. He grew up in a sunken, straw-covered shack with his sister Batyale, who was two years younger than him. Their father Burtzik Schlein owned the shack along with a windmill and a garden. Their mother Chana took care of the family by preparing their meals, washing their clothes, and tending to the garden. In the nearby lake, she soaked flax that she would spin into linen at night. To further supplement the windmill's meager profits, she raised geese that Motele and Batyale lovingly cared for.

Although Motele's family was so poor that they could not afford shoes for him, his childhood was full of fun and affection. He spent his summers playing with his Ukrainian friends, who loved him for his bravery and sense of humor. He, in turn, enjoyed helping them take care of the cows and horses behind the village. As he rode bareback through Krasnovka on the peasants' horses, nobody gave any consideration to the fact that Motele was Jewish.

Most of all, Motele loved music. One of his favorite activities was listening to his mother sing as she worked at her spinning wheel. His favorite song was a ballad about the 1903 massacre of Jews in Kishinev, the capital of the Romanian region of Bessarabia. There was also a blind lyrist who would often visit Krasnovka to beg. While the beggar sat on the ground, singing Ukrainian folksongs and accompanying himself on the lyre, Motele would cry as the music touched his soul. Some days, Motele would walk to the other side of the village to visit the lavish palace of Meir Gershtein, a wealthy plantation owner who was the patriarch of the only other Jewish family in Krasnovka. Peering through the iron fence that surrounded the estate, Motele would spend hours listening with fascination as Meir's daughter Reizele played the piano while her teacher Solomon played the violin.

Motele wanted to make music. He carved a crude

wooden flute, on which he taught himself to imitate bird-calls, to the delight of his friends. He would also try in vain to replicate the wonderful sounds he heard from the Gershtein estate—complex compositions such as a mazurka by Henryk Wieniawski. A handmade flute was the only instrument that Motele could afford, but what he really wanted to play was the violin. "When I grow up, I'm going to learn to play the violin like the plantation owner's teacher," he pledged to Batyale. "I'm going to be a musician."

Motele finally got his chance to learn music in the fall of 1938, when Meir Gershtein's wife—who was Motele's third cousin—invited the eight-year-old boy to live with her family. In the afternoons, after Reizele finished her schooling, she and Solomon would go into the parlor to play music. Motele would become so mesmerized by the sound of Solomon's violin that he would still be staring dreamily at the instrument several moments after they stopped playing.

One time, when Reizele and Solomon were playing a medley of Ukrainian folksongs, Motele started singing along unconsciously. Reizele exchanged a glance with Solomon and whispered, "Pianissimo." As they played softly, Motele's voice resonated throughout the parlor. When they finished, Reizele ran over to Motele and kissed him on the cheek. "What a dear child you are!" she exclaimed. "What a great ear you have for music! Solomon, you must begin teaching him the violin."

And so Motele's dream became a reality. Solomon

started to give him violin lessons on an instrument that Reizele's little brother Shunye had lost interest in playing. Motele quickly proved be a good student. He was intelligent and remarkably talented, he picked things up quickly, and he was always eager to learn. Solomon spent every free moment helping his young prodigy develop his talent, even after Motele decided to move back into his parents' house in the spring of 1939.

Motele's carefree childhood ended on September 1, 1939, when Nazi Germany invaded Poland. As the German army occupied the western part of the country, thousands of Poles, mainly Jews, fled eastward. Several Jewish families escaped to Krasnovka, including one that stayed with Motele's family and told them horrific stories of German atrocities.

In accordance with the Molotov-Ribbentrop Pact, which had secretly divvied up Eastern Europe between Germany and the Soviet Union, the Red Army invaded eastern Poland on September 17. The Soviet occupation brought about many changes in Krasnovka, most notably the nationalization of the Gershtein estate. After the Gershteins were forced to move to a neighboring village, their palace was turned into Krasnovka's first school, which Motele attended. Solomon was retained as one of the teachers. He continued to give Motele violin lessons after lunch.

A period of relative stability ended on June 22, 1941, when Germany violated the Molotov-Ribbentrop Pact by invading Soviet-occupied Eastern Europe. Once again, people started escaping eastward.

"Everyone is fleeing," Motele's mother Chana told his father. "Maybe we should go with them."

"Let's wait awhile," Burtzik responded. But he became less confident in his answer with each passing day. Others were abandoning their houses, but how could he and Chana leave the windmill that his great-grandfather had built? And how would they bring Motele and his little sister Batyale?

By July 1, it was too late. The Germans had occupied Krasnovka. They stormed the town with the roar of engines and the heavy footfalls of boots. They arrested the village chairman and hanged him. They ordered that his body be left swinging from the gallows for three days as an example for the rest of the village. The villagers secreted themselves in their shacks, but the Germans simply went door-to-door, demanding food.

A truck with twelve German soldiers pulled up in Motele's yard. Weapons drawn, they entered the house and sat down at the table. Chana served them eggs, fresh bread, and butter, which they ate without speaking a single word. They just stared at Chana from beneath the steel helmets that they had not even bothered to take off. As Motele and Batyale watched from the cracked door to the adjacent room, the eldest of the Germans suddenly stood up and went into the yard. A few moments later, Motele and Batyale heard several gunshots. The commander came back in and threw to the floor three bloody geese that were still convulsing and flapping their wings.

"These geese must be ready to eat in one hour," he ordered Chana.

Chana just stood there, pale-faced and frozen with horror.

The German grabbed her arm and stared angrily into her frightened eyes. "One hour," he commanded. "Do you understand?"

After the Germans stepped outside, Chana started crying. Wiping away her tears with the side of her head scarf, she started plucking the geese.

Batyale entered the room and hugged her mother from behind. "Don't cry, Mama," she pleaded. "We still have lots of geese."

"I'm not crying because of the geese," Chana answered. "I'm crying over our own fates. God knows if we'll survive these murderers."

Meanwhile, the German commander had ordered Burtzik to wash the dirt and mud off his truck. Burtzik filled a bucket with water and fashioned a brush from straw. When the commander saw Burtzik scrubbing the truck, he became irate.

"You dirty Jew," he shouted, frothing at the mouth. "Why are you ruining the paint on my truck?"

He slapped Burtzik in the face. Then, noticing clean white sheets hanging on a clothesline, he grabbed the laundry, balled it up, and threw it at Burtzik.

"Clean with this, you damned Jew," he spat.

Motele had come running out of the house when the German had started screaming. He watched angrily as his father bit his lip in pain and resumed washing the truck.

The Nazi Occupation of Volhynia

Immediately upon occupying Volhynia, the Germans initiated a plan to completely wipe out its Jewish community. They received ample assistance from local police and townspeople whose anti-Semitism and xenophobia made them willing participants in the genocide. "The element that settled our cities, whether it is Jews or Poles who were brought here from outside the Ukraine, must disappear completely from our cities," declared the editor of the newspaper *Volhyn* on September 1, 1941. "The Jewish problem is already in the process of being solved, and it will be solved in the framework of a general reorganization of the 'New Europe.'"[82]

In the first wave of mass murders, fifteen thousand Jews were killed by the German death squads with the assistance of the Ukrainian police. By October 1941, subsequent waves of killings would result in the deaths of an additional thirty thousand Jews. The slaughters slowed when the Germans realized that they could exploit Jewish laborers rather than kill them. By this time, the vast majority of the surviving Jews of Volhynia had been relocated to cramped ghettos and labor camps, where starvation and disease claimed even more lives.

Although they were the only Jews left in Krasnovka,

Motele's family avoided being banished to a ghetto because Burtzik's work at the windmill had rendered him indispensable to the town. Burtzik was, however, subjected to the Nuremberg Laws. The Nazis confiscated his grain and put severe restrictions on how much he could earn by milling the villagers' grain. He was also required to wear the yellow Star of David, which immediately ostracized him from his fellow villagers.

One of these villagers was Burtzik's closest neighbor Pavlo Fustamit, whose family had lived next to Burtzik's for three generations. Burtzik and Pavlo grew up together, herded cattle together, and served in the military together. As adults, they collected wood together and helped each other buy cattle. They were like brothers. Their wives also became close friends, visiting each other almost hourly to borrow something, seek advice, or just chat. The women would garden together, spin flax together, and help each other with various other chores. When Pavlo's house was burned down by lightning, he and his wife Maria moved in with Burtzik and Chana until Pavlo could build a new home. But after the Nazi occupation, Pavlo and Maria avoided Burtzik and his family. They stopped visiting. They would turn their heads away if they saw them on the street.

Motele was also shunned by his former friends. At the beginning of the school year, he went to Gershtein's former palace to reenroll in classes. Along the way, he passed a group of Ukrainian children playing in a park. As soon as they saw him, they started chanting, "Jew!

Jew!" Motele did not react. He just lowered his head and kept walking.

He walked into the familiar schoolroom and noted a new portrait of Hitler on the wall. "Good morning," he said.

"A Ukrainian doesn't say 'good morning,' but 'glory to Ukraine,'" responded one of the three teachers seated at a round table. None of them bothered to look up from the books they were reading.

"I've come to enroll in this class," Motele mumbled hesitantly.

"What's your name?" one of the teachers asked. Although he was still looking down, Motele recognized him as a geography teacher who had always been mean to him.

"Mordechai Schlein."

The mean teacher jumped up and stared at Motele with hatred. "You zhid!" he shouted. "Who let you in here? Run away quickly. Don't you know that Jews are forbidden from attending school?"

Motele left the room as fast as he could, leaping down two and three steps at a time on his way out of the schoolhouse. He did not stop running until he reached a large field far from the village, where he fell to the ground and sobbed uncontrollably.

That winter was very difficult for Motele's family. They had always lived simply, but they had at least been able to avoid poverty. Now that the Nazis had limited what Burtzik could charge for his services, they barely had enough to survive. To make matters worse, the millstone

in the windmill had worn down and needed to be replaced
if Burtzik was to continue to protect his family by being
useful. To save what little money they earned for the new
millstone, the family ate only potatoes the entire winter.

In addition to nearly starving to death, Motele's family
almost froze. Since the villagers refused to lend Burtzik a
horse, he was unable to get wood for the fire. It was up to
Motele and Batyale to walk two miles to the forest. Dig-
ging through the deep snow with their bare hands, they
would search for twigs that they could load onto their little sled. Crying because they were starving, freezing, and
exhausted, they would endure taunts and insults from
Ukrainian children on their way home.

The Massacres Resume

In the spring of 1942, the ethnic cleansing of Volhynia
resumed with brutal intensity. The Nazis began systematically liquidating the ghettos, starting with women, children, and the elderly who were unfit to work. Close to
twenty thousand Volhynian Jews were killed in the first
stage of these renewed massacres, which commenced in
May and lasted until mid-June. The second phase resulted
in the complete destruction of the ghettos in Rovno and
Olyka and the murder of ten thousand Jews. It was the
third stage that did the most damage. It began in August
and lasted more than two months. The killing teams, often operating in several districts at the same time, murdered 150,000 Jews, effectively obliterating what was left

of Volhynia's once-vibrant Jewish community. A final stage, in November and December 1942, completed the ethnic cleansing by eliminating the 3,500 skilled laborers who had remained in the ghettos. This left alive only a few thousand Jews who had managed to hide or escape to the forests, many of whom would later die of starvation or during partisan battles.

The massacre that took place in the Volhynian city of Korets on May 21, 1942—the eve of the Jewish holiday of Shavuot—resulted in the slaughter of 90 percent of the town's Jewish population. One of the few survivors was a forty-four-year-old civil engineer by the name of Moshe Gildenman, who later related the horror of the Korets massacre in gruesome detail. "Near a pit twenty-by-twenty meters long and three meters deep stood a table with bottles of cognac and food," he recalled. "At the table sat a German with an automatic pistol in his hand. Frightened and despairing Jews were pushed into the pit naked, six at a time. The German ordered them to lie on the ground, face down. Between one sip of cognac and the next he shot them. Among the 2,200 Jews the Germans shot that day were my wife and my thirteen-year-old daughter."

The killings lasted for twelve hours. That evening, Gildenman and the other survivors met in the synagogue to rend their garments and say Kaddish for the dead. While others were mourning, Gildenman's thoughts turned to rage and retribution. He heard a voice cry out from inside himself: "Not with prayers will you assuage our grief for the rivers of innocent blood that was spilled—but with revenge!"

As soon as the Kaddish was over, Gildenman banged the table. "Listen to me, unfortunate, death-condemned Jews!" he called out. "Know that sooner or later we are all doomed. But I shall not go like a sheep to the slaughter!" Gildenman vowed that someday he would exact his revenge.[83]

On September 23, 1942, with the Germans and Ukrainians surrounding the Korets ghetto for its final liquidation, Gildenman, his son, and several other men escaped to the forest. Combining Gildenman's engineering background with their thirst for revenge, the partisans staged a series of sophisticated attacks, killing Nazis and acquiring their weapons. The group's many successes included a number of cleverly engineered attacks on trains, railways, and bridges that prevented the Germans from transporting much-needed reinforcements to the Eastern Front. Taking its name from Gildenman's partisan moniker, the outfit became known as "Uncle Misha's Jewish Group." It would be this partisan brigade that Motele would join in January 1943.

One day, Motele was approaching his family's home when he saw the Nazi-appointed mayor of the village enter the courtyard with four German soldiers. Fearful of coming face-to-face with the Nazis, Motele darted into the windmill. He climbed up to the top floor and looked out a round window at what was happening below.

While the mayor leaned against the well, nonchalantly brushing the dirt off his boots with a twig, the four soldiers entered the house. Suddenly, Motele heard his father cry out. Several gunshots were followed by the heartrending screams of Chana and Batyale.

Then there was silence. A shudder went down Motele's entire body. His hair stood up on end. He knew instantly that his parents and sister were dead. He would be next if he was not careful. He decided to run away as soon as he could get out of the windmill safely.

The mayor walked into the house and reemerged a few minutes later carrying a bloody sheet into which he had packed several stolen items. He walked back to the village, followed by the Nazi murderers.

As Motele continued to watch from his hiding place in the windmill, the neighbor Pavlo Fustamit appeared. Pavlo ran into Motele's house and stuck his head out the window.

"Maria!" he shouted. "Quick, bring a sack!"

Maria walked over with an empty bag and entered the house. After a little while, Pavlo came into the yard with a large featherbed that Motele's mother had painstakingly made. He ripped the quilt apart, dumped out all of the feathers, and took the empty cover back into the house. When he reemerged a few moments later, the quilt cover was filled with stolen items. Maria followed behind him, nearly doubled over under the weight of her heavy sack.

Convulsing with quiet sobs, Motele watched through tearful eyes as the mayor returned.

"Until the regional commander takes over the windmill, it has to be sealed," the mayor explained to Pavlo.

As the mayor walked toward the windmill, Motele

scampered down from the top floor and hid behind an old crate. His heart pounded and his head spun. He felt dizzy.

"Is there anyone here?" the mayor called out, opening the windmill's only door. "Come out, because I'm nailing the door shut."

Motele heard the door close, followed by the hammering of nails. He breathed deeply, but did not leave his hiding place. He lay there for a long time, crying softly.

When night fell, Motele decided to make his escape. He found a rope and tied one end to a post. He pushed the other end through a small hatch on the top floor. He climbed through the hatch and slid down the rope fifty feet to the ground.

Motele's heart pounded as he approached his house. As soon as he walked through the door, he froze. In the moonlight he could see Burtzik lying in the middle of the room, covered in blood. His eyes were still open. Chana was on the bed, one bare foot draped off the side of the bed into a pool of blood. Young Batyale lay nearby, underneath a chair. Her face was flat against the floor. Her little hands were stretched out, frozen in her last moments of desperation.

"Blood . . . blood," Motele said to himself, in shock over what he was seeing. "I no longer have anyone. They've all been murdered. I have to run away from here, as quickly as possible. They'll murder me, as well."

Before he left, he noticed his father's little prayer book on the floor near his feet. He picked it up, pressed it to his lips, and put it in his pocket. He quickly ran out of the house.

He had no sooner reached an old pear tree that stood near the border of the yard than he saw Pavlo coming down the road. Motele quickly scampered up the tree and watched as Pavlo walked to his own house. As Motele climbed down, he suddenly remembered the Gershteins' violin, which he had secreted in the hollow of the very tree in which he was hiding so the Germans would not confiscate it.

Motele grabbed the violin from its hiding place and pressed it to his heart. It was his last reminder of better times. He ran into the dense forest with only one thought in his mind: "Run away, the farther the better. Escape from these evil people."

Motele in the Forest

As Motele would later tell Lionka and the other partisans who would discover him in the woods, he spent the summer after his flight in the forest. Walking eastward, toward Belarus, he lived off wild berries and mushrooms. Whenever he came across a town or village, he would hide in the bushes until it got dark and steal potatoes from a garden on his way out of town. When he needed to sleep, he would build himself a bed out of moss or grass and use his violin case as a pillow. He was initially scared of living in the forest, but he quickly became more confident as he developed his survival skills.

When the autumn brought cold winds and rain, scavenging food became much more difficult. Berries were no longer in season, mushrooms were increasingly hard to find under inches of fallen leaves, and potatoes had already been harvested from their gardens. With only a thin linen shirt, one pair of pants, and no shoes, Motele was also freezing. The weather was even affecting his violin case, which was starting to swell from the moisture. Motele had not played the violin in months, because he was afraid that someone would hear him. He would, however, occasionally open the case and run his hand gently over the strings. Just this small amount of physical contact with his instrument was enough to bring him comfort.

When the cold rain became too much to bear, Motele hid his violin under a fallen tree and walked into a village. He knocked on the first door he came to and was welcomed by an elderly farm woman who found him a job working as a shepherd for the richest farmer in the village. Motele went back into the forest and reclaimed his violin, which he hid under a pile of straw in the woodshed. In return for caring for two oxen, four cows, and ten sheep, Motele was given a jacket, a pair of pants, and a pair of boots.

The rich farmer Karpo was a quiet and kind man who treated Motele well. His wife Christia, on the other hand, was a hateful woman who lorded over Motele and her servant girl Dasha with verbal and physical abuse. Even worse was her son Pyetro, an anti-Semitic policeman from nearby Dombrovitze.

"This is our new shepherd?" Pyetro asked upon seeing Motele. "For some reason, he has very curly hair like a zhid. Come closer to me, boy."

Although his heart was pounding, Motele approached Pyetro with every ounce of courage he could muster. "Glory to Ukraine!" he cheerfully greeted the policeman, using the salutation he had learned from the Nazi schoolteachers in Krasnovka.

Pyetro stared into Motele's shiny black eyes. "The 'Our Father,'" he said, referring to the Christian prayer. "Do you know it?"

Motele had grown up with Christian Ukrainian children. He had learned their customs and their prayers. He recited the prayer in one breath.

"Even though you're a Christian," Pyetro conceded, "you do have the hair of a non-Christian."

That settled the matter until New Year's Eve, when Christia discovered among Motele's belongings the little prayer book that had once belonged to his father.

"You're a zhid!" she said, confronting Motele when he entered the house that night.

"Everybody says that I look like a zhid," Motele responded matter-of-factly. "Even your son Pyetro said that I have the hair of a non-Christian."

"Then what's this?" Christia demanded, triumphantly holding up the prayer book.

"Where did you find Seryozha's little book?" Motele exclaimed, quickly inventing a Jewish friend. "He gave it to me to play with for a day and I lost it. We almost got into a fight over it." He calmly grabbed the book and slid it into his pocket.

"I told you that you are picking on this poor child for

no reason," Karpo scolded his wife. "He's a true Christian soul, and you want to turn him into a Jew."

"Tomorrow our Pyetro will come," Christia responded, not willing to concede defeat. "He'll interrogate the boy as necessary and will establish whether he is a zhid or a Christian."

On New Year's Day, when the family departed for church, they left Motele behind to guard the house. The interrogation would come after the church service. Motele had planned to simply disappear while they were gone, but was overcome with a thirst for revenge. He thought of the Nazi teacher who had humiliated him in Krasnovka and of the beatings he received from Christia. He thought of his old neighbors Pavlo and Maria Fustamit, who had shunned his father and then looted his house. He thought of his murdered family. It was not fair that the self-proclaimed Christians would celebrate their New Year while he would be forced back into the forest. Someone had to pay.

Motele grabbed his violin, climbed into the attic, and set the straw roof on fire. Hiding behind buildings, he quickly made his way through the village and into the forest. As soon as he reached the tree line, he heard screams. The church bells began to sound an alarm. Motele turned around. As he disappeared into the forest, he watched the flames from Karpo's house shoot into the sky.

The servant girl Dasha had told Motele stories of the partisans who had occupied the forests surrounding the village. These brave combatants were killing policemen, ambushing military depots, and sharing their loot with the poorest farmers. Inspired by the tales of their bravery, Motele had made up his mind to find them. After three days of his wandering around in the forest, they found him. And so the boy who called himself Mitka joined Uncle Misha's Jewish Group, which by then was receiving tactical support from the Red Army. Motele proved to be a clever and daring young operative with a knack for intelligence and espionage.

Motele the Young Partisan

Shortly after Motele joined the Jewish Group, Uncle Misha himself sent the boy on a mission. Motele was to spy on a group of Hungarian soldiers who had arrived in Lubin, a village located three miles from their partisan camp.

"When they stop you and ask who you are, what will you say?" Uncle Misha asked Motele before dispatching him.

"I'll tell them that I'm from the village of Kristinovka and that I'm looking for a white cow with red patches and a broken horn," Motele smartly replied, without even thinking about it. "The cow separated from the herd and went in the direction of Lubin."

Barefoot in his short linen pants, with a bag over one shoulder and a whip in his hand, Motele looked every bit the part of a shepherd. He walked right through the village, innocently strolling past the Hungarian soldiers who were going from home to home gathering eggs and cheese.

When he reached the center of the village, he came upon six large wagons. Next to the wagons Motele discovered a fat Hungarian cook, whom he befriended by chopping wood for him and by stirring his soup. While Motele was working on the soup, the cook dozed off. Motele noticed that the cook had left his pistol on a bench and thought to himself, "Once I have a pistol like that, I'll be a real partisan." He quickly removed the cook's pistol from its holster and slid it into his bag.

As Motele was heading out of the village, he happened upon a Hungarian soldier who was mounting a horse. The soldier dropped his whip and signaled to the boy to pick it up for him. To avoid looking suspicious, Motele ignored his pounding heart and calmly handed the whip to its owner. As soon as the soldier rode off, Motele ran quickly back to the forest.

After recounting his experience for Uncle Misha, Motele reached into his bag and dramatically produced a Belgian Colt. "Come to the other side of the marshes," he said gleefully to Lionka, grabbing his new friend by the hand. "You can teach me how to shoot!"

"Wait a second before learning how to shoot!" Uncle Misha interrupted. "You haven't reported to me the findings of your reconnaissance mission. I sent you to Lubin to find out how many Hungarians are there and how they're armed, not to steal pistols from sleeping cooks."

Motele's face turned bright red. "I told you that there were six wagons," he retorted angrily. "If we assume that there are five men to each wagon, then there are thirty

Hungarians. The cook makes thirty-one, and the commander makes thirty-two. There cannot be any more than that because Hungarians are not partisans who are willing to ride ten to a wagon.

"They only have one heavy machine gun, like our Maxim," he continued, referring to the bulky machine gun that took several people to operate. "I saw it on a wagon, hiding under a heavy green tarp. It looks like they came to Lubin to get some wheat because I saw new bags painted with swastikas on one of the wagons."

Within less than an hour, Uncle Misha acted on Motele's report by attacking the Hungarians in Lubin. Just as Motele had calculated, there were thirty of them. Uncle Misha's men killed them all and took their supplies.

One Sunday in the spring of 1943, Motele was sent on a new mission—one considerably more daring than simply spying on a brigade of Hungarians. Whipping a horse that was half dead from starvation and disease, Motele drove a wagon loaded with bran bags toward the village of Bielko. When he was just outside the village, Motele stopped and climbed down from the wagon. Looking around to make sure that he was not being watched, he unscrewed the bolt that secured the right front wheel and threw it into the bushes. He rode into town, announcing his arrival with the loud screeching of the ungreased wheels. He stopped right in front of a large wooden house that was the headquarters of the most powerful police force in the region, including forty Ukrainian policemen and six German soldiers. Six policemen came out of the building to investigate the noise while a German soldier watched from a window, laughing at the young Ukrainian peasant's primitive transportation.

Motele climbed down from the wagon and made a spectacle out of checking the front right side. "I lost the bolt from the front wheel." He started to cry, hitting himself in the head with his fists. "What will I do now? My father is going to kill me!

"The bolt must be in a forest not far from here," he continued. "How will I go on?

"Would you please hold on to my horse while I run and look for the bolt?" he asked the policemen who were standing there poking fun at the weeping boy. Before they could respond, he handed one of them the reins and started back toward the forest. He walked with his head bent down, studying the ground. Every few steps, he would kneel down as if he were searching for something. When he reached the dense forest, he slipped into the woods and disappeared. He ran as fast as he could for five hundred yards and stopped. Putting two fingers in his mouth, he whistled loudly. Immediately, he heard a similar whistle from not too far away. Lionka and two other partisans appeared out of nowhere.

"Did you deliver the present?" Lionka asked.

"I delivered the present not only to the police station, but also to the six policemen and two soldiers who were guarding it," Motele said, laughing. "Oh, did I fool them!" He did two somersaults in celebration.

After Motele had left the police station, the policemen

had continued to stand around, laughing at the poor state of the horse and its driver. When Motele did not return, the policemen decided to move the horse and carriage into their courtyard. Unable to coax the horse into pulling the wagon, one of the policemen started unloading the bran bags. He had gotten two bags on the ground and was unloading the third bag when there was a violent explosion. The bag had been connected to a bomb the partisans had placed at the bottom of the wagon.

The bags, the wagon, and horse entrails went flying through the air. Four of the policemen were killed and the other two were seriously injured. A piece of the wooden wagon struck the German soldier who was standing in the window, gouging out an eye and knocking out all of his teeth. When the peasants came running out of their homes to see what was happening, they saw hundreds of pieces of paper. These were leaflets that had been in the bran bags. They had been hurled into the air by the explosion. The paper slowly floated down, covering the roofs, the yards, and the road like fresh snow. The leaflets, which the Red Army had airlifted to Uncle Misha's Jewish Group just a few nights earlier, boasted of the German defeats on the Eastern Front. They warned the Ukrainians that those who continued to collaborate with the Nazis would be punished by the approaching Red Army.

It was not until May 21, 1943, more than five months after he joined Uncle Misha's Jewish Group, that Motele finally disclosed his true identity to the partisan brigade. His confession came as Uncle Misha was mourning the

262 JAMES A. GRYMES

first anniversary of the murders of his wife and daughter. Uncle Misha, Lionka, and ten other partisans from Korets decided to leave their camp to say Kaddish in private. Noticing that Motele was following them, Uncle Misha ordered him to return to the camp.

"What kind of holiday is today?" the boy asked.

"Today marks exactly one year since the Germans murdered our family," Uncle Misha replied.

"The Germans also murdered my parents."

"But we are Jews and we are going to say a prayer to our God."

"My father told me that all people have one God. I won't bother you. Let me come with you."

Uncle Misha relented.

By the time the partisans reached their destination on the other side of the swamp, the sun had already set. They nailed two rows of candles on a wide tree stump, and lit them. One of the partisans took out a prayer book and led the evening prayer. When that was finished, the mourners tearfully said Kaddish. When the partisans were finished, they heard Motele slowly reciting the last line of the Hebrew prayer: "Peace upon us and upon all Israel, and say Amen."

Astonished, the partisans turned to the boy who was standing in back of the group, holding a small prayer book in his hand. It was the book that Motele had taken from his father's house. He had kept it with him ever since.

Large tears were rolling down Motele's cheeks. He ran

up to Uncle Misha and wrapped his arms around his neck. "Uncle Misha, I'm a Jew, too!" he exclaimed.

The partisans were stunned. Why had the boy lied about his Jewish heritage? There was certainly no stigma for being a Jew in Uncle Misha's Jewish Group.

"First of all, what's your Jewish name?" Lionka demanded, feeling betrayed. "Second, why didn't you tell me that you're a Jew? Do you think that being a Ukrainian is a greater honor?"

"My real name is Motele, which is what I want you to call me from now on," the boy finally divulged. "Secondly, I didn't reveal my Jewish identity because from the day the Germans occupied our territory, I suffered so much as a Jew that I felt safer not identifying myself as one, even when I was among friends. Besides, it seemed to me that as a Ukrainian I would have more opportunities to avenge the deaths of my parents and my only sister."

Fighting alongside the partisans under his true Jewish name, Motele continued to demonstrate astonishing skills and confidence.

On July 6, 1943, Uncle Misha's Jewish Group was attacked by two German fighter planes while attempting to cross a river. When a partisan radio operator named Mania got stranded on a small island in the middle of the river, she shot herself to avoid being taken alive and possibly tortured for her secret codes. As the partisans watched in disbelief, her body fell into the thick undergrowth that surrounded the island and disappeared. Losing Mania meant also losing their radio batteries, which she had packed in a cigar box in her leather satchel. It was through that radio that they received critical tactical information from the Partisan Movement Central Headquarters in Moscow. It was through that radio that they would need to dispatch an SOS signal if they were to have any hopes of surviving the German attack.

"I can swim over to Mania and rescue the satchel containing the batteries," Motele volunteered.

"That's impossible," Uncle Misha replied. "The Germans will see you as soon as you surface."

"They won't see me," Motele said confidently. "I'll swim underwater."

"How will you be able to stay underwater for so long?"

"I can stay underwater for several hours. Let me show you." Motele got undressed, crawled over to the shore, and plucked a reed out of the ground. He put one end in his mouth and blew through the reed as if it were a straw. "I can swim all the way to the Volga with this reed!" he exclaimed.

He climbed into the water and disappeared. All that was left was the other end of the reed, barely sticking out of the water. Uncle Misha and the other partisans watched as the reed made its way across the river. As the Germans surveilled the partisans from the opposite shore, the reed made it to the island. The bushes swayed a bit before going back to being still. Then the reed started working its way back to the partisans. Motele triumphantly emerged from the water with Mania's satchel. An hour later, the

Russians heard the partisans' signal and were able to come to their defense, thanks to Motele's heroic swimming.

Motele Blows Up the Soldiers Club

In August 1943, Uncle Misha's Jewish Group was operating in the dense forests of the northern Ukrainian province of Zhytomyr. Despite growing tired of their grueling life in the woods, the partisans were bolstered by the latest radio reports of the success of the Red Army, which had gained the upper hand on the Eastern Front during the Battle of Kursk just weeks earlier. The Russians were now advancing westward, liberating towns and capturing Germans along the way.

Although the Soviet leaders had ordered the partisan commanders to suspend their sabotage missions until they could be reunited with the Red Army, Uncle Misha was not ready to end his quest for vengeance. He was planning a surprise attack on the nearby city of Ovruch to destroy the train station and the large bridge that served as main gates to the Eastern Front.

From an informant named Karol, Uncle Misha learned that the Orthodox church leaders in Ovruch had convinced the German and Ukrainian police to allow visitors to enter and leave the city without documentation on August 20. This would allow everyone to freely celebrate the First Feast of the Savior. Uncle Misha decided to take advantage of this temporary lapse in security by dispatching several partisans to Ovruch to familiarize themselves with the town, to find out which military units were stationed there, and to assess the residents' allegiances. He also wanted to confirm Karol's report that the police department was prepared to surrender to Uncle Misha's Jewish Group and hand over their weapons.

In addition to the partisan spies, Uncle Misha sent Motele and his violin to Ovruch. While the partisans were gathering intelligence, Motele was to join the group of beggars soliciting alms in front of the church. Posing as a street performer, Motele could surreptitiously observe the spies and immediately report back to Uncle Misha if they were discovered. Motele was even provided with counterfeit documents, forged by a partisan who was a former stampmaker, indicating that he was Dmitri Rubina from the Ukrainian village of Listvin. If he was questioned, Motele would simply reply that he was traveling to the city of Zhytomyr to find his father Ivan, who he had heard was being held in the German prisoner-of-war camp there.

The beggars included a blind man singing psalms while accompanying himself on a lyre, a one-legged veteran of the Russo-Japanese War playing an accordion, an elderly woman with a swollen and bandaged cheek, and several other destitute and handicapped drifters hoping to elicit sympathy from the holiday travelers. Motele sat on a wooden stool at the back of the crowd and placed a clay bowl he had purchased in the market between his feet. He tuned his violin, strummed a few strings, and began to perform one of the many Ukrainian folksongs he had learned in Krasnovka. The folksong was "The Ant," a song about a woman whose work is so underappreciated that she asks God for wings. Motele would sing a stanza and then play the melody on his violin.

Although Uncle Misha had specifically chosen Motele for this assignment because of his ability to blend in with Ukrainians, the beauty of his singing and playing far surpassed that of the other beggars. He quickly attracted a crowd. When he finished the folksong, the onlookers threw coins into his bowl and slipped dumplings into his backpack.

Suddenly, there was a commotion in the back of the crowd. The congregation parted to make way for a German officer who was marching toward Motele. The officer stood in front of the boy. The young violinist was so engrossed with the music that he did not notice him. Finally, the officer tapped Motele on the shoulder with his riding crop. Raising his head and seeing the German uniform, Motele jumped to his feet and bowed.

"Come with me," the officer commanded.

Motele felt his breast pocket to make sure he still had his forged documents. He calmly placed his violin back in its case, collected the coins from his little bowl, and followed the officer.

After walking a few blocks, they arrived at a building that was flanked by several German limousines and motorcycles. They passed an armed guard at the entrance and ascended a flight of stairs to a large restaurant where German officers sat around tables eating, drinking, and talking loudly. The officer marched Motele to the corner of the room, and whispered to an elderly man who was playing the piano.

"Can you read music?" the pianist asked Motele in Russian, assuming that the boy was an ethnic Ukrainian.

"Yes."

The pianist dug through his sheet music and produced the score to Ignacy Jan Paderewski's popular Minuet in G Major, op. 14, no. 1. From a political point of view, the work was an interesting choice for the venue, given that the recently deceased Polish composer had raised money for Hitler's Jewish victims. From a musical standpoint, it was an excellent selection for a pianist attempting to accompany an unknown twelve-year-old street musician. The melody begins simply, moving stepwise in easy rhythms, and only increases in difficulty as the piece unfolds. If the boy stumbled early on, it would have been easy for the pianist to gracefully improvise a quick conclusion to the failed experiment.

But Motele was no ordinary street performer. He was a talented and well-trained violinist who had actually played that very minuet several times before, in the Gershteins' palace with Reizele playing the piano. At first, Motele's new pianist played only the accompaniment part with his left hand, listening intently to the young violinist's playing. As he gained confidence in Motele's abilities, the pianist added more harmonies with his right hand.

The restaurant grew quieter and quieter as the diners interrupted their conversations to listen to the beautiful duet. When Motele and his accompanist finished

the coda—a tour de force of virtuosic passagework—
the diners responded with vigorous applause. The Nazi
officer who had discovered Motele was so pleased with
the violin playing that he offered the boy a position entertaining the guests at the Soldiers Club for two hours
during lunchtime and from seven to eleven in the evening. In return, Motele would receive two reichsmarks a
day, plus lunch and dinner.

Motele protested, returning to his cover story of need-
ing to find his father in Zhytomyr. He added that he would
then have to return to Listvin to care for his sick mother
and three small siblings. When the officer promised to
find out if his father was in Zhytomyr and, if so, have him
transferred to Ovruch, Motele was left with little choice
but to accept the job.

Motele immediately visited Karol and asked him to
convey his predicament to Uncle Misha. The partisan
commander recognized the opportunity and ordered Motele to remain in Ovruch and report everything he ob-
served through Karol.

The Soldiers Club was one of many restaurants that
the Germans had appropriated as havens for soldiers on
their way to the Eastern Front. It was a place where they
could strengthen their resolve with great music, gourmet
food, French wine, and pretty Ukrainian waitresses who
served them in more ways than one. While playing his
violin, Motele was able to track the numbers of units and
the types of uniforms worn by German soldiers on their
way to the front. He also eavesdropped on the conversa-

tions of the few who returned. Between lunch and dinner he surveilled the streets of Ovruch, taking note of everything for his reports to Karol.

Despite impossible conditions, young Motele was somehow able to conceal his disdain for the Nazis. He even earned their trust and friendship. A regional commandant who spent every evening at the Soldiers Club went so far as to have a little German uniform and cap tailored for Motele, to the delight of the other employees at the Soldiers Club.

Motele also discovered that the fat cook would prepare his best dishes in exchange for performances of his favorite song, "Rose-Marie." Motele dined in the kitchen, which was located in the basement of the Soldiers Club. He usually ate his lunch before playing in the afternoon and returned for his dinner after he was done every night.

One day, on his way back upstairs after lunch, Motele noticed that one of the storerooms across the dimly lit hallway from the kitchen had been left open. He peered into the darkness and discovered a large cellar filled with empty wine cases, herring barrels, and other discarded items that had clearly been forgotten.

On the wall opposite the doorway was a jagged crack, presumably the result of a nearby bomb explosion. Motele, who had heard numerous tales of sabotage from other members of Uncle Misha's Jewish Group, stopped in his tracks. He realized that if he filled that crack with explosives he could blow up the Soldiers Club and kill all of the Germans inside. Every time he passed the open storeroom, his resolve became greater. He eventually shared his idea with Karol. Uncle Misha eagerly approved the plan and instructed his explosives expert Popov to work out the details with Motele.

The beginning of the autumn harvest season meant that peasants were traveling between Ovruch and the surrounding fields with increasing frequency. The German soldiers guarding the city had grown tired of searching their wagons and had become less meticulous in their inspections. This allowed Motele to leave the city in Karol's wagon unnoticed under a cartful of straw sheaves for bundling wheat. The German guard who allowed Karol to pass over the bridge out of town never suspected that underneath the heap of straw twists was a Jewish boy who planned to blow up his comrades.

Motele rendezvoused with Popov three miles outside Ovruch. After discussing the thickness of the stone walls and how long the wick would need to be to give Motele ample time to escape, Popov calculated that it would take forty pounds of explosives to bring down the Soldiers Club.

Motele returned to Ovruch in Karol's cart, then snuck out to the forest again a few days later. This time, Popov taught Motele how to construct a bomb and insert a detonator, a lesson that Motele had watched him give before. Popov gave Motele the explosives and sent him back to Ovruch with instructions to hide them at Karol's house.

That evening, after finishing his dinner and saying good night to the cook, Motele crept into the storeroom. He hid his instrument inside an empty barrel and left the Soldiers Club with an empty violin case. When he returned the next day, his case had a few pounds of explosives hidden inside. After his lunch, he snuck into the storeroom and swapped the explosives for his violin.

Motele repeated this process over the next several days, until he had successfully hidden all forty pounds of explosives in the cellar. Whenever he could, Motele would return to the storeroom to break off the stones that surrounded the crack in the wall and replace them with the deadly material. When he had packed all of the explosives into the wall, he inserted the capsule detonator and the long wick that Popov had given him. He hid everything behind a pile of garbage.

At the same time, Motele and Karol were working on an escape plan. Every day, they would visit the river that borders Ovruch, pretending to be fishing or swimming while actually looking for an area that would be shallow enough for Motele to cross during his getaway. On their way to and from the river, they would note the streets and gardens through which Motele would have to run on his flight out of town.

The only aspect of the plan that remained unresolved was when to detonate the bomb. The perfect opportunity finally presented itself when a division of the SS came through Ovruch on its way to try to salvage the increasingly hopeless situation on the Eastern Front. The success of partisan sabotage of the railroad had forced the SS division to abandon the train and instead travel eastward by road, stopping at Ovruch for the night.

At around three in the afternoon, their cars and motor-cycles began to arrive at the Soldiers Club. The restaurant quickly filled with high-ranking SS officers in their formal attire. Motele's violin and the piano accompaniment could barely be heard above the din of clanking dishes, clinking glasses, and loud laughter. Motele and the pianist were for-bidden from taking any breaks as the guests got drunker and as the cigar smoke thickened. The intoxicated officers requested tangos and waltzes, occasionally insisting that the musicians play only "their song." At one point, a red-faced German at one of the tables started screaming wildly, "Play 'Volga, Volga,'" referring to the popular "Volga Song" from an operetta by Franz Léhar. Another officer stumbled around the restaurant hugging a bottle of cognac while tearfully singing, "My father does not know me, my mother does not love me, and I cannot die because I am still young."

Motele's fingers ached from the nonstop playing and his eyes burned from all the cigar smoke. But he contin-ued to play. "I'm playing for you for the last time," he thought to himself as he smiled at his applauding audi-ence. "Eat, drink, and be merry, you accursed Germans. These are your final hours. I'll play so well for you tonight that you'll be blown apart dancing."

It was not until eleven that night that the pianist finally convinced the manager to let him and Motele relinquish the responsibility for entertaining the officers to the guests who could play the piano. Motele went downstairs to the kitchen, where he told the cook that he was too tired to eat his dinner after playing the violin for eight hours straight.

He left the kitchen and entered the hallway. Groping around in the darkness, Motele found the storeroom door and quietly closed it behind him. Using the dim light from a small grated window as a guide, he located the detonator and ignited it. He hastily ran out of the cellar, down the hallway, and up the stairs. Slowing as he approached the soldier who guarded the exit, he extended his right arm and proclaimed a sarcastic "Heil, Hitler!"

The guard, familiar with the affable young violinist in his little soldier's uniform, amusedly responded, "Ach, you little Ukrainian swine!" And Motele vanished into the darkness.

After running for two hundred feet, Motele heard a violent explosion behind him. The ground shook and windowpanes shattered. He heard police whistles and sirens and saw red flares illuminate the sky over Ovruch.

Terrified and euphoric at the same time, Motele hid himself from view by flattening his body against the buildings as he escaped. He ran into the river, holding his violin above his head with both hands to protect it from the cold water that reached up to his neck. Glancing backward, he saw an enormous fireball shooting into the sky.

When Motele reached the other side of the river, five armed partisans from Uncle Misha's Jewish Group plucked him out of the water and into their wagon. They quickly disappeared back into the safety of the woods.

For a few minutes, Motele was speechless, overwhelmed by the success of his mission. Then, raising his clenched

fists to the red sky, he declared in a trembling voice, "That
is for my parents and my little sister Batyale!"

Motele's Last Mission

By October 1943, the male adults in Uncle Misha's Jewish Group had been incorporated into various divisions
of the Red Army and the women and children partisans
had been sent out of harm's way. The Russians wanted
Uncle Misha to stay behind the lines as an engineer, but
he declined. "I have a final account to settle with Hitler
in Berlin," he insisted.[84] He and Lionka became snipers in
the Red Army's 141st Rifle Division.

Motele was also instructed to leave the combat zone.
He, too, refused. "I'm not a child anymore," he argued
tearfully. "I'm already more than twelve years old. I can
act as a small scout in the front and be just as useful as I
was in the forest.

"I'm an orphan," he continued. "And I don't have any-
body other than Uncle Misha and Lionka. I don't want to
part from them."

Uncle Misha was able to intervene on Motele's behalf,
convincing the commanding officers to allow the boy to
stay in his regiment.

On the morning of October 14, Uncle Misha, Lionka,
and Motele found themselves in a trench, pinned down by
a constant barrage of German bullets and mortars. They
had been under attack since the night before, when they
had been discovered laying land mines. By the time dawn

broke, the river embankment in which they had found refuge was littered with the bodies of dead soldiers and horses from the bloody battle.

A little over four hundred yards away, they noticed a group of Russian officers trying to hide in a shallow trench. Every time the officers moved, their golden epaulettes sparkled in the sun.

"Look, Uncle Misha!" Motele exclaimed, pointing toward a cluster of bushes close to the Russians' trench. "Something is stretching along the ground like a blue snake."

Uncle Misha quickly spotted the group of Germans in blue-gray uniforms stealthily crawling through the bushes toward the Russians. The partisans tried to warn the Russians, but their shouts were drowned out by the cracks of gunfire, the whistles of mortars, and the resulting explosions. They could not shoot the Germans, as their automatic weapons only had a range of two hundred yards.

"I'll run to warn them," Motele volunteered.

"Don't talk nonsense," Uncle Misha retorted. "The Germans will see you before you even get a chance to run halfway there."

"They won't notice me. I'm small. I'll run hunched over and hide behind the dead soldiers and horses," Motele responded. "Look! The Germans are already close. I'm going!"

Before Uncle Misha could stop him, Motele leapt out of the trench and darted toward the Russian officers. He zigged and zagged to avoid being targeted. Every twenty-five yards, he threw his body to the ground, waited a few seconds, and then took off running again. When Motele reached the Russian officers, they pulled him into their trench. Seconds later, they opened fire on the bushes where the Germans were hiding.

The Germans started running away. By then they had gotten so close to the Russians that there was nowhere to take cover. One by one, they fell to the ground dead.

The German artillery that had been bombarding the partisans and the Russians relentlessly since the night before changed tactics. They would cease fire every few minutes in an attempt to lure their foes out of their hiding places. After each temporary lull in the action, they would fire two dozen mortars into the area.

During one break from the fighting, Motele climbed out of the Russians' trench and started zigzagging back to the partisans. When he was a little over thirty yards away, there was a sudden burst of fire from a German machine gun that had been camouflaged on a hill.

Motele threw himself to the ground. He waited a few seconds, and then picked himself up.

He had not even taken another step when the machine gun fired again.

Motele screamed and fell to the ground.

Uncle Misha and Lionka ran over to Motele and pulled him back into their trench. They ripped open his bloody shirt and pants and found that the entire right side of Motele's body had been riddled with bullets. They tore off their own shirts and tried to fashion compress bandages that would stop the bleeding, but the damage was too severe.

"I wanted to be with you," Motele explained weakly.

He grew weaker and paler with every passing minute. Uncle Misha held Motele in his arms. Silently crying, Lionka held Motele's left hand and stroked his curly black hair. Uncle Misha and Lionka were so consumed with grief that they barely noticed the German airplanes that had started dropping bombs near their location.

Motele opened his eyes.

"Uncle Misha, when I die, will I be reunited with my parents?" he asked, his voice almost inaudible.

"Don't talk nonsense, my dear child. You're not going to die," Uncle Misha said, trying to console him.

Uncle Misha promised to carry Motele back to the field hospital, where he would be patched up and returned to the regiment. The sadness in Motele's eyes indicated that the boy knew he was dying.

"But when I die . . . will I be reunited . . . with my parents?"

Uncle Misha could not answer him. Tears streamed down his face. This was the first time he had cried in a year and a half. These were the first tears he had shed since his wife and his daughter had been killed during the Korets massacre.

Seeing Uncle Misha's tears, Motele stopped waiting for an answer.

The noise of the artillery suddenly fell silent. A deathly stillness permeated the embankment.

"I will tell . . . my parents . . . and Batyale . . . how I avenged them . . ." Motele groaned quietly.

He did not finish his sentence. His entire body stiffened. With a contented smile on his face, the thirteen-year-old partisan gave up his brave soul.

Motele's Violin

Uncle Misha ultimately underwent officers' training in the Soviet Union. He entered Germany as a captain in the Red Army—bringing with him Motele's violin—and was in Berlin when Hitler committed suicide. After the war, Uncle Misha worked at the Jewish Historical Institute in Poland before immigrating to Paris. In 1951, he moved to Israel, where he died in the city of Nes Ziona in 1957.

Motele's violin was passed down to Lionka, who had become a lieutenant in the Red Army. After the war, Lionka returned to Korets and shot one of the Ukrainians who had assisted with the murder of his mother and sister. Lionka was tried in a military court and sentenced only to a few weeks of duty in a disciplinary battalion.

Lionka immigrated to Israel with his father. He eventually gave Motele's violin to his own son Seffi Hanegbi, a tour guide in Israel's Negev Desert. For many years, the instrument sat between clothes and blankets in the back of Seffi's closet, collecting dust.

In the early 1990s, Seffi happened to meet Amnon, who was accompanying his wife Assi on a visit to the Negev. Seffi asked Amnon what he did for a living.

"I am a violinmaker," Amnon replied. He had not yet started his work of restoring violins from the Holocaust.

"I will have to tell you a beautiful story someday," Seffi promised.

In 1999, Seffi heard a radio program in which Amnon talked about the Wagner Violin and the other German instruments in his collection. This inspired Seffi to visit Amnon's workshop in Tel Aviv and finally tell him the story of Motele Schlein's Violin. Amnon pledged to restore the instrument, which still remained in the battered wooden case that Motele had used to sneak explosives into the storeroom of the Soldiers Club.

"It is a German instrument, very typical of what Jewish people had before the war," Amnon recalls. "The violin was in good condition, because it was kept by the family the whole time."

The only evidence of the instrument's astonishing odyssey from Volhynia to Israel is a fingerprint on the back of the violin where the varnish was stripped off by coming into contact with alcohol. From the position and location of the damage, Amnon has surmised that at some point a drunken German at the Soldiers Club tried to grab the instrument, perhaps to play it himself.

Although Amnon would completely refurbish many of the other Violins of Hope, he decided to leave Motele's instrument relatively unchanged. He made only minor repairs, replacing just the pegs, bridge, and soundpost to make the instrument playable for special occasions. Using prewar materials that he had inherited from his father,

Amnon was able to restore the violin to its original condition.

Seffi subsequently donated the violin to Yad Vashem with the stipulation that it be available for performances. It has since become a permanent feature in Yad Vashem's Holocaust History Museum, in the Resistance and Rescue Gallery, which is dedicated to those who defied the Nazis. Motele Schlein's Violin can be found alongside not only displays about rescue attempts and partisan camps, but also an authentic Schindler's List.

Sixty-five years after Motele played his violin for the last time, the instrument came alive again on September 24, 2008. In a historic concert at the foot of Jerusalem's Old City walls, a twelve-year-old boy named David Strongin was handed Motele Schlein's Violin. He joined a dozen other children performing on the Violins of Hope in front of an audience of three thousand. Fittingly, the young musicians and the audience came together at the end of the concert for a moving rendition of "Hatikvah."

EPILOGUE

———

SHIMON KRONGOLD'S VIOLIN

Shimon Krongold with his violin in his Warsaw apartment, 1924. At the request of Yaakov Zimmerman, Krongold would allow young Jewish violinists to practice in this very room. One was Michel Schwalbé, who survived the Holocaust to eventually become the concertmaster of the Berlin Philharmonic. *(Courtesy of Nadir Krongold.)*

As the world's leading authority on violins of the Holocaust, Amnon is frequently contacted by descendants of Holocaust victims looking for instruments that were once owned by their families. One day in 2008, Dov Brayer brought Amnon a picture of his brother Shevah. The faded black-and-white photograph was taken at the Brayer home in Lwów, Poland, in the mid-1930s, before Shevah was taken to a concentration camp and killed. In the picture, Shevah holds a violin that Dov hopes to reclaim someday.

"This was a professional violin, not just a simple Klezmer," Amnon deduced after looking at the photo. "And it was made in Poland."

"Yes, yes," Dov confirmed excitedly. "It was given to my brother as a gift by a Polish noblewoman. He was a concertmaster. We believe he played it at the entrance to the Janowska concentration camp near Lwów. That is where he died."

Amnon paused for a moment in the memory of yet another violin virtuoso whose life and career were cut tragically short. "We can never understand what happened in the Holocaust," he finally concluded. "But if we can understand what thoughts went through the minds of the people who played music at the entrances to the camps . . . maybe we can understand something. These instruments are a testimony from another world."

Amnon took out a magnifying glass to inspect the photo even further. "The scroll of this violin is extraordinary," he said, pointing to the decorative dog's head that had been carved into the top of the instrument. "I've never seen anything like it.

"The chances of finding it are one in ten million," Amnon warned Dov. "But thanks to this unique scroll, at least it's not impossible.

"And if I do find this violin," he continued, "it will be played in a huge concert."[85]

The Brayers are just one of thousands of Jewish families who lost their violins during the Holocaust. Some instruments were sold for pittances when their owners became desperate for money to feed their families or to emigrate. Others—like the violin that Feivel Wininger left behind in Gura Humorului—were abandoned when their owners were forced from their homes for arrest or deportation. Still others fell into new hands when their owners died in ghettos and concentration camps, as was apparently the case with Shevah Brayer's violin.

Many instruments—like the Amati that Feivel played in Transnistria—were stolen by neighbors, local authorities, and German officials. After initiating a comprehensive campaign to eradicate the Jews in Europe, the Nazis launched a corresponding initiative to destroy all Jewish cultural and economic activities. This started with the confiscation of millions of valuables such as art, jewelry, books, and religious treasures. Over the course of World War II, a special team of Nazi musicologists seized hundreds of thousands of music books, as well as tens of thousands of musical instruments, manuscripts, and music scores from Jewish musicians and music businesses.

Only a small fraction of these stolen items were ever returned to their rightful owners. Many of them were destroyed during the war. The majority of the objects that did survive remained in German hands. Some looted artifacts were given to German soldiers as rewards for their service. Other war booty was reallocated to German families as compensation for belongings that were destroyed during bombings. The items that were ultimately uncovered by the Red Army were shipped to the east. They would never be seen again.

The Western Allies largely failed in their attempts to return the cultural artifacts to their legal owners. It was difficult to track down survivors and witnesses. Records of the stolen instruments were often inaccessible, incomplete, or missing altogether. Those who had just survived the Holocaust were not likely to still have bills of sale, certificates of authenticity, or any other documents that could identify and prove ownership of a rare instrument. Even when there are photographs of owners like Shevah Brayer holding distinctive violins, such records are useless if the instruments themselves remain missing. It is impossible to know whether those violins no longer exist, or whether they remain concealed in secret collections.

Records of the Netherlands' Ministry of Finance include sixty reports of instruments that were stolen from the Netherlands during the Nazi occupation. The claims include valuable violins by Amati and Guarneri as well as instruments by lesser makers that were confiscated by the Germans when their owners were taken prisoner or fled their homes. Most of these thefts were never investigated. Many of the reports lacked descriptions of the instruments that would be detailed enough to easily distinguish that particular instrument from the thousands of others just like it in Nazi collections. Other instruments were simply not valuable enough to pursue. Only one report is marked "Returned to the Netherlands."[86]

Another instrument that has been returned to its owner's family once belonged to Shimon Krongold, an amateur violinist whose accomplished daughter had played with the Warsaw Philharmonic. Shimon's brother Chaim immigrated to Palestine in 1923, never to see Shimon again. Chaim married and raised two children, who knew little about their uncle Shimon beyond what they could glean from an old picture of him holding his beloved violin. Chaim heard that Shimon escaped from Warsaw to Russia and then to Tashkent, Uzbekistan. Later, he learned that Shimon had died of typhus in Tashkent.

In 1946, a man visited Chaim's apartment in Jerusalem. Chaim's daughter-in-law answered the doorbell.

"Are you Krongold?" the stranger asked.

"Yes," she replied.

"Do you have any connection to Shimon Krongold?"

"Yes, of course we knew about him."

"Well, I have something for you from him." The stranger unfolded a shabby blanket that he was carrying in his arms. Inside was a violin. "This violin belonged to Shimon," he explained. He refused to provide any details about how he had come into possession of the instrument.

By this time, Chaim had gotten involved in the conversation. He was a prominent lawyer. He knew his rights. "Okay, if it belonged to him, it belongs to the family," he stated. "So would you please leave the violin with us?"

"Yes, of course," the stranger responded. But only in exchange for money.

"Why should I buy the violin that belonged to him?" Chaim demanded. "Did you buy it from him? Did you pay for this?"

The stranger still would not answer. Instead, he simply turned to walk away with the instrument.

Chaim was outraged by the injustice. He had already lost Shimon, and now a cagey stranger was demanding money to return Shimon's violin, which Chaim felt was his rightful property. He was willing to let the man and the violin go, but his wife intervened. She darted from the kitchen and caught up with the stranger.

"What do you want for it?" she asked.

The man quoted a reasonable price for the instrument, which Chaim's wife agreed to pay. Chaim's son Nadir remembers the amount being around 250 U.S. dollars.

The violin stayed with the Krongold family in Jerusalem as one of their only remembrances of Shimon. Nadir later traveled to Tashkent to try to find his uncle's grave, but even the Jewish community there was unable to uncover any information about him. All that is left of Shimon is the photograph of him with the violin and the instrument itself. "This is the only memory that we have from him," Nadir explains. "The only memory and the only story about his life."[87]

In September 1999, Amnon gave an interview on the radio about Motele Schlein's Violin. He asked listeners to contact him if they knew of any other instruments that were connected to the Holocaust. Nadir and his sister Edna responded by bringing him their uncle's violin. After comparing the photograph of Shimon with the instrument the family had purchased, Amnon was able to verify that this was indeed Shimon Krongold's Violin.

The biggest surprise came when Amnon peered into one of the violin's f-shaped sound holes. Attached to the inside of the instrument is a label that reads, in a combination of Hebrew and Yiddish: "This violin I made to commemorate my loyal friend Mr. Shimon Krongold, Warsaw, 1924." The dedication is signed by Yaakov Zimmerman. Amnon was holding in his hands an instrument that was made by the very same man who had taught his father how to repair violins more than sixty years earlier. The circle was complete.

Unidentified Violins

For every violin that is recovered, there are thousands that may never be returned to the families of their previous owners. This includes dozens of instruments that Amnon has collected while scouring the world for violins with connections to the Holocaust. While the instruments have survived, information about the musicians who once played them has not. There is simply no way of tracking down the original owners—if those violinists or anyone in their family even survived the Holocaust.

While their owners are unknown, the craftsmanship of their construction and the ornate Stars of David they bear indicate that they were once owned by Jewish musicians. Klezmer performers often decorated their instruments with Jewish symbols. The more "Jewish" the violin looked, the more likely that the local rabbi would recommend that its owner be hired to play at weddings—and the more likely that the performer would receive a few extra coins or a little extra food from the celebrants. One of the violins with a Star of David also features a lion's head, to which its owner later added two decorative diamonds that no doubt delighted the children in his audience. A violin by Yaakov Zimmerman—one of three in Amnon's collection, including Shimon Krongold's Violin—is adorned with no fewer than five Stars of David.

Amnon has deduced that some of the unclaimed instruments were played in ghettos and concentration camps, based on distinctive damage to the tops of the violins that comes only from being played outside in the wind, rain, and snow—something no musician would have ever done unless he was forced to do so under extraordinary conditions. Auschwitz Main Camp violinist Teodor Liese once spoke of liters of water pouring out of his instrument while the orchestra was performing in the rain.[88] One of the instruments was damaged beyond repair. Amnon has left it in the ruined state in which he found it, as a testament to the thousands of other instruments and the millions of lives that were shattered in the Holocaust.

Amnon considers the unidentified violins to be the most precious instruments in his collection. They are not expensive instruments like the Ole Bull Guarneri that Ernst Glaser brought to Bergen or the Amati that Feivel Wininger played in Transnistria. They are simple, unsophisticated violins that represent the everyday Jewish lives and the everyday Jewish traditions that were destroyed during the Holocaust. They are artifacts of the Jewish culture that the Nazis tried unsuccessfully to wipe off the planet. To Amnon, the historical and sentimental value of these instruments far surpasses any monetary worth.

Amnon has never known the names of any of his uncles, aunts, and cousins who died in the Holocaust. Since they were buried in mass graves, there are no graveyards to help him piece together his genealogy. There are no family records, nor surviving relatives whom he can visit to learn the stories about the family members that his parents had been too grief-stricken to talk about. His only way of connecting with his family is through the craft his father taught him: repairing violins.

And so Amnon continues to collect and restore instruments that were played by Jewish musicians during the Holocaust. Each violin tells its own story. Each violin is a tombstone for a relative he never knew.

ACKNOWLEDGMENTS

I first became aware of the Violins of Hope in 2008, just after the instruments had been featured in the historic concert at the foot of Jerusalem's Old City walls. At that time, three administrators and colleagues from my university—Ken Lambla (dean of the College of Arts and Architecture at the University of North Carolina at Charlotte), Royce Lumpkin (chair of the Department of Music), and David Russell (Anne R. Belk distinguished professor of violin)—were initiating a plan to bring the Violins of Hope to the Western Hemisphere for the first time. This bold initiative came to fruition in April 2012, when UNC Charlotte and numerous cultural and educational partners came together for an impressive series of exhibitions, performances, lectures, and films.

As my university planned for the events in Charlotte, I grew increasingly fascinated by what I was hearing about Amnon Weinstein. My recent research had focused on music in Hungary before, during, and after the Holocaust, so the Violins of Hope project resonated with me on a human, artistic, and scholarly level—a perfect storm of intellectual curiosity. In February 2011, I spent a week with Amnon and his charming wife Assi in Tel Aviv, seeing the instruments for myself and learning more about Amnon's journey. It was during this trip that I became inspired to write a book about the violins and the musicians who once played them.

Over the course of researching *Violins of Hope*, I have been honored to meet and interview the descendants of several of the figures profiled in this book, including Freddy Davidovitz; Seffi Hanegbi; Nadir Krongold; Berit, Liv, and Ernst Simon Glaser, as well as their stepbrother, Torleif Torgersen; Mona and Solveig Levin; Helen Wininger Livnat; and Ze'ev Weininger. In Norway in particular, I received friendly assistance from Steinar Birkeland and Thomas Hellum (Norwegian Broadcasting Corporation), Hilde Holbæk-Hanssen (Music Information Center), Lorentz Reitan (Bergen Philharmonic Orchestra), and Magne Seland (National Library). Stanley Bergman, John Cox, Susanna Glaser, David Goldman, Mindle Crystel Gross, Joseph Itiel, Martin Jacobs, Henia Lewin, Myra Mniewski, Nofar Moshe, Anne Parelius, and Benjamin Still also provided a great deal of assistance throughout my research. I am especially grateful to my agent, John Rudolph of Dystel & Goderich Literary Management, for believing in this project from the very beginning, as well as to my editor Claire Wachtel and associate editor Hannah Wood at HarperCollins for their expert assistance in seeing the book through to publication.

I would like to express my gratitude to the Ghetto Fighters' House Museum, Israel Philharmonic Orchestra, United States Holocaust Memorial Museum, and Yad

Vashem, as well as to Ernst Simon Glaser, Nadir Krongold, Helen Wininger Livnat, and Amnon Weinstein for giving me permission to reproduce historical photographs from their collections. The views or opinions expressed in this book, and the context in which the images are used, do not necessarily reflect the views or policy of, nor imply approval or endorsement by, those institutions and individuals.

This work was supported in part by funds provided by the University of North Carolina at Charlotte and its College of Arts and Architecture. Invaluable support was also provided by the Lois Lehrman Grass Foundation.

I am very grateful to my father Robert J. Grymes for his assistance and companionship during my research trips to Israel, as well as to my brother Chris for his continual encouragement. Most of all, I must thank my wife Elizabeth and our daughter Helen for their love and patience. I simply could not have written this book without their support.

NOTES

1. Levi, *Music in the Third Reich*, 4.
2. Lühe, *Die Musik war unsere Rettung*, 93.
3. Kater, "Jewish Musicians in the Third Reich," 75.
4. Sommerfeld, "Kein Bier für den Juden dahinte," 202.
5. Ibid., 206.
6. Goldsmith, *The Inextinguishable Symphony*, 299.
7. Otto D. Tolischus, "Bands Rove Cities," *New York Times*, November 11, 1938.
8. Goldsmith, *The Inextinguishable Symphony*, 204.
9. Geissmar, *Two Worlds of Music*, 84.
10. Ibbeken, *An Orchestra Is Born*, 17.
11. "Toscanini to Conduct Concerts of New Orchestra in Palestine," *New York Times*, February 23, 1936.
12. Ibbeken, *An Orchestra Is Born*, 42.
13. Ibid., 18.
14. Lühe, *Die Musik war unsere Rettung*, 88.
15. Toeplitz, *Sipurah*, 59.
16. Sommerfeld, "Kein Bier für den Juden dahinten," 209.
17. Ibbeken, *An Orchestra Is Born*, 19.
18. Ibid., 25.
19. Toeplitz, *Sipurah*, 35–36.
20. Lühe, *Die Musik war unsere Rettung*, 154.
21. Toeplitz, *Sipurah*, 34.
22. Clare, *Last Waltz in Vienna*, 177.
23. Ibid.
24. Sutton, *Bettelheim*, 124.
25. Cummins, *Dachau Song*, 77.

26. Lenk, *The Mauritius Affair*, 24–25.

27. Ibid., 42.

28. Ibid.

29. Beda and Mayer, "In the Eye of the Storm," 26–27.

30. Lenk, *The Mauritius Affair*, 73.

31. Pitot, *The Mauritian Shekel*, 111.

32. Beda and Mayer, "In the Eye of the Storm," 30–31.

33. Pitot, *The Mauritian Shekel*, 122.

34. Makarova, *Boarding Pass to Paradise*, 80.

35. Interview with Ze'ev Weininger, July 15, 2013.

36. Meyer, "Anscheinend ging nichts ohne Musik," 143.

37. Stroumsa, *Violinist in Auschwitz*, 43.

38. Ibid., 45–46.

39. Szczepański, *Häftlings-kapelle*, 18.

40. Laks, *Music of Another World*, 31–32.

41. Ibid., 33–34.

42. Goldsmith, *The Inextinguishable Symphony*, 295; Meyer, "Mußte da auch Musik sein," 34; and Vahl, "'Die Musik hat mich am Leben erhalten!'" 13.

43. Goldsmith, *The Inextinguishable Symphony*, 296.

44. Laks, *Music of Another World*, 37.

45. Ibid., 38.

46. Meyer, "Mußte da auch Musik sein," 35.

47. Shuldman, *Jazz Survivor*, 37–38.

48. Stroumsa, *Violinist in Auschwitz*, 49.

49. Laks, *Music of Another World*, 70.

50. Meyer, "Anscheinend ging nichts ohne Musik," 144.

51. Laks, *Music of Another World*, 99.

52. Ibid., 112–13.

53. Ibid., 124.

54. Rachela Olewski Zelmanowicz, "Crying Is Forbidden Here," 29.

55. Shuldman, *Jazz Survivor*, 44.

56. Ibid., 45.

57. Schumann, *Der Ghetto-Swinger*, 86.

58. Wiesel, *Night*, 49–50. The German word *Kommando* has been changed to "work detail."

59. Ibid., 95.
60. Laks, *Music of Another World*, 115.
61. Levi, *Survival in Auschwitz and The Reawakening*, 50–51. The German abbreviation "Ka-Be" and word "Lager" have been changed to "the infirmary" and "camp," respectively.
62. Sachnowitz, *The Story of "Herman der Norweger,"* 187.
63. Vahl, "'Die Musik hat mich am Leben erhalten!'" 15.
64. Interview with Freddy Davidovitz, March 10, 2012.
65. Unless otherwise noted, all quotes in chapter 4 are from Glaser, interview at the Music Academy in Ålesund.
    Abrahamsen, "The Holocaust in Norway," 139n67.
66. Haugen and Cai, *Ole Bull*, 58.
67. Bull and Crosby, *Ole Bull*, 247
68. "Ole Bulls fele til Bergen idag," *Bergens Tidende*, January 16, 1941.
69. Synnøve Louise Krogness to Alfhild Thallaug Olsen, January 22, 1941, Oslo National Library.
70. Fasting, *Musikselskabet "Harmonien,"* 16.
71. "Da nazistene stoppet en konsert i Harmonien," *Dagen*, January 18, 1946.
72. Krogness to Olsen, January 22, 1941.
73. "En beklagelig demonstrasjon," *Bergens Aftenblad*, January 17, 1941.
74. Hurum, *Musikken under okkupasjonen*, 61.
75. Ulstein, *Jødar på flukt*, 185.
76. Flagstad, *The Flagstad Manuscript*, 139–40.
77. "Da nazistene stoppet en konsert i Harmonien."
78. "Kunstnerparet Glaser," 1–2.
79. Ibid., 2.
80. Unless otherwise noted, all quotes in chapter 5 are from Livnat, *Le-male et ha-zeman be-ḥayim*.
    Carmelly, *Shattered*, 275.
81. Fisher, *Transnistria*, 97.
82. Unless otherwise noted, all quotes in chapter 6 are from Gildenman, *Motele*. Spector, "The Jews of Volhynia," 160.
83. Suhl, *They Fought Back*, 260.

84. Ibid., 261.

85. Leora Eren Frucht, "Breaking the Silence," *Hadassah Magazine* 89, no. 7 (March 2008).

86. De Vries, *Sonderstab Musik*, 168.

87. Interview with Nadir Krongold, March 8, 2012.

88. Szczepański, *Häftlings-kapelle*, 66.

BIBLIOGRAPHY

Prologue: Amnon's Violins

Yitzhak Arad, "Vilna," in *Encyclopedia of the Holocaust*, ed. Israel Gutman, vol. 4 (New York: Macmillan, 1990), 1571–75; Moses Einhorn, ed., *Volkovisker Yisker-bukh* (New York, 1949); Elana Estrin, "Did Jews Invent the Violin?," *Jerusalem Post*, August 20, 2009; Ida Haendel, *Woman with Violin: An Autobiography* (London: Victor Gollancz, 1970); interview with Ida Haendel on October 31, 2012; and Aharon Weiss, "Volkovysk," in *Encyclopedia Judaica*, 2nd ed., ed. Fred Skolnik and Michael Berenbaum, vol. 20 (New York: Macmillan, 2007), 573–74.

1: The Wagner Violin
Music in the Third Reich:
Kurt Baumann, "The Kulturbund—Ghetto and Home," in *Germans No More: Accounts of Jewish Everyday Life, 1933–1938*, ed. Margarete Limberg and Hubert Rübsaat, trans. Alan Nothnagle (New York: Berghahn Books, 2006), 118–27; Berta Geissmar, *Two Worlds of Music* (New York: Da Capo Press, 1975); Martin Goldsmith, *The Inextinguishable Symphony: A True Story of Music and Love in Nazi Germany* (New York: John Wiley & Sons, 2000); Lily E. Hirsch, *A Jewish Orchestra in Nazi Germany: Musical Politics and the Berlin Jewish Culture League* (Ann Arbor: University of Michigan Press, 2010); Michael H. Kater, "Jewish Musicians in the Third Reich: A Tale of Tragedy," in *The Holocaust's Ghost: Writings on Art, Politics, Law and Education*, ed. F. C. Decoste and Bernard Schwartz (Edmonton:

University of Alberta Press, 2000), 75–83; Kater, *The Twisted Muse: Musicians and Their Music in the Third Reich* (New York: Oxford University Press, 1997); Erik Levi, *Music in the Third Reich* (New York: St. Martin's Press, 1994); Nicolas Slonimsky, *Music Since 1900*, 4th ed. (New York: Charles Scribner's Sons, 1971); Kurt Sommerfeld, "Kein Bier für den Juden dahinten!," in *Premiere und Pogrom: Der Jüdische Kulturbund 1933–1941*, ed. Eike Geisel and Henryk M. Broder (Berlin: Siedler Verlag, 1992), 200–209; and Leni Yahil, "Kristallnacht," in *Encyclopedia of the Holocaust*, vol. 2, 836–40.

Music in Palestine:
Philip V. Bohlman, *"The Land Where Two Streams Flow": Music in the German-Jewish Community of Israel* (Urbana: University of Illinois Press, 1989); " 'Divine,' Says Huberman: Palestine Symphony Orchestra's Organizer Acclaims Its Debut," *New York Times*, December 27, 1936; Helmut Goetz, *Bronislaw Huberman and the Unity of Europe* (Rome, 1967); Jehoash Hirshberg, *Music in the Jewish Community of Palestine 1880–1948: A Social History* (Oxford: Clarendon Press, 1995); Ida Ibbeken, *An Orchestra Is Born* (Tel Aviv: Yachdav, 1969); Barbara von der Lühe, *Die Musik war unsere Rettung! Die deutschsprachigen Gründungsmitglieder des Palestine Orchestra* (Tübingen: Mohr Siebeck, 1998); *Orchestra of Exiles*, directed by Josh Aronson (New York: First Run Features, 2012), DVD; "Orchestra of Exiles," *New York Times*, February 9, 1936; Elsa Thalheimer, *Five Years of the Palestine Orchestra* (Tel Aviv: Palestine Orchestra, 1942); Uri [Erich] Toeplitz, *Sipurah shel ha-Tizmoret ha-filharmonit ha-Yisreelit* [The history of the Israel Philharmonic Orchestra] (Tel Aviv: Sifriat Poalim, 1992); "Toscanini to Conduct Concerts of New Orchestra in Palestine," *New York Times*, February 23, 1936; and documents in the private collection of Amnon Weinstein.

2: ERICH WEININGER'S VIOLIN
Austria and Germany:
Yehoshua R. Büchler, "Buchenwald," in *Encyclopedia of the Holocaust*, vol. 1, 254–56; George Clare, *Last Waltz in Vienna: The Rise*

and Destruction of a Family, 1842–1942 (New York: Holt, 1989); Paul Cummins, *Dachau Song: The Twentieth-Century Odyssey of Herbert Zipper*, 3rd ed. (New York: Peter Lang, 2001); Barbara Distel, "Dachau," in *Encyclopedia of the Holocaust*, vol. 1, 339–43; Sarah A. Ogilvie and Scott Miller, *Refuge Denied: The* St. Louis *Passengers and the Holocaust* (Madison: University of Wisconsin Press, 2006); Theron Raines, *Rising to the Light: A Portrait of Bruno Bettelheim* (New York: Alfred A. Knopf, 2002); Hans A. Schmitt, *Quakers and Nazis: Inner Light in Outer Darkness* (Columbia: University of Missouri Press, 1997); and Nina Sutton, *Bettelheim: A Life and a Legacy*, trans. David Sharp (New York: Basic Books, 1996).

Emigration to Palestine:
Joan Campion, *In the Lion's Mouth: Gisi Fleischmann and the Jewish Fight for Survival* (Lanham, MD: University Press of America, 1987); Karl Lenk, *The Mauritius Affair: The Boat People of 1940/41*, trans. and ed. R. S. Lenk (London: Booksprint, 1993); Elena Makarova, *Boarding Pass to Paradise: Peretz Beda Mayer and Fritz Handel* (Jerusalem: Verba, 2005); Munya M. Mardor, *Haganah*, ed. D. R. Elston (New York: New American Library, 1964); Beda and Hannah Mayer, "In the Eye of the Storm," in *Across the Street and Far Away*, ed. Valerie Arnon (Jerusalem: Verba, 2004), 16–49; Geneviève Pitot, *The Mauritian Shekel: The Story of the Jewish Detainees in Mauritius 1940–1945*, trans. Donna Edouard, ed. Helen Trooper (Lanham, MD: Rowman & Littlefield, 2000); and Aaron Zwergbaum, "Exile in Mauritius," *Yad Vashem Studies* 4 (1960): 191–257.

3: THE AUSCHWITZ VIOLIN
Auschwitz:

Jozef Buszko, "Auschwitz," in *Encyclopedia of the Holocaust*, vol. 1, 107–19; Guido Fackler, " 'We all feel this music is infernal . . .': Music on Command in Auschwitz," trans. Corinne Granof, in *The Last Expression: Art and Auschwitz*, ed. David Mickenburg, Corinne Granof, and Peter Hayes (Evanston, IL: Northwestern University Press, 2003), 114–25; and Shirli Gilbert, "Fragments of Humanity: Music in Auschwitz," in *Music in the Holocaust: Confronting Life in the Nazi Ghettos and Camps* (Oxford: Oxford University Press, 2005), 144–95.

Auschwitz Main Camp Orchestra:
Emilio Jani, *My Voice Saved Me: Auschwitz 180046*, trans. Timothy Paterson (Milan: Centauro Editrice, 1961); and Ignacy Szczepański, *Häftlings-kapelle* (Warsaw: Książka i Wiedza, 1990).

Birkenau Men's Camp Orchestra:
Goldsmith, *The Inextinguishable Symphony*; Szymon Laks, *Music of Another World*, trans. Chester A. Kisiel (Evanston, IL: Northwestern University Press, 1989); Henry Meyer "Anscheinend ging nichts ohne Musik," in *Premiere und Pogrom*, 136–45; Henry Meyer, "Mußte da auch Musik sein? Der Weg eines Geigers von Dresden über Auschwitz nach Amerika," in *Musik im Exil: Folgen des Nazismus für die internationale Musikkultur* (Frankfurt am Main: Fischer Taschenbuch), 29–40; Ken Shuldman, *Jazz Survivor: The Story of Louis Bannet, Horn Player of Auschwitz* (London: Vallentine Mitchell, 2005); Jacques Stroumsa, *Violinist in Auschwitz: From Salonica to Jerusalem 1913–1967*, trans. James Stewart Brice, ed. Erhard Roy Wiehn (Konstanz: Hartung-Gorre, 1996); and Barbara-Maria Vahl, " 'Die Musik hat mich am Leben erhalten!' Henry Meyer, zweiter Geiger des LaSalle Quartet, im Gespräch," in *Das Orchester: Zeitschrift für Orchesterkultur und Rundfunk-Chorwesen* 44, no. 3 (1996): 11–15.

Birkenau Women's Camp Orchestra:
Fania Fénelon, with Marcelle Routier, *Playing for Time*, trans. Judith Landry (Syracuse, NY: Syracuse University Press, 1997); Gabriele Knapp, *Das Frauenorchester in Auschwitz: Musikalische Zwangsarbeit und ihre Bewältigung* (Hamburg: Von Bockel, 1996); Anita Lasker-Wallfisch, *Inherit the Truth: A Memoir of Survival and the Holocaust* (New York: St. Martin's Press, 1996); Richard Newman, *Alma Rosé: Vienna to Auschwitz*, with Karen Kirtley (Pompton Plains, NJ: Amadeus Press, 2000); and Rachela Olewski Zelmanowicz, "Crying Is

Forbidden Here!," trans. and ed. Arie Olewski and Jochevet Ritz-Olewski, courtesy of Arie Olewski and Jochevet Ritz-Olewski.

Other Auschwitz Ensembles:
Ruth Elias, *Triumph of Hope: From Theresienstadt and Auschwitz to Israel*, trans. Margot Bettauer Dembo (New York: John Wiley & Sons, 1998); Primo Levi, *Survival in Auschwitz and The Reawakening: Two Memoirs*, trans. Stuart Woolf (New York: Summit Books, 1986); Herman Sachnowitz, *The Story of "Herman der Norweger," Auschwitz Prisoner #79235*, with Arnold Jacoby, trans. Thor Hall (Lanham, MD: University Press of America, 2002); Coco Schumann, *Der Ghetto-Swinger: Eine Jazzlegende erzählt*, ed. Max Christian Graeff and Michaela Haas (Munich: Deutscher Taschenbuch Verlag, 1997); and Elie Wiesel, *Night*, trans. Marion Wiesel (New York: Hill & Wang, 2006).

4: OLE BULL'S VIOLIN
The Holocaust in Norway:
Samuel Abrahamsen, "The Holocaust in Norway," in *Contemporary Views on the Holocaust*, ed. Randolph L. Braham (Boston: Kluwer-Nijhoff, 1983), 109–42; Samuel Abrahamsen, *Norway's Response to the Holocaust* (New York: Holocaust Library, 1991); Maynard M. Cohen, *A Stand Against Tyranny: Norway's Physicians and the Nazis* (Detroit: Wayne State University Press, 1997); Richard Petrow, *The Bitter Years: The Invasion and Occupation of Denmark and Norway, April 1940–May 1945* (New York: William Morrow, 1974); and Sachnowitz, *The Story of "Herman der Norweger."*

Ole Bull:
Sara Chapman Thorp Bull and Alpheus Benning Crosby, *Ole Bull* (Cambridge, MA: Riverside Press, 1883); Einar Haugen and Camilla Cai, *Ole Bull: Norway's Romantic Musician and Cosmopolitan Patriot* (Madison: University of Wisconsin Press, 1993); Mortimer Smith, *The Life of Ole Bull* (Princeton: Princeton University Press, 1943);

and Amnon Weinstein, "Ole Bull: A Renaissance Man," *Journal of the Violin Society of America* 17, no. 1 (2000): 85–125.

Bergen Philharmonic Orchestra:
Hans Jørgen Hurum, *Musikken under okkupasjonen* (Oslo: H. Aschehoug, 1946); Kåre Fasting, *Musikselskabet "Harmonien" gjennom to hundre år 1765–1965* (Bergen: John Grieg, 1965); Olav Mosby, *Musikselskabet Harmonien, 1765–1945*, vol. 2 (Bergen: John Grieg, 1949); and Elef Nesheim, *Et musikkliv i krig: Konserten som politisk arena, Norge 1940–45* (Oslo: Norsk Musikforlag, 2007).

Ernst Glaser:
Newspaper clippings and other documents from the Bergen Philharmonic Orchestra; Ernst Glaser, interview at the Music Academy in Ålesund (typescript), January 14, 1975, courtesy of Ernst Simon Glaser; newspaper clippings and other information from Berit, Liv, and Ernst Simon Glaser, as well as from Torleif Torgersen; interview with Berit, Liv, and Ernst Simon Glaser on January 29, 2012; interview with Solveig and Mona Levin on January 28, 2012; and newspaper clippings and other documents from the Oslo National Library.

Flight and Exile in Sweden:
Kirsten Flagstad, *The Flagstad Manuscript*, ed. Louis Biancolli (New York: G. P. Putnam's Sons, 1952); "Kunstnerparet Glaser: To trofaste norske musikkambassadører i Sverige," *Norsk Musikkliv* 9–10 (1945): 1–5; Robert Levin, *Med livet i hendene*, with Mona Levin (Oslo: J. W. Cappelens, 1983); and Ragnar Ulstein, *Jødar på flukt* (Oslo: Norske samlaget, 1995).

5: FEIVEL WININGER'S VIOLIN
The Holocaust in Romania:
Jean Ancel, *The History of the Holocaust in Romania*, trans. Yaffah Murciano, ed. Leon Volovici, assisted by Miriam Caloianu (Lincoln: University of Nebraska Press, 2011); International Commission on

the Holocaust in Romania, *Final Report* (2004); and Radu Ioanid, *The Holocaust in Romania: The Destruction of Jews and Gypsies Under the Antonescu Regime, 1940–1944* (Chicago: Ivan R. Dee, 2000).

Transnistria:
Felicia Steigman Carmelly, *Shattered! 50 Years of Silence: History and Voices of the Tragedy in Romania and Transnistria* (Scarborough, Ontario: Abbeyfield, 1997); Julius S. Fisher, *Transnistria: The Forgotten Cemetery* (South Brunswick, NJ: A. S. Barnes, 1969); Yosef Govrin, *In the Shadow of Destruction: Recollections of Transnistria and Illegal Immigration to Eretz Israel, 1941–1947* (London: Vallentine Mitchell, 2007); correspondence with Dr. Timor Melamed; Avigdor Shachan, *Burning Ice: The Ghettos of Transnistria*, trans. Schmuel Himelstein (Boulder, CO: East European Monographs, 1996); and Meir Teich, "The Jewish Self-Administration in Ghetto Shargorod (Transnistria)," *Yad Vashem Studies* 2 (1958): 219–54.

Feivel Wininger:
Helen Wininger Livnat, *Le-male et ha-zeman be-ḥayim* [Filling time with life] (Tel Aviv: Ministry of Defense Publishers, 2006); interview with Helen Wininger Livnat, March 7, 2012; and Feivel Wininger, "We were so many and so weak; we remained few but strong and powerful" (unpublished memoirs), translated by Laura and Zvika Livnat, courtesy of Helen Wininger Livnat.

6: Motele Schlein's Violin
The Holocaust in Volhynia:
Wendy Lower, "Facilitating Genocide: Nazi Ghettoization Practices in Occupied Ukraine, 1941–1942," in Eric J. Sterling, ed., *Life in the Ghettos During the Holocaust* (Syracuse, NY: Syracuse University Press, 2005), 120–44; Schmuel Spector, *The Holocaust of Volhynian Jews, 1941–1944*, trans. Jerzy Michalowicz (Jerusalem: Yad Vashem, 1990); and Spector, "The Jews of Volhynia and Their Reaction to Extermination," *Yad Vashem Studies* 15 (1983): 159–86.

Uncle Misha's Jewish Group:
Reuben Ainsztein, *Jewish Resistance in Nazi-Occupied Eastern Europe* (New York: Barnes & Noble, 1974); Interview with Seffi Hanegbi, March 7, 2012; Moshe Kahanovitch, "Moshe Gildenman—Partisan Commander of the 'Yevgrupa,'" *Yad Vashem Bulletin* 3 (1958): 13–14; Allan Levine, *Fugitives of the Forest* (Toronto: Stoddart, 1998); and Yuri Suhl, ed., *They Fought Back: The Story of the Jewish Resistance in Nazi Europe* (New York: Crown, 1967).

Motele Schlein:
Moshe Gildenman, *Motele: Der yunger partizaner* [Motele: The young partisan] (Paris: 1950).

EPILOGUE: SHIMON KRONGOLD'S VIOLIN

Frances Brent, *The Lost Cellos of Lev Aronson* (New York: Atlas, 2009); Howard Reich and William Gaines, "How Nazis Targeted World's Finest Violins," *Chicago Tribune*, August 19, 2001; Carla Shapreau, "The Stolen Instruments of the Third Reich," *The Strad*, December 2009; and Willem de Vries, *Sonderstab Musik: Music Confiscations by the Einsatzstab Reichsleiter Rosenberg under the Nazi Occupation of Europe* (Amsterdam: Amsterdam University Press, 1996).

INDEX

ABOUT THE AUTHOR

James A. Grymes is an internationally respected musicologist and a critically acclaimed author. He holds a bachelor's degree in music education from Virginia Commonwealth University, master's degrees in historical musicology and music performance, and a PhD in historical musicology from Florida State University. His three previous books are about the Hungarian musician Ernst von Donhányi, a forgotten hero of the Holocaust resistance who was later falsely accused of Nazi war crimes. Dr. Grymes is a professor of musicology at the University of North Carolina at Charlotte. www.jamesagrymes.com